NO COVENANT

Eaten by lions - the story behind one of humankind's greatest fears

Jason Swemmer

Original illustrations / Photographs where applicable by Jason Swemmer

Cover illustration: Deadly Shadows *by Sir John Seerey-Lester (1945-2020), original oil on canvas, 12" x 24", with full permission. The painting was one of Sir John's personal favourites and portrayed, he felt, one of our worst nightmares.*

World-renowned artist, the late John Seerey-Lester and award-winning painter Suzie Seerey-Lester are both distinguished wildlife and landscape artists whose works depict large mammals, birds of prey, magnificent underwater creatures and environmentally sensitive tableaus.

"He was a magnificent beast, with a black and tawny mane; in his prime, teeth and claws perfect, with mighty thews, and savage heart. He was lying near a hartebeest on which he had been feasting; his life had been one unbroken career of rapine and violence; and now the maned master of the wilderness, the terror that stalked by night, the grim lord of slaughter, was to meet his doom at the hands of the only foes who dared molest him."

Theodore Roosevelt, March 1910

"…there can be no covenant between men and lions…"

From *The Iliad* by Homer

Dedication

Dedicated to the memory of Peter Hathaway Capstick, whose hauntingly-realistic prose has teleported me many times to the Silent Places;

and to Annelindi, who understands.

Acknowledgements

The author wishes to express his thanks to the following, without whom this manuscript would never have morphed into a book:

Fiona Claire Capstick, a legend I am humbled to call a close friend, for writing the foreword, providing guidance and being so kind, ever since I first called her out of the blue, now many years ago. A researcher of note and renowned author in her own right, I am eternally grateful.

Suzie Seerey-Lester, for permission to use the late, great John Seerey-Lester's remarkable painting as the cover picture. John's works hang in many valuable collections, including that of the White House. I am humbled and honoured.

Robert R. Frump, New York author and executive director of communications, for permission to quote from his research in the chapter on the Kruger lions; the regard in which he is held by colleagues speaks volumes, and is in no way undeserved.

The team at Angel Key Publications, for their guidance and patience.

My family, who have inspired, supported and loved me.

Author's note

The use of the words African, white and black are in the factual context, and are in no way to be construed as racial terms, or slurs. A white man is a white man, a black man is a black man, and a bush African is an African person that lives in rural areas. I have declined to use the terms of the day while recounting some of the events, one of which occurred in the nineteenth century. But I am a white man; it's OK, it's not a racial term. It's what I am.

Contents

1   Foreword

This lucidly written book and its splendidly accessible prose will transport the reader in an instant out of a sanitized, first-world lifestyle with its inevitable self-righteous assertions and ignorance about wildlife and its effective conservation. Deft, often frightening word pictures, based on admirable research and covering many countries and vast regions of African wilderness, will be a sobering, indeed often terrifying introduction to man-eating lions and the worlds they still inhabit in the new millennium.

The author has the advantage of being a son of Africa where he was born and grew into adulthood and where he developed a close, first-hand knowledge of the African bush and of its wildlife, especially concerning large predators such as lion. As a boy of ten, the author remembers reading enthralling material about man-eating lions. Such was the impact of that early experience that the author never let go of his fascination with man as prey, especially concerning lions. As this book will prove in unnerving fashion, 'they're still out there', as Peter Capstick would say.

Lions date back to the early Pleistocene of some 2.6 million years ago. They once roamed from the southernmost tip of Africa right through the continent to the Arabian Peninsula, Turkey, Greece, Asia Minor and India. This riveting book, with excellent and accurate zoological detail, reveals how human population explosions have destroyed much of the natural habitat of lions. This, in turn, has fuelled an upsurge in man-eating as natural prey diminishes and lions lose their innate fear of humans because of ever closer proximity. Predation on livestock has resulted in mass poisoning of lions in places like southern Tanzania where lions are known to even brazenly stalk and kill human prey in daylight.

Several myths about lions are debunked in this authoritative book. Most man-eating lions are not sickly and old but are in their prime. There is even compelling evidence that man-eating is learned behaviour. Cubs will snack on humans if the lioness provides the opportunity. Once a taste for human flesh is cultivated and once lions know the ease with which they can run down and kill humans, as opposed to animal prey, the die is cast and the lions become far more dangerous. The author amply demonstrates this when depicting the plight of the waves of illegal immigrants, fleeing civil war and famine as they crossed into South Africa through the famed Kruger National Park from neighbouring Mozambique. Lions feasted for years on those desperate and despairing people, be they toddlers or adults.

This hugely adventurous book introduces many a legendary character from the annals of African adventure. Among them is the fabled George Rushby of Tanganyika and his nightmares with the man-eating lions of Njombe which were 'like measles in children', such were their numbers. The horrors of the Tsavo man-eaters in British East Africa roar into life on these pages, as does many another tragedy in the African bush. The reader is taken into the murky world of witchcraft and were lions, of lycanthropy and murder, of scandal in colonial society, of the infamous and illegal trade in lion bones for traditional Asian medicines and the appalling 'canned lion' carnage, soaked in human greed and wrongdoing, that masquerades as hunting.

A bold and informed plea is made for better protected reserves in order to conserve lions by separating them effectively from the very humans who are destroying their natural habitat. Informed defence of the proven rule of the ethical hunting industry is stated, as is its vital role in generating funds, providing rural populations with livelihoods and policing the wilderness areas of Africa for the future sustainability of wildlife.

This is no "fluffy love" story, to quote the author. He writes the truth and confronts the misconceptions spewed into the ether by a media-obsessed world walking the politically correct tightrope. He speaks to a world far removed from the often-unnerving realities of the African wilderness, African politics and the daunting difficulties faced by the most vulnerable citizens living in remote regions where lions still roam. And still hunt humans.

Read this book – with the lights on and the doors locked!

Fiona Claire Capstick

Waterkloof

Pretoria

REPUBLIC OF SOUTH AFRICA

2   Introduction

I guess it was two things really; two things that sparked my fascination, that piqued my interest despite the creeping horror that raised the hairs on the back of my neck. The second was profound, life-altering and massive, leaving the all-pervading feeling that this was much bigger than me, bigger than all of us there, bigger even than this entire time: it was the first time I heard a lion roaring at night. It was a pitch-dark night and the sound carried easily across the 3km (2miles) of water between us. Everyone was instantly hushed into an awestruck, respectful silence. No comments, no jokes; just the realisation that we humans are not all that powerful at all. Every other night creature, from crickets to bushbabies, was instantly silent too.

Much has been written about this exact experience over time. I was perhaps the billionth person to experience that feeling, probably more; I certainly wasn't the last. Explorers have written of it since explorers first wrote; tourists have noted the same moment when, having left their protected First-World existences for a safari, or holiday, or charity work to those places that still draw people in spite of - or is that because of? - the very savagery, they heard that awe-inspiring sound; it is a sound unlike any other. Of course, there are people that have lived with that sound their entire lives.

Televised documentaries seem to have diluted the impact a lion's roar has. No television can convey the noise in the same way it hits you in the wild. There are louder sounds. There are more hysterically urgent sounds: a woman screaming for instance; a sickly infant in desperate discomfort. But the roar of a lion – or indeed, that of a tiger in Asia – has the impact that it has because it travels across the eons from a time when we were living helpless, in constant terror of being eaten. It literally hits you because much of the effect is caused by the vibrating waves of sound that resonate in your chest cavity, freezing you in mid-step and leaving you speechless.

Eaten. It seems absurd; I'm writing this in the second decade of the twenty-first century. This is now, modern times, Cloud computing and Google glasses and touchscreen televisions; we can see people on the beach from space. We message relatives in real time across the planet. We Skype them and speak as if they are before us, not time zones distant. And yet, there are places where people are eaten by animals, every day. America's Summer of the Shark (mid 2001) was well-documented and followed by Australia's own version (late 2008 to early 2009). It reminded people that sharks are out there, and attacks do occur, and some are fatal, and yes, some are even predatory.

This doesn't affect a majority of people; the vast majority of the earth's population do not live in coastal cities and towns (around a billion do, around 6 billion don't). Funnily enough, this is the very factor that results in the word "shark" having the biggest impact of any on the human mind: as we have progressed and developed over time, we have managed to eliminate or cage almost every large animal that can bite us. We have grizzlies, lions, tigers and more in reserves. They stare back at us through zoo cage barriers. But we can't know, let alone often even see, when a shark might be swimming ten feet away from us.

So, many would reason, that's an easy sum to work out: stay out of the ocean. Fair enough, but there are also many terrestrial places where we haven't quite managed to place enough of a barrier between ourselves and the things that bite. Humankind is pro-creating at an exponential rate. We are approaching eight billion people on this planet. Space to move – and there is still a lot of it – is decreasing and in many underdeveloped countries, this fact combined with a lack of infrastructure due to weak economies means that people and wild animals are sharing space again. And the old cycle is relaunched almost daily.

When people started eating meat - which accelerated our brain development enormously - and we became the dominant predator, it was inevitable that we would clash with the existing predators. And we have over time emerged victorious. Our greater intelligence led to strategic planning and our population growth spelled doom for most large predatory competitors. But there's a different dimension to be considered here; we weren't just competition. We were food; and this goes some way to explaining the spine-chilling awe one feels when that lion roar is heard in the wild places.

The first thing that sparked my interest, by the way, was something that came from The Picture Box. Back in the hazy mists of the 1970s - and to a lesser extent, the 1980s - where I grew up in Pretoria, South Africa, the world was not yet privy to such fantastic inventions as Google, the internet, even the home computer. We had several series of excellent encyclopaedia which assisted us greatly at school, where research was required. But sheer number of topics meant that these books could only cover any given subject for a few pages at best, more often a few paragraphs.

So, my mother had taken it upon herself to keep newspaper and magazine articles and pictures, and store these willy-nilly in The Picture Box. In actual fact, The Picture Box was two boxes. They were large, coral pink in colour, originally from some clothing boutique, and were oddly shaped, for containers. Largely square, they weren't very deep in the third dimension, perhaps three or four inches. They did, however, contain a staggering assortment of papers, pictures, articles, pamphlets, whole magazines and other bric-a-brac that my mother had managed to squirrel away over the years.

Happily, much of their contents centred around one of my most burning passions, Africa's wildlife, my mother not unreasonably adjudging this sort of thing to likely make good subject matter for future school projects. And in the depths of one of the boxes lay a catalyst, a gem to a ten-year-old boy with a passion for such things. It was a faded light-blue tri-fold in A5-size, and on the front was emblazoned the head of a full-maned male lion, snarling its very obvious displeasure. That alone would have gotten my attention, but the words below, in large capital letters, clinched it: MAN-EATERS. It was disturbing and horrific, especially to a ten-year-old; but ghoulishly attractive in some way, probably the same reaction that makes people stare at a road traffic accident. You want to look away, but you're compelled to look.

I'm not sure if it was a Readers Digest supplement – which seems likely – or came with one of the topical TV magazines of the day. It doesn't say; but inside were three colour plates, prints of larger paintings by Penny Miller (who is credited on the cover) and for each, an explanatory paragraph provided by South African author Tom Bulpin. Thomas Victor Bulpin, I later found out, was a prolific writer and many of his works are much sought-after Africana today. The three instances were 1) the Tsavo man-eating lions, 2) the 1903 attack on Harry Wolhuter, one of the rangers of what became the Kruger Park, and 3) the Njombe man-eaters.

Over the next several years this pamphlet germinated in my young mind, ably abetted by the series of young adventurer books by Willard Price. These focus on the fictional characters of Hal Hunt and his brother Roger, who travel the globe collecting wild animals for zoos and circuses. How many children must have over time had their budding inner adventurer-naturalist sparked into life by those stories; Willard Price set out to inspire that in children, and to his memory I say, job done! The places they go to are very real and if one has the inclination, can be found over time. I had the

13

inclination! I eventually added the works referred to in the pamphlet to my library. Then I added many more.

And so over time I have collected and avidly devoured the pages of many works by the old hunter-explorers, the adventurers; I have delved into the municipal records of remote towns in far-off places; I have read biographies and autobiographies of rangers, researchers and acquaintances. The works of Wolhuter, Capstick, Bulpin and Frump share space in my library with those of such great ivory hunters as Stigand, Lyell, Bell, Sutherland and Neumann. The legendary Roosevelt, Selous, Corbett and Hemingway sit opposite the stories by Kloppers, Taylor, Patterson and Ruark. As did the fictional Hunt brothers, I grew to love critters from all four corners of the globe, but being African, it was the denizens of that wonderful, maddening, visceral continent that spoke the loudest to my soul.

I was born in Africa and have spent most of my life there, where access to animals and game-reserves is wonderfully easy. Like many South Africans, I spent much time in the reserves, soaking up the wonders of the bush. I visited many of the places recounted in this book. The more I delved, the more I uncovered, and with the advent of the internet, a whole new dimension opened up to assist me in trying to understand why and how lions hunt and consume human beings. Children's books and indeed, much adult literature from days gone, seem to have painted man-eating lions as real outcasts, exceptions; bad apples and in the vast minority. I have come to realise that they are anything but uncommon.

The effect on the human psyche that man-eaters can have is staggering, and understandably so. What exacerbates this is the fact that so many of the large-scale man-eating outbreaks have occurred in the less-developed and poorer parts of our planet, as conditions there are more conducive to such an outbreak than in First-World countries, and where superstition and mythology are rife. Add in the luck that some man-eaters have had, which at times has literally seemed to border on the supernatural, and the sheer helpless terror of the people living in those areas can only be imagined. With no recourse, it must be truly dreadful to experience.

An oft-quoted "fact" among those in the know is that more people fall prey to lions in current times than was the case a century ago. This likely just appears to be the case because 1) people are more populous now, and 2) we are better at recording it now. That said, as of the current time, into the second decade of the 21st century, lions still eat over a hundred people each year in Tanzania alone, probably five hundred across Africa each year. This is reality, daily life for thousands of people all throughout Africa. The fact isn't advertised and many of these killings are not reported, for the same reason the mayor in the 1975 film *Jaws* needed the reality hidden: potentially losing tourist dollars. People are less likely to flock to areas to visit reserves, perform charity work or back-pack if they know they might actually be killed and consumed for their troubles.

Modern terminology nowadays tends towards "human-animal conflict", "human-carnivore conflict" and "human-lion conflict", suggesting that the term "man-eater" is dramatist and perpetuates a stereotype. It is what it is; try telling the man whose wife is killed by a lion before his eyes, or the mother whose child is taken in the night, that they should be politically correct. The act is violent, bestial, and no amount of diplomatic window-dressing will alter that. The term "man-eater" will appear throughout, because that is what it is.

We desperately need to conserve wild lions, which are disappearing from this planet at an alarming rate, but we need to save people from such basic horrors as being consumed too: man-eating in Africa is rife, and far more so than people are aware of, or would like to admit. It looks like we still have lots to do.
Here then are some of the things I have found; many are well-known, some are downright household names in some quarters; others are not. I have endeavoured to recall as many of the legendary cases from the past, as well as some of the very newest concepts and theories, into a single reference work. I hope you enjoy reading as much as I enjoyed delving and compiling.

- Jason Swemmer, Brisbane, Australia, 2022.

3   The animal

Consider a lion: it is a cat, the world's second largest. Only the tiger is bigger, or more specifically, longer and heavier; the biggest lions are taller than the biggest Bengal tigers, on average apparently by 14cm (5.5 in). The biggest Siberian tigers are so large as to defy comprehension; they commonly exceed 660 pounds (300kg) and the record weight for that striped gentleman of the snows is a scarcely credible 1,025 pounds (465kg)! That is twice the weight of a big male lion, so I've used the Bengal tiger as reference. Lions seem to have a more regal upright stance than a tiger, a defiance in them that spawned the term lion-hearted. Sir Alfred Edward Pease wrote in 1914 that the animal has always stood as the emblem of concentrated courage and terrific power. The number of royal banners, coats of arms, town crests and sporting club badges that are adorned by lions is immeasurable.

He is the classic game animal, the ultimate sporting conquest and great adversary of people since time immemorial, an animal to both venerate and dread. A lion sells his life dearly. He won't go looking for trouble, but as Winston Churchill wrote, when he is bayed he will fight to the death. He can have broken limbs, a broken jaw, lungs shot through, even a destroyed heart, but only instant death to the creature will save a man when attacked, as the cat charges all the way. Sir Alfred Pease felt that aside from the tiger, no other game animal renders the improvement in modern rifles and ammunition so irrelevant. A shot needs to be fatal, or regardless how severely wounded, a lion will make sure he gets to you.

A lion can be the epitome of peaceable relaxation, but when its blood is up the cat seems to draw on energy born of limitless hate, a violent fury. A full-grown male lion walks with the unconscious swagger that comes from the innate knowledge of superior power. They have attitude, a confidence born of existing in relative safety and having come through the harsh school of physical violence, which contrasts starkly with the vulnerability that comes with being a lion cub. Modern filmmaking has shown this swagger brilliantly, the massive slabs of muscle shaking as the great shaggy-maned beasts plod about, patrolling their domain and daring a challenge.

The first impression when right next to a lion is the sheer size of it; even a 6-month old cub is enormous and daunting, a full-grown male simply terrifying. You are acutely aware that it could destroy you with ease, and there's that nagging fear that it will *eat* you.

Some uncomfortable and ancient knowledge which has morphed into instinct? Probably; I think so anyway. The next thing is the coarseness of the hair. Touch a clean lion at a game farm where relatively tame lions can be viewed and the fur can in places be surprisingly soft, but in rural areas out in the wild the hair is rough, like sisal. Touch a bit firmer though, beneath the fur, and the massive muscles are obvious. This is an animal of real power; its muscles when in use are like steel bands. The next impression is one of sheer weight. Muscle is heavy and this is just more evidence of what lies beneath a lion's skin. They feel like they weigh a ton, even when relatively little.

In South Africa, powerful guard dogs known as *Boerboels* (old Dutch for "farm dog") have been bred to protect homes and farms, and early versions accompanied the Dutch pioneers that forged the northern regions of South Africa out of virgin wilderness when they left the Cape to escape British rule. They are the only breed of dog in the world bred from scratch to be watchdogs, and are now recognised internationally. They are probably 20 percent bigger than a Rottweiler or large German Shepherd and the males can grow to 80kg and more. A Boerboel is a mobile mastiff and there are records of individuals fighting and killing leopards.

I actually owned one, a beautiful female that weighed 63kg at the age of 12 months, and went on to top out at 75kg, which is a very fine female specimen indeed. I also owned a male which was a Boerboel-Rottweiler cross. He peaked at some 60-odd kg. The impression I remember most about the Boerboel was the sheer weight of muscle. They were so much heavier than our previous dogs, and it's this impression that I got when I have handled lions. They are as heavy as lead. Of course, there is no real similarity between lions and Boerboels, other than that they share the same tawny colour and the fact that they each have four legs: a male lion weighs as much as three of the very biggest Boerboels. Add in the factor that a lion is a cat, and thus amazingly fast and powerful for its size, and you have a formidable animal in anyone's terms.

I suppose some people imagine they could bravely fight a lion off with their bare hands, should the very obviously-life-and-death situation ever arise. It has been suggested in films and picture stories, albeit Tarzan films and comic pulp such as Conan. A leopard, maybe. It has been done and recorded. But a lion? Handle a real one, an adult one, and answer me that question. Then remember that a real attack from a lion doesn't involve them lolling on you in a friendly manner. What then occurs is upward of 200kg hurtling at you at a speed that has been reliably measured as Bloody Fast, and that hurtling 200+kg is a hardened package which has been conditioned to strike such mobile fortresses as Cape buffalo at full tilt. Add in the two-inch hooks for claws and the three-inch teeth that can penetrate the skulls of large herbivores, and the net result is a human being that is turned into a reddish jelly, but *quickly*.

Incidentally, a reliable measure of a lion's top speed when charging is yet to be made and will vary due to the animal, how irate it is, whether or not it's wounded and the terrain. There has been much speculation and even reasonable logical deductions made based on distance covered and time taken to do so. At least 60km/h (around 40mph) is possible and I have seen 80km/h quoted (50mph) for a short burst. It's actually irrelevant, really; no person under the sun can smell these figures, so running is the most pointless exercise when charged by a lion. The speed is daunting and the animal keeps low, coming so fast that even though he runs straight, your first shot has to be right or your second may not anchor him before he hits you. And there's usually only one outcome to that scenario: the reddish jelly alluded to earlier. As if this pleasant thought isn't enough, the animal exudes a series of unnerving grunts, and if wounded, vocal mayhem that has to be heard to be believed. So even when armed with the most potent rifle in the world, when a lion starts a full, going-all-the-way charge, you have perhaps three seconds to kill him, and sometimes as little as one second, depending on the visibility and denseness of bush, or you will be checking out.

The bite force of a lion and its three-inch canines add up to a bite in the chest for a human ending fatally. In all my trawling, I have uncovered just one case of a full bite in the thoracic area - not the shoulder - by an adult lion where the person survived. Bite force in an adult lion is enormous; Dereck and Beverley Joubert recorded male lions biting down on hyenas until bones audibly cracked, in the late 1980s in Botswana's Savuti area. Hyenas are a bit harder than humans. The male lion that most often engaged in this practice, incidentally, seemed to relish biting hyenas and commonly confronted other species as well, among them bull elephants. The Jouberts named him *Ntchwaidumela* – 'He who Greets with Fire' in Setswana – and he features in one of the most famous and spectacular pieces of footage on inter-species conflict ever filmed. It was actually on Christmas Day in 1990 when he chased down a matriarch hyena and killed her, covering an enormous distance at full speed to get to her. The footage was included in the Jouberts' famous 1992 documentary *Eternal Enemies: Lions and Hyenas*.

It was around this time that the Jouberts realised that perhaps we humans don't have the monopoly on emotions that we think we have; some animals will be more vigorous than others, just as some humans are fitter and more energised than others, and there will even be lazy individuals, just as in people. There will be some that show obvious displeasure towards other species, and that displeasure can be so latent that there can be no other word to use when describing it but hatred. That this male lion - *Ntchwaidumela* - would go to such extraordinary lengths to kill hyenas with no subsequent consumption of the kill, shows without a doubt that he hated them. Any dog or cat owner will confirm that their pet likes and dislikes different people or animals, and sometimes to extremes.

Just by the way, the occasion where the human survived a bite in the chest from an adult lion happened to Dr W. Brandon Macomber, a famous plastic surgeon from the US, in northern Botswana in 1968. When Dr Macomber and his professional hunter were both mauled by an unwounded lion, the good doctor suffered a large bite through his chest and back that resulted in crushed ribs which threatened to puncture his lungs. He was fortunate in that the lion bit once and left. Humans may have survived big body-bites by adult lions on other occasions, but they strangely aren't advertised, and are the extreme exception.

Lions first appeared sometime during the early Pleistocene. The Pleistocene covers a time some 2.6 million years ago until approximately 11,700 years ago. This means that lions have probably been around for some two-and-a-half million years. Large parts of Africa, incidentally, still exist under conditions certainly similar to the late Pleistocene, while Europe modernised much more quickly. In Africa, huge herbivores still roam the plains while powerful predators stalk the shadows. Of course, this is one of the attractions of Africa, and why millions of First-World tourists flock there every year: to sample the wildness that is long-gone from Europe, the US and other advanced places.

Lions were found throughout Africa (except the Sahara desert and the rainforests of the central areas), the coastal areas of the Arabian peninsula, Greece, Turkey, Asia-Minor and right down to the southern tip of India, and are thought to have even populated Italy, France, Spain, Britain and other parts of Europe, the last

European one probably killed between AD80 and AD100. They are considered to have been the most widespread large land mammal after humans until around 10,000 years ago. They now survive in pockets of Africa, mostly in reserves, and in the Gir Forest in Gujarat, on the northwest coast of India. As of 2018 the species is still classified as 'Vulnerable' on the Red List of Threatened Species as compiled by the International Union for Conservation of Nature (IUCN), and has been for some years. The 'Vulnerable' classification falls under the blanket-classification of 'Threatened'. Following this, there is 'Endangered', then 'Critically Endangered' and beyond that, the animal will be extinct.

Carl Linnaeus, the Swede who laid the foundations for the modern scheme of naming species, allocated the scientific name *Panthera Leo* to the lion in 1758. A large lion in the books and writings of early writers carried a default weight of 500lb (227kg), but this is a very large one; a male of 400lb (180kg) is a big animal. Full-grown females average 275lb (125kg) and are considerably shorter on all-fours than males; very large females of up to 400lb (180kg) have however been recorded and are not uncommon in some sub-species. Cage-fat animals can weigh far more than the averages, but in the wild, lions have to work for their meals and do occasionally have to go for some time without food. A weight of 550lb (250kg) for a wild lion is exceptional and larger ones are extremely unusual.

The biggest wild lion ever reliably recorded was shot at Hectorspruit, just south of the Kruger National Park, in South Africa's Eastern Transvaal (now Mpumalanga) in 1936. He weighed 690lb (313kg). I have often been struck by how big the adult male Kruger lions can get, and this must have been a gigantic animal. Incidentally, this huge male was reportedly a man-eater. There is of course the nagging and distinctly uncomfortable possibility that 500lb (227kg) was indeed once an average adult male weight, and hunting in its many forms – trophy shooting, poaching, capture for the Roman games – has eliminated large individuals to the point that 400lb (180kg) is large today.

In defence of humans, though, Sir Alfred Pease wrote in 1914 – when lions were still considered vermin – that a male lion exceeding 400lb (180kg) in weight was very heavy and a 500lb (227kg) specimen uncommon. Still, the mass-exterminations of the past may have had an effect. This would be the same reason that huge tuskers are far rarer in modern times than they were a century or two ago. That said, nature knows how to replenish itself and although the world-record tusk sizes are from a long time ago, the biggest elephants themselves, at least, are still being recorded in modern times: the record elephant in body size was shot in Angola in 1956. In this same vein, there are enormous lions about in Botswana, and in Kruger, to this day.

Lions are primarily nocturnal, but are often crepuscular (primarily active around dawn and dusk). In East Africa, they commonly operate by day or night, with hyenas seeming to rule the night in areas, whereas in Botswana and in South Africa, lions are mostly nocturnal. Again, they are adaptable, and unique regional circumstances further affect this. By night they transform and back down for nothing, where by day they may give way to people and other species. It is a well-documented, interesting and disturbing transformation. There were originally thought to be twelve recent sub-species, based on old zoo classifications that tended towards physical appearance. Before 2017, eight were recognised:

- *Panthera leo persica (the Asiatic Lion or Indian lion) - once widespread from Turkey, across Southwest Asia, to Pakistan, India, and even as far as Bangladesh. Around 400 remain in and near the Gir Forest of far northwest India. Their ancestors are thought to have split from the ancestors of sub-Saharan African lions between 203 thousand and 74 thousand years ago, according to genetic evidence; the default-quoted time is 100 thousand years back.*
- *P. l. leo (the Barbary lion) - originally ranged from Morocco to Egypt. Hunted to extinction in the wild, the Romans took literally thousands from the wilds for their gladiator games. The last wild one was killed in Morocco in 1922. This was thought to be the largest of the lion sub-species, with reported lengths of 3.0–3.3m (10–11ft) and weights exceeding 440lb (200kg) for males. They appear to be more closely related to the Asiatic rather than sub-Saharan lions. There are some in captivity, particularly the 90 animals descended from the Moroccan Royal collection at Rabat Zoo, and these have been subjected to intensive DNA research.*
- *P. l. senegalensis (the West African lion) - found in western Africa, this sub-species ranges from*

Senegal to the Central African Republic. Early in 2014, the BBC carried an article suggesting that this once-widespread sub-species is now critically endangered.

- *P. l. azandica (the northeast Congo Lion) - rare, dwells in the north-eastern parts of the Congo.*
- *P. l. nubica (the East African, Nubian or Maasai lion) - found from Ethiopia and Kenya down throughout Tanzania and to Mozambique; the Tsavo lions are a local population of these.*
- *P. l. bleyenberghi (the South West African or Katanga lion) - ranges from south-western Africa, Namibia, Botswana, Angola, Katanga (Democratic Republic of the Congo), to Zambia and Zimbabwe. These are large well-muscled lions, especially in Botswana's Okavango region where they often need to swim short distances in the wet season and where buffalo form a large part of their diet. It is also these lions that occasionally prey on elephants.*
- *P. l. krugeri (the Transvaal or southeast African lion) - found in the Transvaal region of south-eastern Africa, including the Kruger National Park. These too are robust animals; the largest wild lion ever measured was one of these.*
- *P. l. melanochaita (the Cape lion) became extinct in the wild around 1860. Recent DNA research indicates that this is not actually a distinct subspecies. What was thought to be the Cape lion was likely the southernmost population of P. l. krugeri.*

So, the eighth sub-species isn't considered distinct, which leaves seven. In their defence though, Per Christiansen found that using skull morphology allowed him to identify the subspecies krugeri, nubica, persica, and senegalensis, while there was overlap between bleyenberghi with senegalensis and krugeri. The Asiatic lion (persica) was the most distinctive, and *the Cape lion had characteristics allying it more with P. l. persica than the other sub-Saharan lions* (my italics). He had analysed 58 lion skulls in three European museums. So the seven sub-species may be eight anyway, and could soon become nine: In late 2012, researchers studying fifteen lions in captivity in Addis Ababa (Ethiopia) determined them to be genetically unique and that this likely extended to their wild source population. These lions - the males apparently have a distinctly dark and luxuriant mane - were incidentally owned by the late Haile Selassie I of Ethiopia. Of note, one of these killed their keeper on 16 September 2013. The BBC reported it online on the following day. The keeper, a 51-year-old man, had forgotten to close the door to the inner cage where the seven-year-old lion sleeps. This was apparently the second such occurrence in the past seventeen years.

Then in 2017, The Cat Classification Taskforce of the Cat Specialist Group decided that the Asian population, the West, Central and North African lions could be grouped together as *P.l. leo*, grouping the Southern and East African populations together as *P.l. melanochaita*. This is based on genetic research and now differentiates between the following:

- *North African lion (leo) – comprised of the nubica and somaliensis sub-species;*
- *Asiatic lion (leo) – formerly known as persica;*
- *West African lion (leo) – formerly senegalensis;*
- *Central African lion (leo) – formerly azandica;*
- *leo-cross-melanochaita – genetically mixed populations from northern Kenya and Northeast Africa;*
- *The (now extinct) Cape lion – melanochaita;*
- *East African lion (melanochaita) – formerly massaica, sabakiensis, roosevelti, nyanzae, hollisteri and webbiensis; and*
- *Southern African lion (melanochaita) – formerly bleyenberghi and krugeri.*

Confused yet? Me too; or rather, not confused, but baffled as to why…obviously all lion subspecies eventually roll up to *P.l. leo*, right? So, will this process be undertaken again every few years, until we either do indeed roll them all up – which sadly as the wild populations diminish, may be most reflective (look, there's a lion!); or we drill down into the minutest details to differentiate between a lion within its territory, which is minisculely different to the one in the next county, due to the different minerals in the soil in this valley as opposed to that in the one alongside, and thus causing tiny differences due to the minerals ingested via the prey species?

Leave it be now, for Pete's sake! In fairness, this does make scientific sense at least; genetic connection would be closest, and it stands to reason that the Kruger and Katanga lions for instance are most closely related, as they are easily and visibly the biggest sub-species.

The footage and photographs I have seen of Barbary lions seem to indicate that they can have large measurements – tall, almost gangly stance at times, and considerable length – but tend not to match the bulk of the Kruger and Katanga lions. This may be a feature of their distribution: desert elephants tend to be tall, to be that slight bit above the heat of the desert floor, whereas forest species are small so as to better negotiate the hemmed-in jungle paths. The Barbary lions lived in the semi-desert areas. They did occasionally have immense manes, which is strange: recent study shows that the maneless Tsavo lions appear to have lost their manes over time as an adaptation to the heat, not the thorn scrub they frequent. The Kruger lions are at times truly massive, with 500lb (227kg) males and 400lb (180kg) females commonplace, while the documentaries by Dereck and Beverley Joubert show the lion prides in the north of Botswana to be extremely well-muscled. These Okavango and Chobe lions spend considerable time negotiating their way between islands in the wet season of the delta, often swimming, and commonly hunt buffalo. Some even take elephants and the less-bulky lions elsewhere would never risk that. Again, the species adapts to local conditions.

When I left school, two friends and I spent some weeks in the world-famous Kruger National Park. One day at a remote waterhole – I have no recall of which one – we were delighted to see, perhaps just ten meters (33ft) from our car, a lioness and a large cub. They were lying between us and the water's edge. The clump of shrubbery in which they were lying was slightly elevated above the water, which was perhaps 15-20 metres (50-66ft) further from us, beyond the lions. A herd of waterbuck were lazily traipsing by, meandering in that way antelope have when they are relaxed and contentedly feeding. The lioness appeared to be teaching the cub to hunt, as it was of an age that would suggest that, being large but still young. The inexperienced cub rushed out and spooked the waterbuck, clumsily and noisily betraying its presence way too soon. The lioness was visibly annoyed, castigating the cub in sneering snarls of lionese and even cuffing it.

After a while everything settled again. Knowing that we may see a predation, we sat tight. The tension became more and more tangible. I don't quite recall what we did, perhaps switching the engine on, maybe rustling a food packet, either of which would have admittedly been careless; I'd like to imagine that we weren't that stupid and a shift in a seating position resulted in a creak or bump. Regardless, it was us that broke the tension the second time. I will never forget the look the lioness shot at us. It positively dripped distaste. Sheer hatred would be a better description. To be fair, she may have been battling all day before our arrival to teach the wayward cub and by then had been thoroughly fed-up. But it was more than disdain or irritation. She seemed to look right through us while looking at us. I had heard the term and read of it in books, but until that day had never experienced it.

Gordon Cundill, the prolific lion hunter and safari operator, wrote that "*a lion will often not deign to recognise your presence. He seems to look right past you, and if he does look at you, it seems that he is focussed on an object some distance behind you. If you are foolish enough to provoke him, it is his eyes that you will remember if you are fortunate enough to survive the experience*". How right he was; the stare can be casual or relaxed, but when they give you THAT stare, the predatory stare, the one that has your spine crawling, it says only one thing: that animal is going to kill me, and probably eat me. Is this yet another legacy that harks back to the distant, frightening past? I think so; Gerrie Camacho, renowned carnivore scientist at Mpumalanga Parks Board in South Africa, says that you *know* when they look at you when they want you for food. It is a petrifying feeling.

Many naturalists, particularly in recent times, have dismissed the lion as a mean, dirty, unimpressive animal, especially those people actually studying other species in the field. This is understandable. Lions don't have the glossy coats of leopards, for instance, due to several factors. Pride life means competition for food, which gets heated over a kill. Scratches, cuts and the like proliferate on a lion's coat. Leopards - those quintessential cats - spend considerable time in trees, especially where they share areas with lions. This ability to rise above that leopards possess, means that lions also tend to fight more with hyenas than leopards do. The increased exposure to thorn scrub takes its toll on lion skin too. They have been described as the dog of the cat family, and tend to care less about their grooming than do other cats. Life as a lion is hard: fewer than 50 percent survive their first year.

Another factor is that lions tend to remove competition, being the top predator, so people studying hyenas, wild dogs, leopards, cheetahs (and certainly the prey animals), can and often do see their subject killed before their eyes. It's our human reaction to a perceived bully; noble kings of beasts are not the description that many such naturalists would attribute to lions. With the hunting of lions much scarcer nowadays, far fewer naturalists get to see the animal's true fighting spirit. This is a defining factor, and has resulted in the lion's stock dropping exponentially over the past 20-30 years. Study lions though, and one's respect for them increases exponentially. They have a truly tough life, males especially. Dereck Joubert noted that what seems to be a needless collage of hardships is just another part of the life of lions. When ejected from a pride, males wander for several years, usually from the age of 18 months or two years old, until they take over their own pride, aged five or six years.

This interim period is immensely tough and many don't survive it. If they are sufficiently lucky to be two, three or more individuals of the same age when ejected, they can band together and eventually have a far greater chance of ensuring a takeover based on numbers alone. Naturally, two lions are better than one, and three better than two. That relation can't however go on forever; where four lions take over a pride with two or three pride males, for instance, the four often split again into two pairs and set up their own prides. But it is during these tough bachelor years that a male does the hard yards, where he earns the right to appear lazy once he is at the helm of his own pride. Young males have to endure attacks by hyena clans and other prides. Without the protection of a pride and the hunting benefits of the group, they have to learn to hunt and learn fast, just to survive.

And hunt they can; a common misconception is that large male lions are too big and heavy to hunt. This is utter nonsense. In a pride they tend to let the lionesses hunt, and this appears to be what humans would consider lazy, but it's really just efficiency, and perhaps fuelled by memories of suffering as a wandering young lion, males may feel they earn the free meals for the protection they provide. I have come across a giraffe with four young males feeding on it, having pulled it down. This is no easy task. Males do contribute to the hunting; in Botswana the males help the pride when the buffalo herds return to the area. The size and power of the males make a visible difference when one watches these hunts and are often the difference between a large buffalo bull going down or not.

The other crucial male function – aside from keeping the boisterous teenagers in line – is protecting the pride against hyenas and attempted takeovers by rival males; it is well-documented how new males bring the females into oestrus by killing existing cubs. So male lions earn their stripes, one might say, although they will never get to wear them. An interesting aside to this time in a young male's life, is how many man-eaters are of this age, and not the old infirm lions of legend. Starving yes; that often brings the animal to sample a person. But old and injured? Not often. Harry Wolhuter noted in his brilliant *Memories of a Game Ranger* (compiled into book form from his diary field notes in 1948) when dealing with two man-eaters near Skukuza – the capital of the Kruger National Park – that he was surprised to discover that both were two young lions not yet in their prime.

He felt sure that the reason they killed their victim – an elderly woman – was that she had blundered into them on exiting her hut, and in their excitement, having tasted blood, they ate her. Wolhuter remarked that had they not been eliminated immediately (he shot both), that they would have become two immensely dangerous animals. This supports the argument that once the initial fear of man is overcome and the ease noted with which the meal was gathered, the animal becomes deadly-dangerous. Although he was found to have an abscess beneath a molar, the Rufiji lion of Tanzania was found to be just three and a half when shot. His pain may have added to his crankiness but his youth suggests that he may have started killing people in this starving young lion phase.

Thus, hunger can contribute to people-processing by these young male lions, near fully-grown and thus easily able to overpower a person, and desperate enough to try anything. Affecting a lion's prey animal populations, by whichever means, can thus greatly add to this danger. Lions are now that endangered that all wild ones (indeed, all big cat species) need to be protected as a priority. The situation is approaching that which exists for the great tuskers in the Kruger and other reserves: a few rangers monitor them by staying reasonably close, 24 hours a day. All wild prides should enjoy similar monitoring. Happily, many already do. This cannot be funded by the current game reserve financial budgetary setup. The protection of such organisations as LIONAID and PAWCT is crucial now. But it isn't enough. Private funding is desperately needed. There is another solution, and it's covered in the next chapter.

4   How does a lion become a man-eater?

Man-eating in lions appears to be initiated by one or more of several means. The traditional view, to this day in some circles, is that man-eating lions (as well as tigers, leopards, bears, and any other large terrestrial predator) are crippled, injured, old, toothless or otherwise worn-down lumps that can't hunt their natural prey, often due to nasty hunters putting a bullet into them. When John Henry Patterson published *The Man-Eaters of Tsavo* in 1907 many of these theorists started to shift uncomfortably in their seats. The Tsavo lions were both maneless males, in tremendous shape, in the blush of youth and featuring glossy coats, a feature that has since been noted of regular man-eaters.

Peter Hathaway Capstick, the American professional hunter, animal cropping officer and renowned author, wrote in his celebrated first book, *Death in the Long Grass* (St. Martin's Press, 1977) that one reason for early explorers considering man-eaters to be "mangy brutes" had more to do with human psychology than fact. Most people have considerable difficulty processing the thought that mere animals actually consider us as food on a regular basis. As Capstick goes on to show, research on the health of known lion man-eaters by Peter Turnbull-Kemp, the South African writer and ex-ranger, indicated that 91 percent of the killers were in "good" or "fair" condition when killed, regardless of age. Just over 13 percent were "aged", and fewer than 5 percent were "aged" AND "injured" in any way. Infirm animals may well turn to people as easier to catch; but it isn't the deciding factor.

Jim Corbett, who shot the two cats with the greatest totals of human victims in India in the early part of the 20th century (a tigress and a leopard, among several others), can lay claim to being the greatest hunter and killer of man-eating cats in history. He was a gentleman and a master woodsman, having grown up in Nepal and the hill country of northern India, and wrote several excellent books on his exploits. A common theme running through his *Man-Eaters of Kumaon* (first published in India in 1944) is that so many of the tigers that became man-eaters had porcupine quills lodged in their chests, jaws and forepaws. This appears to have perpetuated the theory, not least because it is cited as a direct cause for the onset of the bouts of people-processing.

Far be it for me to contradict Corbett, who doubtless saw and experienced this feature of many of the tigers he had to shoot, when they developed a taste for the good citizens of the area. It may be that porcupines are common in Nepal and Northern India. It may be that, at least at that time, the tigers in the area were so fond of them that they risked attacking them more often than in other areas. I don't know; but there have been such terrific scores of people racked up by tigers in India over the centuries that this cannot have been the case for a majority of man-eating tigers. It is more likely just one of several reasons why tigers would start to prey on people.

Corbett theorised that healthy tigers don't consume people as a rule. This sounds sensible. Regardless, it does illustrate the distinct difference between tigers - which are largely solitary - and lions, which at times thrive as a collective, but seem to suffer exponentially during lean times. With lions, many seem to start eating people in times of extreme hunger, whereas Corbett clearly conveys in all his books how tigers are largely peaceable until wounds by gunshot or porcupine flick a switch, as it were. The human population explosion – and India is fabled for a huge, burgeoning population – appears to have put the squeeze on tigers until something inevitably snapped. This encroachment by people on the territories of carnivores is probably the overriding catalyst to inevitable clashes; habitat preservation and the elimination of contact between people and large predatory animals is the only way to keep both safe.

Carnivores are opportunists. When I was a child I kept a small brown house snake for a Boy Scout project. I had to keep it for several weeks, feed it, record its habits, maintain a photograph record of it and the like. As the snake is indigenous to South Africa I was able to catch its food outside, mostly juvenile skinks and geckos. Ideally, the little snake was to eat perhaps once a week. I became quite adept at hitting the little lizards, just enough to stun them so that they were still alive, but that I could grab them, to be carried to the container where the baby snake lay waiting.

One day I managed to catch four lizards, maybe an hour apart. So, all four went down the hatch; the snake ate all four. Animals don't plan shopping lists, so they have to eat when opportunities present themselves. The point I'm trying to make, is that carnivorous animals will eat when they can. And the great cats are master opportunists. Leopards in particular survive to this day in far greater numbers than the documentaries would have you believe, even in large cities. Lions have the curiosity and opportunistic mind specific to all cats, and will take advantage of chaos and chance, especially if something's going to walk down their throats.

In days gone, people weren't always buried deep in the ground, or incinerated. In poorer communities in particular, corpses were often just left in the bush, to be cleaned up by hyenas and vultures. Many still are, to this day. Lions aren't averse to scavenging, and doubtless they have done their share of corpse-disposal. When Arab traders discovered Africa's East coast and the slave trade opened up, perhaps in spates even thousands of years ago, the number of people who died along the route will have been staggering. Slave traders traversed great distances inland to feed the demand for labour and few of those that died *en route*, if any, will have been interred at all. Dennis Ikanda, a researcher from northern Tanzania who worked with lion expert Craig Packer, believes that the first slave caravans moved through the area around 2AD and that because of this, humans have formed part of the natural prey for lions in the area for centuries.

All of these factors amount to teaching wild animals that people are food. It won't take a lion very long to work out that the moving, ambulatory versions of *Homo sapiens* are edible too. People often come across lions in the bush and are killed for a number of reasons. A lioness with cubs, for instance, has no sense of humour and will naturally attack people that she perceives pose a threat. A mating pair of lions is also extremely volatile and likely to attack. Usually, these attacks are for protection or out of fear, but should a lion happen to be extremely hungry, it may take a bite (Sir Alfred Pease wrote most entertainingly in his early-1900s prose that *"...a lion when he is hungry is so very dreadfully hungry – the awful ravening pangs of his inside pass man's understanding..."*). Does this mean that all lions are man-eaters? Of course not. Does it make all lions *potential* man-eaters? Absolutely.

Lions, like many animals, can adapt to conditions and events, and have some capacity to learn. A term common in many studies of man-eating by various species, is "lost their fear of man". This is indeed a critical factor. The late Australian "Crocodile Hunter" and conservationist, Steve Irwin, considered that of all his large saltwater crocodiles at Australia Zoo, in Queensland's Beerwah area to the north of Brisbane, the most dangerous was the one he'd helped hatch himself decades before, a large male who'd never been afraid of Steve. They say familiarity breeds contempt, and nowhere is this more the case than with large predatory animals and people.

While I was writing this, a case was reported in the major media networks in March 2013 where a 24-year-old volunteer intern at a private big cat park had been killed by a four-year-old male lion near Fresno, California. The poor woman was doing her dream job, according to her father. The lion broke her neck with his initial swipe and the animal had to be shot after further mauling her. The lion - named Couscous - had been raised at the sanctuary since he was eight weeks old. The intern was not allowed inside the lion's cage but apparently the animal slipped a paw under a gate that was not completely shut, and lifted it easily. Would a wild lion have done this? Maybe; even probably. But this one was used to humans, and it did.

Where did this original fear come from? Before primitive humans and lions started to compete for food and space, when we were still very much on the menu, our larger brain was the key to survival and eventual pre-eminence as the dominant species on the planet. Primitive man devised weapons and tactics to defend himself and his family. These methods were refined but largely remained the same for centuries, and centred on such stabbing and thrusting weapons as spears, lances, swords and arrows. Over time lions grew to recognise people as dangerous and we moved down the menu, if not completely off it. With the invention of firearms our position was further strengthened.

I have myself watched what can only be described as naked panic on the part of lions, when they see Maasai approaching in Kenya's Maasai Mara. The very sight of the red blankets worn by the *morani* (warriors) injects an urgency into the lions which is admirable, considering their default daytime lethargy, and I have seen the same in countless documentaries in Tanzania's Serengeti. This can only be brought about by the knowledge that these upright red beings are *coming*, that this is no idle threat; they are going to plunge steel lances into the body that burn like fire and eventually kill.

A breakthrough occurred in 1904 in the mystery as to why lions may eat us: the first signs that man-eating may result from specific conditions that people may be able to affect and change, appeared. In Rutshuru, near the Congo's (now the Democratic Republic of the Congo) eastern border with Uganda, a prevalence of man-eating lions coincided with a marked reduction in herds of topi and kob, antelope that are endemic to the area and which form a large part of the diet of lions in that part of Africa. It makes sense that depletion of natural prey species in a given area may induce an increase in man-eating, but it was documented and proven here for the first time.

In South Africa's Kruger National Park, man-eating by lions can over time only be described as prolific. That is detailed in its own chapter; but certain activities seem to have tipped the odds in the lions' favour. Back when the reach for empire was at its peak, the colonial powers declared lions and leopards as vermin, to be shot on sight due to the damage – actual or perceived – that they wrought on the livestock of the budding colonies of farmers. South Africa was no different. In fairness, the damage was more real than perceived. Stock animals are far easier to catch than antelope, and they are neatly stored in *kraals* for easy shopping convenience!

During 1922, large-scale cattle-farming was commenced north of the Sabi River, on a block of farms known as the Sabi Ranch, in the far northeast of the country. In 1926, the Kruger National Park was created from the merging of the Sabi and Shingwedzi Game Reserves. The first rangers had their work cut out protecting the cattle from the depredations of lions: the park boundaries were demarcated by occasional piles of stones. The great park warden James Stevenson-Hamilton hired the assistance of among others, the phenomenal Harold Trollope – more on him later – to control the depredations.

Trollope was that effective that he eliminated lions from entire regions. For extended periods of time thereafter, relative calm reigned. The lions learned to scoot when they spotted people. Have we, in our modern throes of preservation, actually made it worse for ourselves by eroding the reasons that lions fear people? Circumstances would suggest so. For the record, a preservationist allows nothing to be killed. Everything survives in a utopia. A conservationist actively manages areas for the common good. The old migratory routes are forever closed to animals. The seven billion-plus people on planet earth are here to stay, and increase. Wild animals now survive in pockets. These pockets need active human management, conservation; without it, the animals populating these pockets die out.

Man-eating activity by lions appears to worsen during rainy weather. When there are pools of standing water, the game herds don't accumulate around the usual watering spots and lions have to work harder for their food. This is further exacerbated in areas that are thinly wooded, or with extensive large plains, as herd animals can spot predators from far away and avoid them. In desperation, those lions that may never have considered man-eating can be forced into the practice. A recent study in Tanzania showed the attacks on people spiking with the rainy weather.

There is also a possibility that some lions are casual man-eaters; that would mean an animal that includes an occasional human in its diet. In rainy weather, such casual killers may find it easy to drop by a village for a snack. This is a known and documented dietary possibility for man-eating leopards, the ultimate opportunistic feline predator. They seem to continue eating their usual fare after becoming known people-eaters. It does however seem less likely with lions, as historical tendencies seem to suggest that once a lion becomes a man-eater, he seems to prefer human flesh to any other.

This can be partly explained by the fact that a lion is lazy; lions spend 18-20 hours out of each day sleeping. Perhaps 'lazy' isn't the right word though. Their high-protein meat diet means they spend far less time foraging than herbivores do. Energy-efficient may be a better description. Or just plain intelligent. Look at it this way; why would you risk life and limb tackling such formidable foes as buffalo when there is much softer fare freely available that put up very little comparable resistance? There are of course just as many stories of emaciated and injured lions that had easy access to people and never even made an attack from easy proximity, let alone took a bite. Different strokes, I guess…call it lucky for us.

Recent research in East Africa indicates that darkness plays a huge part in man-eating activity. Ecologist Craig Packer, a lion expert from the University of Minnesota (Twin Cities) and probably the world's foremost lion conservationist, pored over data compiled from 1978 until well into the new century, on attacks by lions on people in Tanzania. He and his team visited 450 sites and interviewed survivors and families of deceased victims. Nearly all attacks occurred after dark, 60% of these having taken place between 6pm and 9.45pm. But most striking was that attacks were up to four times more likely on the 10 nights after full-moon.

This goes some way to explaining our fear of the dark and the mythology surrounding the full moon. But it also clearly shows the adaptability and learning ability of big cats that hunt people. Between 6pm and 9.45pm it is dark, but people are still active. So, attacks then are understandable; but such a spike in the dark nights is impressive. To support this theory, a study of depredations by tigers on people in Nepal was carried out by Charles McDougal, biologist for the International Trust for Nature Conservation (UK), over the past three decades. It revealed that most attacks occur *by day*, because people in Nepal - not unreasonably - flatly avoid the forests by night! Further south however, in India, a rash of man-eating by leopards followed the same patterns of darkness in the ten days following full moon.

Interesting developments came to light in National Geographic Channel's recent series of documentaries, *Maneater Manhunt*. One of these centred on the Rufiji lion, which racked up a tally of at least 40 souls before being anchored in 2004. What researcher Gordon Buchanan found on his motion-tripped video cameras was that a lot of the crop-raiding in the area is perpetrated by bush pigs. These are definitely potential lion prey and can explain why lions might be in the crop fields, only to suddenly be encountered by people shouting, clanging pots and clutching firebrands. This will usually work to frighten off lions as well as bush pigs, but for a lion that is already a man-eater, it is akin to ringing the dinner bell. Lions will quickly learn that crop-raiding bush pigs lead to human prey. Even for lions that aren't man-eaters, a sudden appearance of shouting people can illicit an attack out of fear, and presto, you have a man-killer, as distinct from a man-eater.

From this, one of two things can lead to the next step of consumption; the animal may be extremely hungry, and start feeding, or it may kill then run, remembering just how easy it was to overcome a person. But another key factor that dawned on scientists and was later mentioned by Buchanan was that large areas of Tanzania – and many other African countries – are Islamist. So bush pigs, which elsewhere in Africa would form part of local people's diet, are strictly taboo as stock animals for consumption. They are therefore far more common in the Rufiji area than in many other parts of rural Africa, and their nightly search for food results in them raiding crops more often. Trailing behind them are large groups of lions.

One exception I do however take with the National Geographic series, is their insistence that predation on humans is abnormal behaviour. They are a conservation / preservation network and exist because of the fluffy love they help generate for the world's wildlife, so I get why. But as this book will show, consuming humans is far more normal behaviour than anyone would like to admit. As

I've tried to stress before, a lion - like any predator - is adaptable, opportunistic and able to learn. Consider, for instance, the habits of lions in different regions of Africa. In Botswana, there are prides that hunt hippos. This can only be learned from previous generations, as most other lions throughout Africa don't hunt hippo. There are even prides that specialise in hunting elephants in Botswana, and not just the babies. The world-renowned filmmakers Dereck and Beverley Joubert first documented this and showed it to a sceptical public. It was true, and shocking, but again is uncommon in most of Africa.

African fatalism is another contributing factor to predation on people by lions. The bush African has a baffling propensity to shrug and say, "It was his time" when a community member is killed by wildlife. Throughout Africa, the number of people taken by crocodiles from river banks is immeasurable, every year. As crocs usually take their prey into the water, no trace is ever found of hundreds, perhaps thousands, of people annually. From the banks of the swirling, gurgling coffee-brown waters of the Umfolozi (in South Africa's KwaZulu-Natal region) to the Nile, people will regularly go to fill buckets from the very spot where a relative was killed just days before. Likewise, people are often lax when a man-eating cat is about.

This boggles the Western mind, but to be fair to the rural people for whom the natural water sources take the place of taps and indoor plumbing in Western homes, what else can they do? It does however make the job of a man-eating animal easier. One would think that watching, hearing or even hearing of the death of an immediate community member would bring about some radical behavioural changes to avoid a repeat. Avoiding the exact spot where a croc has just taken someone would be a good start. They should certainly be more disciplined about building secure doors and keeping them shut, as well as not spending too much time out after dark. To the uninitiated, this is just another dose of Africa, I guess...

We are fed hour after successive hour of preservationist rot on the satellite documentary channels on what sweet, gentle and loving animals the large predators are. There are scores of big cats in captivity and held as pets in the United States alone, often more than the entire surviving wild populations. Tigers, for instance, are considered to number between just 3,000 and 4,000 individuals in the wild (down from 100,000 at the start of the 20th century), and

China alone has more than 4,000 specimens officially in captivity. Add the illegal tiger farms and the number swells to over 10,000.

The USA in 2005 had an estimated 4,692 captive tigers. A 2011 census by the US-based Feline Conservation Federation counted 2,884 tigers in 468 American facilities. There are thought to be over 1,000 lions in similar captivity, but judging by the number of captive tigers, this figure seems conservative. Provided they are official, and properly funded and run, these institutions are unquestionably essential in the survival of the world's big cat populations, especially those in serious risk of extinction such as the Amur leopard and Siberian tiger. But part of this situation at least has been caused by the constant panic-stricken message of impending extinction. People try anything to save the creature from dying out.

The documentary channels show programs where big cat rescue teams relieve obviously cash-strapped owners of their "pet" charges and relocate them to properly-equipped conservation institutions. Many of these owners refuse the assistance, claiming that their "babies" won't be able to survive without them. As post-scripts to the shows, most note that within a couple of months the owners almost always relent, and allow the cats to be transferred. Just as well, as the pigheadedness of some of the owners is just plain infuriating. Two things are disturbing here: one, the tendency of people to consider these large predatory carnivores as pets; and two, that they are able to acquire them in the first place.

I myself investigated the possible purchase of a leopard, largely in jest in conjunction with my daughter in order to torment my wife, when we were considering a move to the United Arab Emirates; but eventually I was curious to see how feasible it was. There are several sites on the internet where buying such exotic animals as big cats, monkeys, antelope, crocodiles, even elephants, is possible. This is in addition to the usual fare of just about any species of snake or lizard you'd fancy, from the largest constrictors to such lethal venomous niceties as cobras and mambas. No problem, was the general reply; if you have the money, the formalities are easily attended to. This sort of demand also fuels the illicit trade in exotic animals, which is rightly banned. Consider the realities of this; based on documentaries, baby leopards are exceedingly cute and of course can develop into a loving, faithful pet. Right? Maybe not; I spoke with an acquaintance who shall remain nameless, who kept a baby leopard and eventually had to hand it over to a game farm. It ribboned the inside of his house; bit and tore and chewed *everything*.

In the past, leopards, of all the big cats, were thought to make the worst pets as they were thought to eventually turn savage. This was actually good. Recent documentaries have shown that leopards can be peaceable companions, often for many years. But any animal can have a bad day and play too rough. And with big cats, that only needs to happen once. At least 27 people were killed or injured by tigers in the United States between 1998 and 2001. The bottom line is, these animals are born killers, and are not pets by any stretch of the imagination. The only advantage we have over them is an in-bred fear of us that the cats have from time immemorial. Once that is eroded, or dispelled, and they realise what physical jokes we are, the ruse is over.

David Doubilet, the famous underwater photographer whose work has often adorned the pages of the National Geographic among others, said during the documentary on Great White sharks *Great White Deep Trouble* (2000) that we humans love our monsters. Again, this is a good thing and in stark contrast to the fear-driven reaction to exterminate the things that bite which pervaded in colonial times. But protecting them does not mean getting too close and trying to make pets of these animals. The point I'm trying to make is that we mustn't stumble over ourselves to throw our arms around these creatures, desperate to protect them, and then wonder why we occasionally have our heads removed. Robert Frump wrote in *The Man-eaters of Eden* (2006) that a hundred years ago, lions were considered God-cursed in South Africa's Kruger National Park; the danger now is the swing to the opposite end: today they are seen as blessed by God and ready to lie down with lambs. Good luck to the lambs…

In August 2013 a tragic story played out wherein two little brothers, aged 6 and 4, were killed by a 4.3m (14ft) African rock python in Campbellton, New Brunswick, in Canada. The boys were sleeping in the living room of a friend above a pet shop and the serpent was initially thought to have escaped its cage. It later turned out the creature was a pet and the investigation is underway as I write this. The bottom line is that two little boys are now dead; no play over, no start again; dead. And if the snake was a pet, that just underlines my point: large predatory animals are indeed beautiful, are indeed stunning to look at, and are impressive and spectacular. But they are NOT pets. They are hardwired to kill. The two little guys were buried in a single casket as their parents wanted the "inseparable" pair buried together.

The people who know me may laugh at this next statement, but it should be illegal for ordinary citizens to keep large predatory animals as pets, large constrictors included, worldwide. The reason some may find this rich, is that we ourselves kept a Burmese python as a pet. But I can make that statement with inside knowledge; Burmese pythons are popular among herpetologists as they are docile, breed well in captivity and are quite frankly, stunningly beautiful. But there's a catch; with large predators there's always a catch. Burmese pythons grow to over 6 metres (20ft) in length and over 100kg in weight (220lb). In captivity, they have even been known to reach 7m (23ft). As in all the large constrictor species, the females are larger than the males.

When we bought our python, she was 48cm long and just 2 weeks old. We wanted a female because large female Burmese can lay as many as 100 eggs at a time. It's a lucrative business: the babies sell like wildfire, especially in Africa with its high crime rate, where they make excellent 'watchdogs': most people are petrified of snakes. When we had friends visit, or people viewing the house when we sold it, people often refused to enter our home, because there was a snake inside, caged though she always was. We sold her at the age of 19 months. She was 2.7m (9ft) long and already, when returning her to her glass cage after feeding, she showed occasional signs of extreme crankiness. We had two small children in the house and had two small dogs as well, and we made the executive decision to sell her before we regretted it.

The whole joke around owning reptiles is the number of loopholes around the laws. In Africa, no license is required for non-indigenous animals. So, we couldn't own an African rock python, for instance, as that was indigenous, but could get a Burmese (or an anaconda, or a reticulated python) as these aren't indigenous. As the ongoing disaster in the Florida everglades has shown, people often dump large exotic (non-indigenous) constrictors that grow too large to handle, into the (foreign) environment. The everglades are inundated with Burmese pythons. They have no natural enemies there. As a result, they are thriving and consuming local wildlife at a rapid rate.

Regardless, what is in place to prevent accidents once the animals grow big enough to kill people? The green anaconda and reticulated python are the two biggest constrictors in the world and are also the crankiest. Keeping one as a pet is an accident waiting to happen. True, most would rightly say that the owners of huge constrictors are foolish and deserve what's coming to them, they

39

know the risks. But they should not be allowed to obtain them in the first place. No little child deserves to pay for a parent's stupidity or rashness, surely. Preserving or conserving predators by clutching them close to our breasts does not work, and merely endangers us. There are more intelligent ways, and more effective methods, to ensure the survival of people and carnivores.

The hunting of big game has developed into one of the world's most controversial subjects. Contrary to popular pulp documentaries, controlled hunting is actually the most effective mechanism of animal conservation. By the time he wrote his fourth book (*Safari: the Last Adventure*, St Martin's Press, 1984) Peter Capstick found that he didn't have to sell hunting anything like as much as he had in his first two books. By 1984 it was a widely-acknowledged fact that properly-controlled hunting was justifiable as the proven best method of conservation. Sadly, in this Google generation, I feel I may have to sell it again, although most readers of this genre won't require convincing.

So, hear me out, for those new to the concept. It is a fact that hunting conserves ecosystems and species infinitely better than preservation. It has been proven throughout Africa a thousand times and it continues to be proven on an ongoing basis. Kenya banned commercial hunting in 1973, and the poaching of elephants sky-rocketed to levels previously not seen. Why? Because commercial hunting assists conservation as does no other practice, and the banning thereof can be catastrophic. And here's another strange but compelling argument; *controlled, ethical* hunting helps to save predator populations, and even assists in preventing man-eating. It works as follows:

The government - or other landowner - grants a large piece of land, known as a hunting concession, to an operator. This can be done in "blocks" of time - where the operating safari firm leases hunting rights to companies - or to a single concessionaire over a period. The block system survives in bits in Tanzania but is largely no longer used. These concepts involve the leasing of a large portion of land to provide economic benefit, in other words they are the utilisation of a resource. The ultimate such scenario is to ensure that the resource is sustainable, much like commercial farming. The lessee naturally pays an enormous amount for this right, usually in the form of an annual fee to the government or other owner, and a percentage of profits from the activities conducted. The concessionaire has to maintain roads and prevent poaching, much like an extension of the game department. Most often the owner is the operator as well, where the landowner owns the game. These are common in South Africa and are known as *jagplase* in Afrikaans - hunting ranches.

Many of these in South Africa – which ran and still runs the practice more successfully than any other African nation – were originally private commercial farms, parts of which have been reclaimed for wildlife management. Yes, the wealthy farmers were usually the only individuals with the wherewithal and under the white-minority South African government in place from 1948–1994, the only ones granted such land. But they were also the only ones capable of successfully running such a venture from an economic perspective. They too have evolved to benefit rural development and Afrocentric approaches to sustained communities. This is critical in making the entire system beneficial to all parties involved, animals included.

The concession farmers then populate the area with game, such as many antelope species, giraffe, zebras, and the "Big 5" classic game animals. These last-mentioned are not the biggest animals, but rather the five considered the most dangerous to hunt by the old explorers, ivory hunters and professional hunters: the lion, leopard, elephant, black rhinoceros and Cape buffalo. Originally, this list was actually a Big 4, the leopard not even considered a dangerous game animal until ethical hunting standards were introduced. Under these conditions, where the animal has a sporting chance, the leopard is a very dangerous prospect indeed.

Such wildlife ranches are vital in game conservation. The buffalo in the Kruger National Park, for instance, were ravaged by bovine tuberculosis (TB) and foot-and-mouth disease. Discovered in buffalo in Kruger in 1990, bovine TB is an airborne bacterial disease that devastates buffalo herds, which carry it for long periods. It widely contaminates other species, including lion, leopard, baboon, cheetah, eland, oryx, bongo, waterbuck, sable and kudu. Bovine TB probably arrived with the European settlers as it was first reported in domestic cattle in 1880 and in wildlife in the Eastern Cape in 1928. Lindsay Hunt, a hunter turned conservationist, now breeds TB-free buffalo at two separate locations in South Africa for relocation and sale into Kruger and other areas. He has managed to establish TB-free herds in all nine South African provinces. Many others do similar work on other species.

As regards hunting, let me clarify *ethical* hunting. The world's large hunting bodies dictate ethical standards, which condemn canned hunting, hunting at night with powerful spot-lights, hunting from the back of vehicles and the like. These ethical standards are strictly adhered to by professional hunters. As Capstick wrote in his foreword to *Death in the Long Grass*, anyone can murder a bull elephant from 200 yards using telescopic sights over open ground. Ditto any of the other members of the Big 5. But get into the sort of cover that can be found throughout Africa, where visibility is down to feet, not metres, and the odds, dear reader, are most distinctly with the animal.

The anti-hunting fraternity condemn hunting as perpetrated by murderers with high-powered rifles; in an interview with the great hunter, author and host of hunting safaris, Gordon Cundill, which incidentally found its way into Sportsmen on Film's *Hunting the African Lion* in the Capstick series, Peter Capstick mentioned this comment while noting sardonically that the rifles always seemed to be high-powered, never low-powered. Cundill, that master linguist, had the perfect answer: "My response to that is to invite them to try it." What most people don't realise is that the hunting of big game, and in particular the Big 5, is a situation in which the human being, even armed with a modern rifle, is at a distinct *disadvantage*, under ethical hunting conditions. It is the hunting of a lightning-quick and lethal animal on the animal's terms and in the animal's territory.

Any of the Big 5 can move far faster than any human ever will, and when they reach you, well that is generally that. So why hunt, I hear the preservationists howl? Because it is the placing of oneself in harm's way, the ultimate challenge against your own wits, courage and reactions, which you are counting on to save your life. As people climb mountains or traverse the Antarctic, hunting provides one of the last great challenges on earth. Ah, but none of these others involve hurting, killing or executing a poor animal. Back to the hunting concession then…and to the term *ethical hunting*…

African countries have experienced population explosions and this shows scant chance of changing in the future. The areas populated by wildlife are dwindling exponentially, to the point where most are now isolated reserves and concession farms. When these are not managed, the game animals are poached to extinction in short order. This is a constantly-proven and indisputable fact. The areas have no form of income, and in those that do such as game reserves, corrupt officials siphoning funds result in the upkeep of basic logistics - such as fencing - falling by the wayside. There is less money for rangers and field security. The burgeoning populations do the rest. And, as previously noted, one of the factors leading lions to consume human beings is the decimation of their natural prey species.

The Big 5 in particular command massive fees as hunting trophies. A scan of the websites of organisations offering hunting safaris reveals that a male lion can command a price of R500,000 or more (approximately US$50,000). The funds generated by controlled hunting easily make the hunting concession a viable sustainable economic entity. Animals no longer have unbroken access to their age-old migratory routes. The fenced conservation areas are thus by their very nature unnatural, and require active management to avoid the destruction or failure of the area, most often from the very creatures within its borders that the area is trying to protect. A golden rule of wildlife management is, the smaller the area involved, the greater the intensity of wildlife management required.

Weighed up against these figures are the (seemingly) even more-impressive ones to be earned from keeping the animals alive. In mid-1980s US Dollar terms, it was thought that a leopard in Londolozi Game Reserve in South Africa would bring in $50,000 a year, which equates to half a million if the cat lived a decade. A lion would bring in $120,000 in ten years. These figures are however relative; a large, well-financed business such as Londolozi can afford to run on a long-term basis. Many of the animals die well short of ten years, due to various reasons. Most of the smaller game farms and hunting concessions – not to mention the odd farmer – don't have the luxury of nurturing an entire ecosystem over several decades, and as is the case in the world of business, some players just aren't planning long-term ventures. Set off against these income figures are the extrapolated costs of maintaining the *status-quo* so that the animals can survive, including staff salaries, fencing and so on.

For example, in South Africa in 1959 and 1960, severe drought in a *mopane veld* area of the old Northern Transvaal (thereafter named the Northern Province, now Limpopo) resulted in the deaths of an average over seven species of 76 percent of the animal populations (sable antelope, blue wildebeest, impala, Burchell's zebra, warthog, kudu and waterbuck). It was shown that incompetent wildlife management resulted in a temporary build-up of populations to such levels that they could not be maintained in the years of lower rainfall. This is obviously catastrophic and indicated that managing the populations would have to be undertaken to make the operations sustainable. One option is pure meat production. But a far more lucrative income-producing avenue is controlled hunting.

As a direct result of safari hunting in the 1990s, Zimbabwe yielded more than US$700 per family per year in the rural communities involved. This is in communities where the average household income is well below US$700 per annum. In 1990, 25 percent of Zimbabwe's total income from agricultural products was from wildlife, alone or in combination with livestock farming. This was of course before the Mugabe factor really began to bite around 1995...

A study of data gathered from South Africa's Limpopo province between 1995 and 1998 for a 4600ha cattle ranch in the *mopane veld* region showed an annual gross income of R4.50 per kg of meat, but a wildlife production system generated R9.88 per kg from hunting, live sales and tourism. The wildlife industry's pinnacle is trophy hunting. South African figures from 1990 show that the 4,000 foreign trophy hunters that visited South Africa each spent an average of R26,000 there. The Limpopo Province alone contributed R48 million a year from foreign trophy hunters between 1983 and 1998. During the year 2000 in South Africa, wild animals to the value of R63 million were sold at auctions, and in 2001 this figure rose to R87 million.

In 1998, South Africa's income from foreign hunters alone was R55 million. Germans, Spanish, Japanese, Italian and American hunters make up the vast majority of the annual migration to sample African big game hunting, with the Americans providing the bulk of this. The most sought-after animals to hunt are in order of preference (excluding antelope): lion, elephant, leopard, black rhinoceros and curiously, crocodile. The annual turnover of the entire hunting industry in 2001 was R840 million, a huge figure. Around 60 percent of this was generated by local hunters. By 2009, the figures were even more impressive: around 9,500 foreign hunters come to South Africa each year. Approximately 9,000 privately-owned ranches employing 70,000 people cater to foreign hunters, generating one billion rand annually for the economy. That is well over US$100 million. The industry is unquestionably a productive one.

And here's the beauty of wildlife management: the game is farmed. That means harvesting systems are put in place. A sustained harvesting programme has the explicit aim of removing a fixed annual quota or sustained yield from the population without resulting in a continual decline in that population. This holds for the utilisation of animals to yield venison, or as a source of hunting, or live sales. This is exactly the same as cattle ranching. It just happens to be much more lucrative as it has a trophy hunting aspect as well. By choosing to charge money *for a section of the population that has to be removed anyway*, the game rancher ensures the area's very existence.

Its weak point is human greed; these vast sums erode the boundaries of ethics and people that perhaps would think twice under normal circumstances, exceed quotas and stage canned or arranged hunts. One unethical setup in the US bred jaguars – much like a puppy mill breeds dogs – and arranged jaguar hunts down in Central America. As the hunter stepped off his small charter plane, he'd be informed that he was fabulously lucky, the hunting dogs had just treed a jaguar. The hunter shot it, then returned to the US, often on the very same charter flight! The confused jaguar, to all intents and purposes an animal that had lived all its short life in captivity, had been flown down just before the hunter, released in the concession and naturally made for the safety of the trees when confronted by a pack of hunting dogs.

This was lucrative and most hunters were fooled, but some read the game; the operation was swiftly shut down. Real jaguar hunting requires people with experienced dogs tracking the cat and even so, many of the dogs will be lost to a real, wild jaguar that stretches out the pack and kills his antagonists one by one. Many similar lion hunts have been set up in South Africa, especially as the (usually overzealous) customer is none the wiser. Real lion hunting involves tracking on foot and there is every chance the hunter can be fatally injured. Using game ranches to breed lions that don't hunt but are regularly fed, then provided to clients as wild, is despicable. Gordon Cundill wrote of just such an experience and it smacks of disgrace and poor taste.

The problem seems to be that despite the sky-high hunting fees, lion populations continue to decline. Setting aside tracts of wilderness is the most vital act, which costs far more; and these must then be policed and managed. In late 2013, Botswana announced that hunting would cease, commencing early 2014. This is actually what the wild lion populations most need: five or ten years to recover; but then they will need to be minutely managed, or the numbers will again go into freefall. The possible outcomes from the ban are twofold: 1) driving the "practice" underground (read: poaching), with the rampant market for tiger bones in Asia meaning that countless lions die as a substitute; and 2) the breeding programs flourishing in South Africa especially, where lions are bred for canned hunting. Volunteers are actually lured to Africa to "pat wild lion cubs". Most of these cubs – being familiarised to humans, as well as fed by them, remember – end up being shot in small enclosed areas, from whence the term "canned".

Obviously, no program is sustainable if for instance, a game ranch allowed five lions to be shot each year, in a population of 100 animals, and allowed these to be the five breeding males. There is an exact science in determining quotas, and it must yield the largest possible sustained production. The maximum number of animals allowed to be harvested is known as the maximum sustained yield. Throw in the options of recreation, such as tourism, photographic safaris and green hunting (darting safaris), and the maximum sustained yield is adjusted and extended to become the optimum sustained production or yield. For example, a population with a growth rate of 10 percent a year can endure the removal of 5 percent and still grow at 5 percent a year. This must take into account natural mortalities, including those caused by predators if these are present on a game ranch.

To just know the fixed percentage that can be harvested annually from an animal population is insufficient, however, as this figure will vary from year to year. The number of animals present, their reproductive capacity and mortalities and the habitat's conditions all influence this figure. But all these factors are actually reflected in a population's growth rate, so the growth rate is used to calculate the harvesting quotas. To ensure the maximum sustained yield, it is advisable that herd animals, for instance, not be harvested immediately before, during, or just after the lambing / calving season. Certain facets to this industry, such as this last-mentioned one, are just plain common sense.

For larger mammals, there is proof that keeping populations below the ecological capacity through harvesting results in each remaining member having more environmental resources to utilise during the critical periods of any given year. This improves productivity and further chances of survival for each surviving animal. On a macro level, this same advanced level of game management is employed in the larger game reserves. When it is not properly managed, and corruption results in much-needed funding not being ploughed back into the business, a less-committed workforce that is poorly trained and poorly armed, and indeed smaller than it would ideally be, the animal populations that can be sustained in a given area fall out of synchrony. Animals starve when their population outgrows the area. Poaching inevitably increases as the upkeep of fencing (an extremely costly ongoing expense) is discarded.

In larger reserves, elephants require relocation, and eventually require culling as they destroy vast tracts of wilderness. In the past this was able to recover as their vast migratory routes allowed plenty of time for the bush to grow again. Elephants decimate an enclosed area if left unmanaged. This has a direct influence on the other animal populations in a given area. They can die in huge numbers when their environment is radically altered. As shown earlier, just one of the spin-off problems of that situation is an escalation in attacks by predators on people. It is a fair argument to state that a wounded lion would be a holy terror to people, so hunting can theoretically lead to attacks on people; but hunting ethics demand that wounded animals be followed up and killed immediately, for this very reason. Hunting ethics are imperative, and as already mentioned, the large hunting bodies prescribe these and ensure they are rigidly adhered to. Lions must be wild and must be tracked on foot; any other way of hunting them is totally abhorrent and unacceptable.

It has been argued that the hunting quota system is not an exact science, that the quotas are often exceeded which damages the population. As can be seen from the above, it *is* an exact science, and provided the quotas are adhered to, the system works perfectly. The world's foremost lion conservationist, Craig Packer, has been arguing this exact point for decades, and has been trying - with some success - to convince the governments of East African nations to consider joint ventures and programmes where controlled hunting is used to better conserve game populations, and prevent poaching. A BBC report in March 2013 reported Packer as saying that all wild lions should be fenced, and thus in reserves. I fully concur, as the alternative in southern Tanzania and northern Mozambique, for instance, where wild lions are still found in some numbers outside of reserves, will result in people eventually eradicating the lions while a lot of people will die first. For now, only Botswana seems to be able to sustain its wild lion populations, mainly due to their remoteness.

As with so many things in life, the fact or the answer is usually somewhere in the middle; Craig Packer himself has stated that the hunting fees for the Big 5 – which seem impressive in isolation – are a mere pittance in the grand scheme of things. The sums required to preserve huge tracts of land far outweigh the annual fees for all members of the Big 5, ethically harvested, in any area for a given year. Remember too, that from those fees must then be subtracted the hunter's slice, the employees' slices, vehicle costs, aircraft maintenance and all the other myriad expenses involved in running a hunting safari operation. Very little is left in relative terms to purchase land, and over time as already alluded to, repeatedly skimming the best genetics off a population can't possibly be healthy in the longer term. The answer is preserving land, and urgently, against Africa's staggering human population explosion. Conserving land, overseas donations and educating people are vital, but in the short term, hunting must be included to uplift pockets, if only for set periods of time, before allowing populations to recover.

In Zambia's Luangwa River Valley, the hunting concessions established the Luangwa Integrated Resource Development Project in conjunction with the area's tribal chieftains and ruling councils. The income from the concession's controlled harvesting established economic infrastructure and directly resulted in one of Africa's highest rural standards of living. By 1991 – a mere four years into the initiative – the loss of elephants to poaching was a *total* of 120 animals, where before 1987, the *annual* toll was 3,600. The herd increased by 500 animals a year. The population took pride in resource protection and against poaching, and is a glowing working example of the concession idea, executed properly. So, all this shoots down – excuse the pun – every argument the anti-hunting preservationist-pacifist can muster. Conservation works, preservation does not. Yes, it's ascribing an economic value to something that shouldn't have one, but this is the reality that is modern Africa. This is the real world here and now. Without this, the animals will be gone in a matter of years.

What is vital is the preservation and management of land. Pete Swanepoel of hunting authority *SafariBwana* says the problem is our Western Civilisation's need for space to drive cars, install mobile phone towers and build office blocks. We then sit in our air-conditioned buildings and form animal welfare organisations, gathering donations! The infuriating thing, Pete continues, is the audacity of the eco-activists sitting in Malibu, Palm Beach or even Cape Town, who castigate Africans for poisoning the predators that are consuming their livestock and eating their children. Such people have no right to judge unless they are prepared to go and live among these cats, to know what it feels like to be trapped in a flimsy mud hut with two 500lb predators trying to get in, because you are meat and they want to eat you. As he says, this isn't Hollywood, there is no last-minute rescue, they will kill and eat you.

One stickler however remains; in a society where we try to rehabilitate human mass-murderers, trying to understand their psychology, thereby often subjecting innocent people to further horror, the refusal to kill anything is becoming irrational. Many people say to me, that - proven economic sustainability aside - they couldn't pull the trigger, the killing of another living being in this day and age proving too much for most. Well, that's a personal issue. This book is not intended to convert non-hunters to hunting, any more than their opinions will sway many others away from hunting. But to ensure the survivability of species - such as the wild lion populations - and the economic existence and sustainability of rural communities, does hunting actually work better than pure preservation? Yes; this is not emotion, it's an established and proven economic fact. As an incidental spin-off, does hunting actually help prevent man-eating by lions? To the astonishment of many, by contributing to better wildlife economies and limiting the contact between people and wild lions to fenced reserves and concessions, at least indirectly, yes it does.

5 Tsavo – the cats that halted the Realm

Much has been written about the famous Tsavo lions. With good reason; in the worlds of man-eating, general naturalism and African adventure, they loom large in the nightmares as killers so brazen and so prolific that they became the first animals discussed in the House of Lords. For a few weeks in December 1898, they even brought a halt to the progress of no lesser adversary than the British Empire, which was at the time the world's most powerful. Several events and circumstances surrounding the Tsavo lions dispelled old myths and beliefs. For one, they were maneless males, a phenomenon which is almost unique to the Tsavo region and has since been found to relate to the climate, not as a result of the thorny *nyika* thickets through which Tsavo lions often have to crawl. To this day the area is rock, red sand and thorns, and so hot that breathing is a chore. Secondly, they were relatively young, generally in fine condition and hunted in tandem. Prior to this, man-eating lions were thought to be old, injured and alone, a type of rogue or social outcast, the lion equivalent of a human socially-undesirable.

Most of the story occurred at Tsavo on the Tsavo River in what is now southern Kenya, where the railway would cross by means of a bridge. Today the bridge is still there, and to see it is an anti-climax. To think that so many perished at this juncture, for what by modern standards is a plain little structure, seems to worsen the feeling (the actual bridge itself was blown up by the Germans during the First World War; it was subsequently rebuilt). It is well documented that the name Tsavo means *place of slaughter*, a *Kikimba* word given to the place after massive tribal conflicts resulted in the deaths of many. Disease and fever exacted a toll later, and then the slave caravan leaders noticed the unnerving loss of porters, always in this area.

The terrain is ideal hunting area for lions and they doubtless made a decent living, eating herd animals and people, long before the two Tsavo man-eaters leapt onto Patterson's pages and on to world fame, or rather notoriety. Their story has spawned films, books and research and made a world-wide celebrity of their eventual vanquisher, an Irish military engineer who would actually go on to achieve far greater things, but forever be remembered for this alone. John Henry Patterson was actually instrumental in the eventual formation of Israel by leading their armed forces and fighting for their independence. He was also, just incidentally, very likely a murderer. This may seem a little harsh on the character of the Patterson of legend, but legend can often tint things with rose-coloured glasses.

The incident referred to is known as the Blyth Affair and it has been smeared closed, so to speak, for many decades. It was 1908; Patterson was world-famous by then and the Tsavo lions had garnered him many high-powered friends, not least of which was Theodore Roosevelt, the American ex-president, himself about to undertake a safari that would birth an industry. Another was the great hunter Frederick Courtney Selous, who wrote the foreword to Patterson's *The Man-eaters of Tsavo*, published in 1907 by Macmillan. Ernest Hemingway's famed story, *The short happy life of Francis Macomber*, as well as the film *The Macomber Affair*, are rumoured to be based on the event. This is the official story:

Patterson returned to Africa in 1906 and a year later was made Chief Ranger for the East African Protectorate. He recounted the tale in his second book, *In the grip of the Nyika* (1910). In early 1908 Patterson was sent to perform the initial survey to eventually establish the northern boundary of the Northern Frontier District. He had two high-ranking guests who wished to hunt, James and Ethel Blyth. James's father was the Lord Blyth while Ethel's father was a powerful politician.

James was injured and ill, so he had to be carried and constantly treated, and Patterson soon resented his companions, who were a drag on his official tasks. As Ethel had sat up for several nights with her husband, Patterson had her sleep in his tent to prevent her too perhaps falling ill, while he - Patterson - sat up with James Blyth. Patterson supposedly left the tent when he heard lions, and after checking about he spoke with the headman of the party. Then a shot was heard from Blyth's tent and upon rushing there, Blyth was found with a revolver in his hand and a bullet in his head, victim (supposedly) of his own delirious fever.

The body was interred in the wilderness under heavy stones to prevent predation by scavengers. Following this, Patterson continued on to Marsabit to finish his work, rather than decamp to Nairobi. That April, after an inquest in Nairobi, Patterson was sent home to the UK with enteritis. When the case went before the House of Lords in 1909, Patterson was exonerated. In 1908, a year after *The Man-eaters of Tsavo* had been published, Patterson was invited to New York, the personal guest of Roosevelt, and his letters show that the ex-president's support meant a great deal to him at this time.

Here's the actual version: Patterson's appointment as Chief Ranger in itself raises a red flag, or at least an eyebrow, as his assistant was the then-equally famous Blayney Percival, who was overlooked in favour of Patterson despite being far more qualified for the job. Indeed, he was Kenya's most famed hunter at the time, a time when legendary hunters abounded. This already indicates that political decisions heavily influenced the appointment. Patterson was no hunter, despite having killed the Tsavo lions; his ineptitude at times during that episode beggars belief and he was extremely lucky, on several occasions. Patterson's account of the events is largely as it was, except that rumours abounded of a possible love affair between Patterson and Mrs Blyth, and that Patterson may have had a hand in James Blyth's death. These rumours reached the police, who sent an officer to backtrack the safari.

With the help of the trackers and other staff that were on safari with the party, the body was found and exhumed. The wound in the *back* of the skull was caused by a heavy-calibre hunting rifle, indicating murder, and in no way a suicide. There was no court case and both Patterson and Ethel had - somewhat conveniently - already left the country. In his 1990 book *Into Africa: the story of the East African safari*, Kenneth Cameron wrote that Ernest Hemingway's famous professional hunter in 1933, Philip Percival, told Hemingway the story incriminating Patterson, which prompted the writing of *The short happy life of Francis Macomber* (nothing to do with the Dr Macomber who was mauled in 1968, incidentally). Philip Percival was the younger brother of Blayney. Was this an attempt to ruin Patterson by a man bearing a grudge, a man who had been made subservient to someone infinitely less qualified? Perhaps; but the skull wound is most damning evidence. To this day there is no reason why the police or the British Government laid no charges. The glory of Empire, and all that...

Back to the lions; the Uganda Railway (fondly known as the Lunatic Line or Lunatic Express) was built between 1896 and 1901, starting from Mombasa on the east coast, through British East Africa, to Uganda. An Imperial project built during the mad colonial scramble for Africa, it allowed Britain a strategic foothold. It was named for its ultimate destination but its 1,000+km (actual length 660miles) traversed entirely through what would become Kenya, and ended at Kisumu on the shore of Lake Victoria. It helped suppress slavery by vastly reducing the need to utilise manpower in transporting goods, but on the other hand was utilised for the ivory trade. By 1898, the line reached Tsavo.

In writing the introduction to the October 1996 reprint of *The Man-eaters of Tsavo* by Pocket Books, Jeanne Dixon commended Patterson for his account of the lion details in his book. At the time, the tendencies of hunting writers were mostly to recount their adventures in unassuming, modest prose. If anything, they watered down the dangers, the statistics and the hardships encountered. Any attempts to be more descriptive, or to describe in flowery prose what had happened, were dismissed as bombastic, boorish, self-centred and clumsy. Dixon, who had access to Patterson's diaries and letters, noted that Patterson did omit his softer side from the book, which is a pity as it is very much in evidence in his private writings. Modern readers would perhaps warm to him more, whereas he comes across as far less engaging. The time, however, demanded it.

His account of his labourers' uprisings and squabbles make for interesting reading and by today's standards, make him seem cruel, ruthless and severe. Remember however that these events happened in 1898, when there were defined masters and labourers, in no uncertain terms. But both Dixon and Selous note that the book's account on the habits and details of the lions match his diary and if anything, are conservative. Recent research on the Tsavo man-eaters considers the total deaths to be nowhere near the 100-140 often quoted, considering this to merely be part of the legend, and place it at around 35 souls, excluding the native victims. Regardless, far fewer than 130 total. Patterson quotes 28 Indian victims and "scores of African natives of whom no record was kept."

I disagree with this modern line of thinking. The number could well be as high as it was originally thought, due to two crystal-clear reasons: one, no-one actually knows how many people such prolific killers disposed of, as record-keeping in virgin territory back in 1898 was impossible, and as Capstick so often emphasised, the very nature of man-eating means that your evidence is often removed altogether. Secondly, modern scholars openly admit to the key words "excluding native victims." Read the book, and the sheer number of nights where Patterson mentions attacks and killings make the total likely to exceed a hundred people. Having just made a serious dent in the credibility of Patterson's overall character in previous paragraphs, let me bat for his side by also stating that

Selous – and if anyone in history knew of such matters, it was him – considered none of it to be far-fetched.

Wikipedia contains the two following fascinating paragraphs regarding the number of victims:

The two lion specimens in Chicago's Field Museum are known as FMNH 23970 (killed December 9, 1898) and FMNH 23969 (killed December 29, 1898). Recent studies have been made upon the isotopic signature analysis of Δ13C and Nitrogen-15 in their bone collagen and hair keratin and published in the Proceedings of the National Academy of Sciences USA. Using realistic assumptions on the consumable tissue per victim, lion energetic needs, and their assimilation efficiencies, researchers compared the man-eaters' Δ13C signatures to various reference standards: Tsavo lions with normal (wildlife) diets, grazers and browsers from Tsavo East and Tsavo West, and the skeletal remains of Taita people from the early 20th century. This analysis estimated that FMNH 23969 ate the equivalent of 10.5 humans and that FMNH 23970 ate 24.2 humans. This leads to the conclusion that the lower number of 35 victims is more likely and that Patterson exaggerated his claims (though this claim doesn't take into account the people that were killed, but not eaten by the animals).

However, an earlier (2001) study by Tom Gnoske and Julian Kerbis Peterhans, published in the Journal of the East African Natural History Society, contended that a human toll of 100 or more was possible. The diet of the victims would also affect their isotopic signature. A low meat diet would produce a signature more typical of herbivores in the victims, affecting the outcome of the test. This research also excludes, but does not disprove, the claims that the lions were not eating the victims they killed but merely killing just to be killing. Similar claims have been made of other wildlife predators.

Just incidentally, Peterhans and Gnoske consider the main reasons that lions eat people to be because 1) they can, and 2) they always have. This reflects the opinion of Dennis Ikanda, who maintains that we have formed part of the diet of lions since we started sharing space with them. I can't argue.

Consider the observations of John Taylor in *Maneaters and Marauders* (published in 1959 by Frederick Muller, reprinted by Safari Press in 2005); all the way up Africa's east coast – from Mozambique in the south east, up through Tanzania and then Kenya beyond that – there runs a belt of impenetrable thorn scrub.

There are occasional gaps, especially where the burgeoning population has claimed land for cultivation, but any lapse in the agriculture results in nature rapidly reclaiming the land for this thorn belt. As there is precious-little grass in this area, it is not game-rich. Bushbuck and bush pigs proliferate, but not much else. Oh, and there are lions; lots of them. Lions love pigs. But what mystified Taylor was the fact that, were the lions to merely move a few miles inland, they would have a rich selection of plentiful game. Instead, as Taylor mentions, they regularly take to man-eating. This shows disturbing support for the theory of Peterhans and Gnoske. No stretch of this thorn belt is free of man-eating lions for long.

It is also obvious from Patterson's book that the two Tsavo culprits started out as reasonably inexperienced man-eaters and learned over time to be lethally effective. Initially, one of the two would snatch a person from the dwelling compound, and the other joined him to feed outside, but later, the second one would make its own kills as well. Their fine condition when eventually shot, lends further credibility to the theory of young wandering males that adapt to a food source over time. As for many other man-eating cats in history, these too may have had their careers curtailed far earlier had they not been possessed of some incredible luck. It also gives a chilling insight into what can develop if known man-eaters are not eliminated immediately. Add the more superstitious time and population involved, and the two were readily accorded the endearing term of *shaitani*, or devils. The term *the ghost and the darkness* – also the title of the 1996 Paramount Pictures film starring Michael Douglas and Val Kilmer – seems to have been given to the two as one was light coloured, the other darker. There is no such evidence in Patterson's books and the term must have arisen as pulp fiction. The skins on the mounts in the field museum are no darker or lighter than the average lions.

An interesting new dimension to the causes of man-eating activity emerged with the Tsavo lions. The first two possible causes were well known, the third an intriguing addition. Firstly, the 1898 *rinderpest* epidemic, or cattle plague, devastated the region's herd animals. The second factor – the dead from the slave caravans being dumped at the crossing of the River Tsavo – has been mentioned. Third, the dead of the Hindu railroad workers usually being granted abbreviated cremation, was akin to serving dinner to hungry lions. The practice involves placing a live coal in the mouth of the deceased, and taking for granted that the corpse will self-cremate. Of course, it doesn't, and just abetted the lions to consume more people. It is also a sad factor in the staggering numbers of people killed and eaten in India by tigers and leopards.

Patterson noted another interesting point that was verified by several people at the time, and since: the habit of a man-eating lion to lick the skin off a human victim with its rasp-like tongue, so as to access the fresh blood beneath. The animal then tends to suck the blood out of the muscles. This is disturbing enough, but another observation he made is positively chilling: lions obviously so enjoy soft human flesh once conditioned to it that they purr in pleasure as they crunch human bones. To the listening labourers, unarmed and helpless to do anything other than wait their turn, this must have been mortifying to listen to.

Whatever his failings, Patterson was unquestionably a brave man. Since night-time pursuit was out of the question, he spent days following up the lions through the man-high thorn scrub, many times having to be extracted when hopelessly entangled, by his men. One glance at this area will tell anyone at all that a lion holds all the cards here. To merely say that hunting a lion in Tsavo is difficult as everything is in the animal's favour, just doesn't do it justice. In places it is a maze, with visibility down to a few feet. What's more, Patterson wasn't just after two mere lions, but two confirmed man-eaters that showed no fear or respect of people. That fear can give the hunter the edge, the millisecond of time he needs. It is perhaps as well for Patterson that he never got near enough for a proper confrontation.

Patterson sat up nights in trees, in shelters, in railway wagons. Nothing would work, and the simple act of always avoiding him added to the supernatural aura surrounding the lions. In practical terms though, the work area and railhead were so far removed from the dwelling tents that one man could never hope to cover the distance, and with their brilliant night-vision, the lions could avoid him easily on those nights when they happened upon him. The film *The Ghost and the Darkness* has a chilling sequence where the view is afforded from the lion's perspective. The night is well-lit by moonlight, but there is a blanket of fog about, just to exacerbate matters. The men have a baboon tied to a stake, firstly to warn them of the approaching lion, and secondly so that the lion will grab it in their stead should it attack, based on the theory that lions detest the noise a baboon makes.

The sequence never took place in actual fact, although the theory is sound, but it's the lion's night vision that is the most noteworthy.

A baboon has daytime vision equivalent to eight-power binoculars, although its night vision is not much better than ours. In the film it can see as much as the men, that being very little, while the lion looks on with every detail stark, defined and obvious. Although it's only a supposed equivalent of what a lion might see, it can't be far from the actual and would be sobering in the extreme for anyone watching the film, before heading out into lion country at night. On 1 December 1898, tired of being eaten, the majority of the workers stopped the next train out of Tsavo and left.

Using a railway coach, and following a short period of respite from the lions, Patterson set about building an ingenious trap. He divided the coach into two sections, a sliding door entrance at the one end to admit men, and a veritable wall of iron rails only three inches apart cutting them off from the other section, which was to admit the lion. Once he entered, a trip-wire would cause a barrier of rails six inches apart to fall into a groove between two rails behind him, with the rails embedded in the ground. He could thus not reopen the door. Patterson then completed the ruse by pitching a tent over the coach and building a strong *boma* – thorn barricade – to channel the lion toward the entrance. All went to plan, Patterson spending some fruitless nights in the bait / hunter side, before two of his men were cured of indigestion for life while spending their time in the trap: one of the lions tripped the wire.

Each of the two *sepoys* had been provided with a Martini rifle (a powerful British colonial service weapon in circulation in the late 1800s, of heavy .577 calibre necked down to .450, to lower the powder pressure) and sufficient rounds. So unnerved were they when the lion launched himself against the bars though, that for several minutes they declined to fire. They seemed to come to their senses when shouted upon however, but began to fire wildly, even at right-angles to the lion, Patterson and his companion having bullets whizz by them outside. At length and after a fair bombardment, one of their bullets struck the suspended rail door behind the man-eater, knocking a bar off and the lion, no fool he, departed. He had been lightly wounded while caught like a rat in a trap, a bit of blood on the ground outside reflecting this. The flames of supernatural belief were obviously fanned that night!

This sort of escape seems to characterise many of the prolific man-eating cats of the past centuries. Some of the good fortune enjoyed by the Rudraprayag leopard that Jim Corbett eventually shot, for instance, was downright spooky. As often alluded to, the cats seem to be able to adapt to the prey being hunted, and since we are cleverer in our avoidance than their standard fare, they become cleverer in their means around that. Whatever the reason, Patterson had been ridiculed by several supposed experts upon constructing his trap, and although it had worked, he still had two lions at large. As Michael Douglas' character in the 1996 film remarks, it - the trap - was still a good idea.

If the workers thought the lions were spirits, Patterson himself began to wonder after his next foray. He endured a misfire with a borrowed rifle while literally metres from one of the two lions, but was spared when the approaching beaters' cacophony scared the cat off before it could turn him into victim number next. Too late Patterson realised he had a second barrel and fired it as an afterthought, actually hitting the lion but not seriously. How well was the message drummed into an extremely lucky Patterson: never use an untried weapon when hunting, on any game, much less on two of the very deadliest animals in the world. Patterson eventually managed to kill the first lion on 9 December 1898. It was that very night after his misfire, and his luck changed, although he had to endure an even more drawn-out agony of fear before he could at last celebrate.

Patterson built a *machan*, a shooting platform often used in India, and sat up over the carcass of a partially-eaten donkey. The night was, of course, again an inky black. It was a risky move to put it mildly; he was basically human bait, as any man-eating lion will prefer human flesh to animal if given the choice. Also, a *machan* has to be small enough to be practical, but the 12-foot (3.5 metres) tall structure is the height of a large male lion's reach without even leaping. Before long Patterson was to regret his exposed position as the lion spotted him, evidenced by a blood-curdling snarl. It then spent some considerable time circling the scaffolding - Patterson mentions two hours - no doubt trying to work this new structure out. If the lion had known how flimsy the perch was, Patterson Sahib would have been another name on the list of victims and we'd have read someone else's book. Even ten minutes would be a lifetime in this situation, so if Patterson did overestimate the time, one could forgive him. If not, well then raise your hats to the man.

At length he could just make out a tawny blob and pulled the trigger, the roars and general mayhem accompanied by wild leaps telling him that he'd hit the target. He blazed away at the spot where the lion disappeared into the undergrowth and eventually felt that the groans and sighs indicated its likely demise. The labourers shouted to Patterson after the shooting had stopped, and he told them –

somewhat prematurely, I felt, given previous events – that one of the lions was dead. The men came bearing torches and singing, bowing and dancing and generally exalting Patterson. He wouldn't let them follow up the lion until morning, which was wise, but when they did they found the first Tsavo man-eater, stone-dead. He was nine feet, eight inches (293cm) long and three feet, nine inches (115cm) tall at the shoulder, a big lion.

The other lion showed himself again in the next few weeks and seemed keen to appease his taste for Uganda Railway workers. When he attacked a tree with several of Patterson's men in it, Patterson fired in the general direction, as the night was its usual shade of impossible-to-see. The lion left and Patterson sat up in the same tree the next night, with Mahina, his gun-bearer. Mercifully, it was a cloudless, moonlit night and far easier to see than the few previous. Patterson took first watch and then woke Mahina for his turn, dozing off himself shortly afterward, only to awaken to a strange feeling that something was wrong. Many have written of this sixth sense in the presence of dangerous game, another reference back to the days when we were just prey. Military personnel in the combat zones develop the sense too but it's much more prevalent in the bush around animals.

Capstick opined that the sense appears to be advanced in people after only a short time in the bush, and much more so than in animals. I have experienced it several times; as Capstick says, it's seldom if ever wrong and I have always found it profoundly disturbing, mainly because I know that when I feel it, there's a problem. John Taylor wrote in *Maneaters and Marauders* that this sense was always accurate, provided one took heed of it and acted on it. He had never known it to fail, and after years of experience even relied upon the sense to direct exactly where the danger was situated. Interestingly, Taylor considered the sense to be highly developed in white men after a time in the bush, while the Africans usually seemed blissfully unaware of danger.

To his credit, Mahina was wide-awake and had not noticed anything. Patterson looked too and saw nothing, and was about to settle back when he spotted the second lion. It was using every scrap of cover and Patterson couldn't help but marvel at the liquid muscle despite the bats fluttering in his stomach and the horror creeping up his spine to settle with a tingling in his scalp. He waited, wisely, until it was just 20 yards (18 metres) distant before firing his .303, the bullet audibly smacking into the lion's chest. To his surprise, the cat merely growled and bounded away, and Patterson shot thrice more, the last bullet too hitting home as evidenced by another growl.

When dawn broke they followed him up, the blood spoor plentiful and easy to track. After 400 meters or so (a quarter-mile or 440 yards) they received a snarl and Patterson fired three more times as soon as he could see the lion. The second shot bowled the cat over but he was immediately on his feet again, and kept coming. Reaching for the heavier Martini carbine, Patterson aged another few years in a moment when his fist closed on thin air: it transpired that Mahina was already up a tree, shaken at the lion's ability to absorb rounds and continue his attack.

Patterson joined him and again his luck was in, this time definitively: one of his shots had broken a hind leg, failing which he'd have been a dead man. He made it up the tree not a moment too soon. The lion turned for the cover again but Patterson had by now seized the Martini and dropped the lion at its first shot. For some unexplained reason he then approached the animal, and when it sprang back up and made for him yet again, he anchored it with two more shots. This second lion was even bigger, and in total it had taken ten bullets to kill him. He was two inches shorter in length than the first but over two inches taller at the shoulder and far heavier. Like his companion his skin was luxuriant, but deeply scored by *boma* thorns. To Patterson's amazement, and the workers' horror, these two lions had time and again managed to get through impassable *bomas* without a sound, and back again with a human body in tow.

It was all Patterson could do to prevent the ecstatic workers from tearing the animal into tiny chunks. The consternation, terror, loss and hatred the labourers must have felt could finally be put to rest. The majority of the labourers returned and it was just as well: the works had been stalled for three weeks and were completed just before the rains came. Patterson watched with a sense of pride as the temporary crossings were washed downriver, only a day or so after the bridge was finished. The whole project was that close to being ruined, and the loss of life would have been for nothing.

Patterson kept the skulls and the skins of the two man-eaters of Tsavo for 25 years, finally selling them to the Field Museum in Chicago for US$5,000 in 1924 (an equivalent in 2012 to US$66,500). Given the taxidermy of the day, and the fact that the skins were understandably tatty after a quarter-century as carpets, the museum had to make do when mounting them. They were put on display in 1928 and have been a major drawcard for the museum ever since. The result seems disappointing and is far smaller than the real animals were. At least we have Patterson's photos, which give better perspective. They were large, deadly animals. Even in their deaths they make a statement as to their grisly careers: it is likely that every visible millimetre on these two cats is recycled human protein.

6   Njombe – the most prolific killers

Whereas the Tsavo lions are world-famous and have been for over a century, the Njombe man-eaters have only recently started to gain the recognition that is due them. Their story is truly and frighteningly African, even for people that have lived on that continent for all their lives. It features not only some concentrated man-eating activity by an entire pride of lions, compared to which even the Tsavo lions were truly amateurs, but also the mysterious black-magic of lycanthropy. It is a hunting experience without parallel in history and leaves you with a crawling sense of dread, because some of the events are quite unexplainable. This is what happened.

When George Rushby marched into the warden's office at the game department in Arusha in October 1938, it was to accept a post of ranger on elephant control in Tanganyika's Eastern Province. George was thirty-eight and in those short years had already accomplished enough to fill three lives. The warden, Philip Teare, was on leave but he met with the deputy warden, Major Jock Minnery. Minnery explained what the job would entail and gave George his first task, a small sideline issue of containing the *rinderpest* epidemic at Iringa in the Southern Province. The South Africans and Rhodesians were concerned that the outbreak would spread south and infect the domestic herds. Minnery told Rushby to have a good look at the game, destroy anything that looked sick and report back to the game department. He then rounded the discussion off with the following interesting sentences:

The proper ranger of the Southern Province, Dusty Arundell, is away on leave. In any case, this type of work is not really a ranger's affair. A ranger is fully employed on his normal duties. Arundell also has some special problems on his hands in the Njombe district. The lions there seem to have a tendency to eat people.

Although the Second World War would interrupt before George could get to the Njombe district, his life was about to reach a high-point, which in a life of high points would mean a considerable zenith.

* * *

George Rushby was born in Nottingham, England in February 1900. The family moved to Eastwood where his father died while George was still an infant. His mother remarried but his step-father was a drunk and a bully, whom Rushby hated. He largely grew up with a band of gypsies that camped on their grounds. The men taught him to box, and to poach game. His father had left him some wildlife books on Africa and the young George developed a dream to go and hunt there. He found himself in South Africa in May 1920, made his way to Durban in time for his twenty-first birthday and after a short period without work was employed as an electrical mechanic. Two months later he took work up the east coast in Lourenço Marques (now Maputo). Just two months on again, he made for Beira, the next major port up the coast.

It was here that he first hunted, providing meat for the constructors building the railway, then for the British-controlled Sena Sugar Estate. When he came across his first elephants, he was hypnotised. They were so interesting to watch that George was fascinated. When he shot a human night intruder dead, the local estate manager thought it prudent if George disappeared into Nyasaland (now Malawi) for a time, despite George being totally justified and acting in self-defence. The Portuguese officials were rather prickly to Brits at the time and were likely to make life difficult for him. George did as advised. To support himself, he shot a few elephants for their ivory and then started providing colobus monkey skins to a trader. When the pelt market collapsed, George tried his luck in the Congo as an ivory hunter, effectively poaching; the annual permitted haul was insufficient to survive on.

He then became a barman / bouncer before returning to England for a few weeks to see his family. By May 1923 he was back in Africa, and en route to the Lupa Goldfields. He took a Tanganyika Government license to help control elephants, a relaxed attempt at limiting hunters while cropping the vast and damaging elephant herds. For some years George was a successful ivory hunter, evading officials easily enough and well-liked by the locals to whom his haul of tuskers provided copious piles of meat. Suffering eventually from a heavy dose of Blackwater fever – a legacy of constant repeated sessions of malaria – George made once more for England, eventually recovering sufficiently to realise that he was no longer an Englishman at heart. He needed to get back to Africa.

Waiting for his ship to Cape Town, George met Eileen Graham who had come to England from Cape Town itself to study music. She gave him details of someone there and mentioned the meeting to her contact as well, so George couldn't wheedle out of meeting her! He was to eventually prove grateful: the contact was Eleanor Leslie, a pretty girl who was waiting to meet him when he docked in June 1930. They had a whirlwind romance and after breaking the news to her difficult father, intended getting married and farming coffee in the Mbeya area of Tanganyika. This was the only career that the formidable George Rushby was to be less than successful at, but the weather and the world market prices were more at fault than he was.

The farm Mchewe Estate was pleasant enough but any farming is risky and George's Blue Mountain seedlings – one of the very best types of coffee – endured borer beetles, drought and other difficulties before George had to supplement his dwindling funds by providing his services as a white hunter. By now George and Eleanor had grown into a little family and George moved them all up to the Lupa Goldfields for a time. Next the enterprising George tried his hand at guano gathering. With malaria a constant threat, the three children accompanied Eleanor to Cape Town in 1937, eldest daughter Ann and George Jnr staying with Eleanor's parents until the end of the year while Eleanor returned to Mbeya with Kate. George's mother arrived from England at the end of 1937 to take the two eldest children over to the Old Country with her.

And so on to Arusha in 1938 where George took work as a Tanganyikan ranger. George's first duty in 1938 was to visit the Dar es Salaam rural district commissioner. The records at Nzasa made for interesting reading, not least for the general concession regarding man-eating cats. There were nine known man-eating lions operating in that area in 1936, six were speared or shot to death, a seventh killed by a trap gun. There is no mention of the other two lions; presumably they were still at large at the time the report was written. But the way Tom Bulpin conveys the general feeling in the game department at the time in his excellent book on the episode, *The Hunter is Death* (Nelson, 1962), is interesting, and is not necessarily mere African fatalism: man-eating is a ranger's constant bugbear, and "like measles in children" he wrote, is almost to be expected, at least in small doses, as long as lions, leopards and people share space.

The Second World War was declared in 1939 and after some weeks of mobilisation, duties returned to what they had been, sub-Saharan Africa at least terrestrially being one of the few places on the globe that was largely unaffected by the conflict. George and his little family actually spent a pleasant time in Tanganyika during the war years; George had managed to effectively run his district, whipping his rangers into shape and working well with the local communities. The little European community were friendly and from about 1943, once he had a handle on what needed doing, George could actually take the family on his wide-ranging patrols. These veritable safaris were thoroughly enjoyed by the children with the parents' only regret being that the eldest children could not join them.

That was indeed the only blight on that period in their lives, the war making a visit to England quite impossible, and even a trip down Africa's east coast a dangerous gamble: German submarines took a heavy toll on Allied merchant shipping. One of George's duties in 1943 was to report on the chimpanzees at Lake Tanganyika, whose habitat was being decimated by deforestation and logging. His report resulted in the establishment of the Gombe Stream Reserve, later a National Park and subsequently made famous by Jane Goodall's studies of chimpanzees.

The War ended and Captain Monty Moore, a VC no less (recipient of the Victoria Cross, the British Empire's highest award for valour), was made warden for Tanganyika, a job George had stood in for a while. George was given the Southern Highlands Province as his new district, replacing Dusty Arundell. Arundell, Moore told George, couldn't take the festivities that marked the end of the War! That must have been quite a party, although somewhat understandably. Tanganyika, incidentally, was named by the Arabs in Zanzibar – an ages-old slave-trading point – and appropriately means "Where you travel through the wilderness". George Rushby's already massively-eventful life was about to enter its defining phase; when Moore mentioned the area had no relief, George – always up for a new adventure and challenge – mentioned that his district was quiet. Moore bit; the range would be George's.

Right away, George Rushby realised that this was no ordinary assignment. Moore told him about the problems in the district regarding the Njombe man-eating lions, a point George remembered being told from the day he joined back in 1938. The problem originally arose as far back as 1932 and for an incredible nine years, nothing was done about it. Arundell always seemed to be called away to other duties, just as his next task was to shoot the pride responsible. But that was only part of the problem; as Moore told George, lions consuming people was clear-cut. These however seemed to be mixed up "with some jiggery-pokery – witchcraft and all that sort of thing." Moore wasn't fully up to speed on all the details and felt George had better investigate urgently, involving the police if need be. Oh, and he might drop by Singida to find out what he could about the lion-men…

Ah, Africa; the fun never ends. When George had been a forestry officer at Mbulu he had been exposed to the hyena cult of the Mbugwe people; witches owned these animals, rode them by night and even took them as their lovers, some said. So far, to the Western mind, this is all a load of rot, yes? George recounted shooting a few of these animals that seemed to carry some human interference and ornamentation, beads braided into their fur for instance and cut marks in a ritual form. While George was at Mbulu those few years previously, an elderly Indian trader had visited his camp one evening and sought his advice. The Indian kept chickens and one night was aroused by a disturbance in his yard. Finding a hyena that had forced its way through the fence of his chicken coop and was in the process of enjoying its midnight snack, he shot the animal, twice, before returning to his slumbers.

The trouble started the following morning; the trader was awakened to the sounds of loud lamentations and upon going out, discovered an old woman, a well-known local witch, crying over the hyena's body, pouring dust over her head and wailing piteously. When she saw the trader she lost it, generally throwing all proverbial toys and eventually turning the hyena over to reveal her ownership mark on its shoulder. She demanded the trader explain what the creature had done to warrant having to shoot it. The Indian replied that it had been consuming his chickens. The witch threatened to kill him by witchcraft, loudly berating him, as she considered the loss of mere chickens as nigh-irrelevant. She would happily have compensated him ten-fold had she known. The little old woman was so beside herself that the Indian had to laugh at her.

At length the old crone gathered the hyena up into her arms – no mean feat in itself – and staggered off, sobbing, down the road. The local people told the trader a short time later that she was half-dead with grief, and the trader laughing at her just conveyed that her magic had no power against his own charms. The Indian wondered what advice George could give him, but George was at a loss. The Mbugwe people that occupied the alkaline flats below the Ufiyome Mountain were considered primitive even by their tribal neighbours, but this gives some idea of just how primitive. A ranger in the area had even shot a hyena that was *wearing a pair of men's khaki shorts*. This seems surreal, but it actually happened.

The Singida district; this area to the south of Mbulu has always been a hotbed of a specific type of *mbojo* – black magic – but not just any old magic. This was lycanthropy, the changing of man into animal and back. Africa has a spate of lycanthropy in its history and from several places on that vast continent. Again, a wily witchdoctor or murderer can easily exploit a situation to suit him by having rivals disappear and getting the word out that a possessed animal under his control was responsible. It's a whole new dimension of magic if one can become that animal, at will. The vast majority of the general populace is so superstitious that one's job is half-done. When I kept a pet python in South Africa around the turn of the century, the indigenous people were petrified. When we helped them conquer their fear, holding the snake so they might touch it and feel the cool, smooth scales – most people still expect a snake to be slimy – they were most concerned that the animal in no way be allowed to look at them, for fear it may curse and hypnotise them. This was *now*, the year 2001.

The famous Tintin series features an interesting piece in the second album ever released, the still-rare *Tintin in the Congo* (Hergé, 1930). Tintin is stalked by a witchdoctor who moonlights as an Aniota, or leopard-man. Hergé used the mount in the Tevuren Museum in Belgium as his guide when drawing the Aniota. The Leopard Society is also covered in Willard Price's *African Adventure* (1963). It was basically a group of hired killers who would hide their deeds by using leopard paws attached to the feet to leave tracks, and steel claws on the hands so that attacks would look like the work of a leopard. The Society was strong in the Congo and all through West Africa, particularly in the regions that are now Nigeria and Sierra Leone. These gang members would go so far as to actually believe that they *were* leopards and could change back and forth at will. Much of this initiation and training may of course have involved ample quantities of dubious herbal substances, either ingested or smoked. Apparently, the cultists believe a special elixir made from their victims' intestines and known as *borfima*, enables them to transform.

Ideally in the lion-human association, the overriding characteristic is an enlightened transformation. The human subject is "lionised", imbued with elevated and ennobling qualities of majesty and rulership: heroism, bravery, the ability to discern love and truth, and of course lion-heartedness. This is however the ideal; human nature being what it is, some accounts are ominous. The transformed can also use his powers towards evil ends. The Africanist researchers Georges Balandier and Jacques Macquet spent years researching a lion-man cult in Chad, in the Sara territory during the 1950s. The cult was named *Ngue tel bogue*, literally "those who change into lions". The initiation was described thus:

Before putting on lion skins, arming themselves with lion claws or hunting harpoons and roaring into their calabash resonators, they had to eat dog meat. An intoxicating drink made them unrecognisable and turned them, in their own and everyone else's estimation, into wild beasts. Some had an additional power, which was acquired by undergoing a more strenuous initiation than that demanded of other lion-men: with the aid of a magic bracelet (and presumably by spreading some vegetable ingredients on the ground, as some Ubangi tribes do), they were able to control real lions at long range, or even cause them to be born. Thus, bolinga, the lion bracelet, supplemented the action of bol-tel, the person "changed" into a lion.

This was therianthropic – half-man half-beast – consciousness at its most primal. In stark contrast to the ennobling qualities of leonine metamorphosis, the tendency has often been towards murder and cannibalism instead. Balandier and Macquet wrote that a candidate could only be accepted if he sacrificed a member of his family - wife, child or relative - to the community. The victim would be dragged down some lonely path, and his throat cut with an iron claw. Some body parts were then set aside for a communal feast. Animal footprints were made around the remains to complete the ruse that an animal had been responsible, and the terror spread by the sect silenced the uninitiated.

Incidentally, Gordon Cundill noted in his book *Some Lions I Have Met* (Rowland Ward, 2007) that the word lycanthropy was unknown to him until he read of it in Peter Capstick's *Maneaters* (St. Martin's Press, 1981). Capstick actually took the word from *The Hunter is Death*, by Bulpin. This is odd because Cundill - a highly educated man and superb linguist - actually mentions that work, but erroneously calls it *Death is the Hunter*, a mistake I've seen several people make. Cundill correctly mentions that the word lycanthropy is technically incorrect when describing human-lion transformation, as the term was coined in Europe for supposed human-wolf transformations. Cundill then said he'd sit back and await Fiona Capstick's response! I'm not sure if Fiona ever did respond, but the actual definition is "a delusion in which one imagines oneself to be a wolf *or other wild animal*" (my italics). The word is thus correctly used and as mentioned, was used by Tom Bulpin nearly twenty years before Capstick did.

Back to the Singida district; the Turu tribe from that area were also primitive and marked by superstition and apathy. The area is characterised by thorn trees with the occasional thorn scrub, ideal lion habitat. Way back before anyone could remember it starting, the usual fare of lions killing people started to be supplemented by a more-or-less constant stream of vicious murders committed by an animalist perversion known as *SimbaMtu*, *MtuSimba* or collectively as *WatuSimba* – lion-men. This was accepted as just part of the community by the twentieth century, and it was widely known that anyone who needed a grudge settled could hire such a killer from its controller. The key to the process is the controller, a witchdoctor or witch. Naturally this extends to witchdoctors that control actual lions. All this had been accepted as normal around Singida but occasionally the murders attracted attention for their sheer number.

In 1920, the world first was alerted to the extent of the problem; over two hundred killings occurred, largely in the Usure (pronounced Oo-soo-reh) area directly next to Singida. The political officer in the area wrote some years later under the name of Captain W. Hichens in the *Wide World* magazine, contributing to the popular feature "The Queer Side of Things". He wrote three articles which gave the lion-men international renown. *Wide World* was an illustrated British monthly publication that was produced from 1898 to 1965. Incidentally, the March 1936 edition featured an article on the leopard-men; a picture of the cover of that edition is included in the photo pages. Hichens wrote that after shooting eight confirmed man-eating lions he came across the phenomenon of witchdoctors practising extortion over the local population, by claiming to control real lions and having murders committed by lion-men to prove their point.

Hichens tracked down a lion after an attack and it turned out to be "a sturdy youth dressed in a lion skin", with lion paws over his hands and feet. He appeared to be heavily drugged with hashish (marijuana). A local witch hired him out for five shillings a murder. He would spring upon a victim, knife them through the heart and then claw the body to resemble a lion attack. The party attacked remained convinced that a real lion had perpetrated the deed. Many people told Hichens that lions were tracked after attacks and the pursuit abandoned in terror when the pug-marks seemingly inexplicably turned to human footprints. In actual fact, lions often use paths frequented by people and *vice-versa*, so the overlapping of prints is not only possible, it's likely. Add the drugged state of the witchdoctors' lackeys, and much of this is just hocus-pocus, right? Hold on a second; there's more, much more…

Consider this little gem from *The Hunter is Death*; it comes from a time long before George Rushby had anything to do with lions, when he was an accomplished ivory hunter. Aside from shooting the odd lion that maybe ventured too close to him or his men, George was otherwise occupied gathering ivory. He actually spent contemporary time with Jim Sutherland, the greatest ivory hunter by volume in history, even surpassing the master for quantity in 1928. Before you balk, remember that this is long before CITES, an over-developed sense of self-righteous morals or modern conservation methods. Ivory hunting was strictly for profit and most of the great ivory hunters – admittedly somewhat ironically – later became the greatest protectors of the great elephant herds. It was in 1926 and George was in the Congo, halfway between Albertville and Kabalo on the Lualaba River. He was thinking about how easily he and other ivory hunters merged into the primitive world around them.

Witchcraft becomes much more potent when you live with it. To his own amusement, George found himself quite believing in paganism while in the bush, shedding it just as easily again when back in civilisation. In his defence though, three times in his career did he have his rifles ritually blessed by the local witchdoctor, and all three times he immediately enjoyed the most fantastic good luck. He mused that the Africans went through the same process in reverse when they returned to the wilderness from the outside world. George noted though that it didn't matter how blasé one might be about it, something always took place that made you wonder…one day sitting at base camp on the Lualaba River, he had a clear view of the circular, well-built hut immediately in front of him, attached to a half-enclosed compound.

In the compound, just 50 feet (15 metres) from George, there squatted a middle-aged man, who faced a wooden idol. The man was quite oblivious of his European observer, fully intent on his supplication. The idol was on a small mat and surrounded by the usual dishes of offerings. As George sipped his tea in his camp chair, he suddenly noticed the idol move its head to the left. After 30 seconds or so it moved its head to the front again. George leaned forward in his chair and watched more intently; twice more the idol looked left, then after a time looked back again. The light was bright; there were no shadows, and no cause for optical illusion. George imagined the head to be movable and possibly turned by an attachment, although he could see no strings and the man was perfectly still, his hands out before him.

After 15 minutes or so the man stood up, rolled up his own mat, picked up the idol with its mat and offerings and made to leave. George wandered over and greeted him, enquiring if something was wrong. The man nodded; his wife was ill, and he had prayed for her healing. George asked to see the idol and the man agreed. The idol was made of solid wood; there was no way the head could have moved, but George was willing to swear before any court of law that he'd clearly seen it move on several occasions. He returned to his camp shaken; he had no fever, his eyes were excellent and his strongest drink in camp was tea. Neither he nor author Bulpin could possibly gain anything from lying about this; how many extra books would one sell based on that information? Nice place, Africa…

George was thoroughly intrigued by Moore's story about the Southern Highlands Province and he firmly believed that well-placed bullets would be the best antidote to these lions. He relished the challenge. He broke the news to Eleanor and to his relief she was happy with the idea, having enjoyed her first home in Tanganyika, despite being terrorised by leopards some nights when George was away. She would be happy to return to the area; the ranger home was in Mbeya. The first problem he encountered was a tendency to stone-faced silence on the part of everyone from scouts to villagers. So petrified was the local population that the lions were not even referred to by that name, in case mentioning them brought them down on the person that had dared breathe their name as the next victim. The scouts never mentioned them unless George pointedly quizzed them on the matter and Dusty Arundell was a particularly poor record-keeper, even by remote government-official standards.

The scouts called them the insects of the bush – *dudu ya porini*. This alerted George that this pride was anything other than the usual fare. If one couldn't even mouth the word "lion", something had to be very wrong. The area terrorised by the Njombe man-eating lions basically was immediately north-east of the very northern tip of Lake Malawi. Where Zambia, Malawi and Tanzania converge, the Great North Road runs in a north-easterly direction (!) from Tunduma to Iringa. The first large town after Tunduma is Mbeya at the foot of the Mbeya Mountains. East of Mbeya is the Kinga Plateau. Immediately to the east of this is a large heart-shaped area, bordered by the Great Ruvaha River to the northwest, the Buhoro Flats in the north, the village of Njombe in the south and the Kipengere Range to the south-west. It was here that the Njombe lions plied their deadly trade for fifteen years.

George was still finding his feet in his new job. He was sifting through what records Dusty Arundell hadn't thrown away in the dusty little office (when Arundell's files filled, he'd simply throw out the oldest documents), when a disturbing telegram arrived from W. Wenban-Smith, the District Commissioner of the Njombe district. George remembered him as the assistant district commissioner at the Dar-es-Salaam rural office when George had taken over the Eastern Province in late 1938. He was level-headed and not prone to exaggeration, so the telegram spoke volumes in two short sentences: "*I beg you to apply earliest attention to man-eaters stop Conditions in this district pathetic.*"

George was wondering why there was such a dearth of information on the man-eaters in his office, while Wenban-Smith found the situation sufficiently desperate as to send so urgent a telegram. He was still wondering when a rude interjection from a dusty, wiry stranger broke his train of thought. The man practically burst into the office, almost shouting abuse at George about the general tendency of game department employees to draw their salaries while doing little else. The man turned out to be the road foreman maintaining the Great North Road, an Afrikaner named Watermeyer, and he calmed down and apologised when he realised that George was not Dusty Arundell. It was perhaps as well for him, as George - who could look after himself - was contemplating clouting the rude fellow in the chops, but on the other hand a fight would perhaps have been most unproductive to both parties: the Afrikaners are not noted for being soft.

Half of Watermeyer's workforce had been eaten by lions and the other half, not surprisingly, had downed tools. Watermeyer almost felt the Government intended keeping the lions alive to keep the human population down; it was now thirteen years since the trouble began and the Njombe man-eaters were still rife, and happily productive. Watermeyer reckoned that the roads department had lost seventeen maintenance staff on the Great North Road in the Njombe district, with no pending replacements. Even people who were looking for work would rather scratch a living than join the maintenance gangs in that area, and somewhat understandably so. George assured Watermeyer that the lions would receive immediate attention.

George knew the Buhoro Flats well and was looking forward to getting stuck into the lions; the rot had continued long enough. One day, he and his orderly Mabemba picked up two elderly African hitch-hikers, always a good source of information, particularly if the travellers are older and knowledgeable in local matters. Mabemba knew the score; when searching for poachers in the Eastern Province, he and George had often used this method to glean information. While George took one of the men into the driving cab, Mabemba took up station in the rear of the truck with the second man. Even if the man with George was shy of Europeans, perhaps Mabemba would have more luck. After the usual small talk, George casually asked whether it was dangerous walking in that area, due to the presence of "creatures of the bush".

Those who have lived in Africa can relate; when a bush African closes his mind to an outsider, it is curious, and not a little annoying, to see the almost physical process. The man's reaction to George's question was a slight hint of fear, and then his face went blank. All he would say was that such things were further on, beyond the Ruvaha River, and that they would not walk there. He seemed to give an almost imperceptible little shudder, so George left it at that. Mabemba too met with a veritable steel-shuttered countenance. It was obvious why the men had reacted in this way; if the man-eaters were indeed were-lions, there was no way of knowing who they were when in human form. An African man would not even discuss such things with his own wife for fear that she may be a were-lion (as in werewolf), and exact revenge on the person mentioning her deeds. Asking the question was dangerous, and the average African would know this; hence the travellers' caution, and guarded response.

At length George decided to make for the Njombe administrative station for information, placed in a most idyllic spot some 80km (50 miles) down a branch track that ran south off the Great North Road. The station was originally founded by *Jumbe* Northcote, and he had been inspired. The little settlement was 6,000 feet (1,800 metres) above sea level, in a world of green grass and misty hills, with a waterfall marking the centre. For a second George thought he was in a European hamlet, but any delusions were shattered upon meeting W. Wenban-Smith; the man's relief that the game department had finally sent assistance was palpable. He unrolled a map of the district and at long last, George could soak up some information. The story was a dismal one.

To Wenban-Smith's knowledge, the killings had started around 1932, and there was no single event to mark this commencement; perhaps a lioness had turned to eating people by chance or due to incapacitation. She could then have passed the taste for people on to successive generations of her cubs. The stories about black magic and lycanthropy were common knowledge, but investigating police had never found any indication that the killers had been anything other than real lions. The remains were indicative of known man-eating by lions, the skin and meat literally licked away by the rasp-like tongues. Since the trouble started, successive district commissioners had done what they could; four well-armed African game scouts were permanently stationed at Njombe. African police also often patrolled the area. But for all that, no lion had yet been shot since the outbreak began.

The terror that permeated the place had infected the game scouts too; when questioned about how no lion was ever successfully followed up and shot, they reported the tracks turning into those of humans, and they would then track no further. The police too had no positive outcomes to their investigations. Wenban-Smith told George that Dusty Arundell had tried to get a hold on the situation, but had been called away on some urgent business, every single time. It was uncanny, as if pre-determined by fate. George's take on the situation was that any witchdoctor could exploit this situation to his heart's content. Then George and Wenban-Smith tried to calculate how many people had already fallen prey to the Njombe man-eaters, and the result was staggering.

It would be difficult to get anything like an accurate figure, but going on what was known, the men tried to piece a total together. It seemed the killings had taken place in three sub-chiefdoms, all three equally troubled over the same time-period: Mtwango, Rujewa and Wangingombe. This covered some 1,500 square miles (3,800 square km), mostly small family units over a spread-out area, with no accurate administration to record casualties. Over time these units banded together into villages for a modicum of protection, even if it was only perceived. The difficulty of determining figures was compounded by the reluctance to talk. Only sub-chief Jifiki – at Wangingombe – kept any sort of record. He was the least superstitious and the best-educated of the three sub-chiefs. Between 1932 and 1940, no record was kept. After an inexplicable lull in the killing in 1940, the lions returned with a vengeance in 1941, and Jifiki started recording the casualties.

Wenban-Smith handed the list to George: in Wangingombe alone, from 1941 to late 1945, there were 230 names on the list. George, not a man to be easily shocked, was staggered. The list excluded casual visitors and travellers, which would have been the easiest to consume, and of which there would be no record. Jifiki considered the eight years before he kept any record to have been equally bad. The neighbouring sub-chiefdoms were at least as heavily-hit, with Rujewa thought to have suffered slightly more than the other two. All of this meant that the total of 1,500 *known* victims had been reached and breached some time before. When the district commissioner saw the expression on George's face, he mentioned that perhaps now George understood the urgency of his telegram. He also hoped aloud that George wouldn't suddenly remember a more pressing appointment...

A shocked George Rushby assured Wenban-Smith that no more important task existed, and none would divert him from addressing the man-eaters of Njombe. The very next day he started a tour of the affected area, intending on gleaning as much information as he could and planning his strategy to kill the pride. For two weeks he traversed the district, driving mostly by night to hopefully get a glimpse of the cats in his headlights, but he never even saw a track. While details of the lions were impossible to obtain from the local populace, the missionaries were a veritable mine of information. Both the Reverend Nordfeldt from the Swedish Lutheran station at Ilembula and the commandant of the Kidugala mission, a Mr Wagner, had vivid tales of the killings, Nordfeldt having even kept a record of the victims. It covered only the previous two years but contained over two hundred names.

One thing the Reverend Nordfeldt mentioned to George resonated: they may look like lions; the Reverend supposed they were lions; but they do not behave like them. Incidentally, just a month previously, a member of the mission had been carried off by a lion in broad daylight. The animal dragged the man into a thorn thicket, where by sheer chance a thorn embedded itself in the lion's face. With a yowl of discomfort, the lion dropped its victim, pawing madly at its face to dislodge the errant thorn. Until then the man had been petrified with shock but when dropped, he began to screech and holler so loudly that the man-eater "took fright and bolted". Not many people have been saved while literally in the jaws of death, by a thorn. While circumstance and the law of averages suggest that there must have been at least some survivors of attacks by the

Njombe lions, there couldn't have been many, and how many of those could attribute their salvation to a thorn can be imagined.

At the Kidugala mission – converted during the Second World War into a Polish refugee camp – people had at least made an attempt to hunt the lions. Two of the Italian prisoners of war were sufficiently trusted to allow them to be armed, and they often sat up nights with Mr Wagner, in tree-*machans*. Wagner had sat up at least two nights each week over an extended period but the only time the lions ever showed up was one night when Wagner was away. When the man-eaters started to climb the tree, the Italians' nerve went and they scrambled into the upper branches, dropping their torches, rifles and other *bric-a-brac* onto the heads of the astonished cats. Wagner rescued them the following morning, still treed and still terrified half to death.

The African population however, had done precisely nothing to fight back against the killers, despite being reasonably well-armed. This infuriated George, the apathy and acceptance that many Africans have totally out of step with a modern Western sense of justice and self-preservation. The one man who attempted to fight back told George that his beloved wife had been killed one evening; a lion brazenly clattered into a group of women in the village street, knocking them flying, and grabbing his wife. It then dragged her into a thicket where several lions set about consuming her. Enraged and grieving, the man grabbed his Tower musket, a muzzle-loading weapon much in use during the British reach for Empire. Not surprisingly, his shout for help from his neighbours fell on deaf ears, so he bravely approached the thicket, from whence emanated the spirit-destroying sounds of his wife being torn to pieces.

Suddenly, a large lioness advanced toward him, with his wife's neatly-severed leg in her mouth, defiance writ large all over her gory countenance as she glared at him with that baleful yellow stare. The man stared back, horrified, and he trembled so much that the percussion cap fell off the old smooth-bore, rendering it useless. The lioness slowly turned her back on him and walked off. As if any were needed, the population considered that as more than enough evidence that these lions were invincible. Panic and fear are crippling and over time can develop into a type of disease; Njombe's residents were slowly dying of it, paralysed into dysfunction. Even the community leaders who would speak of the lions were adamant that hunting them was pointless; not only would no African raise a finger to help, but the people felt that violence against the man-eaters was certain to provoke the cats - or whatever they were - to hideous retribution.

The only sensible African of senior ilk seemed to be Jifiki. Although he believed in the black magic, Wenban-Smith thought that he was younger and better-educated than the other sub-chiefs, and that George should press him for information. One night, in Wangingombe, in the room in which Jifiki held court, George learned the inside story. The trouble had indeed started in 1932; in that year, the headman of Iyayi, a village on the Great North Road, was deposed by his tribal chief on corruption charges. This headman was also a witchdoctor of some repute; his name was Matamula Mangera. It wasn't known whether the man-eating outbreak had already started by then, but complaints only surfaced after the deposition. In short order, a story began circulating on the Buhoro Flats that Matamula owned the lions. They were supposedly kept in a secret place between Igawa and Rujewa, herded by an assistant named Mkakiwa while a second man, Hamisi Sayidi, would take selected lions to commit the killings when instructed by Matamula. The terror would continue until Matamula was reinstated.

Matamula did not claim this to be the situation publically, but every tribesman believed it with absolute conviction. People offered Matamula gifts, currency, anything for mercy; supposedly he'd become enriched by the long-suffering residents, but some were offering sums to have the killing directed against enemies. The lions could not be opposed; they were *simba ya mtu*, were-lions. Some were converted from human beings, others were resurrected corpses. That was the end of Jifiki's tale; he would say no more. When George mentioned the number of victims, and specifically when Wangingombe enjoyed a hiatus in the killings in 1940, Jifiki became hesitant and distant. George pressed him but Jifiki, visibly frightened, left to retire to bed. George returned to Mbeya the following morning with his head full of ideas to eradicate the lions, but he declined to drop by Matamula *en route*; that would be a public acknowledgement of the man's power, confirming it to the people.

As soon as he got to Mbeya, George sent telegrams to all the far reaches of his district, calling in whatever game scouts could be spared. He then wired Monty Moore at game department headquarters, indicating the actual extent of the disaster and requesting as many trap guns as could be obtained. He also told Moore that he would hunt the man-eaters full-time until they were destroyed. A short time later, though, there was one more telegram that he had to send; that was to Wenban-Smith, telling him with deep regret that right on cue he – George – had just received a Government order. It was to drop everything, and attend to an outbreak of locusts in the Rukwa valley. He had to assist the International Red Locust Organisation, and the order was categorical. George had no option.

George was able to return at last by mid-January 1946, two months of locust control now behind him. He selected six of his best scouts to tackle the Njombe man-eaters; two were posted at Wangingombe, two others at a small hamlet called Jumbe Musa's, and the remaining two as floating mercenaries, following up leads on the lions' whereabouts. Meanwhile, twenty trap-guns had arrived from headquarters and George erected them all over the district. They were cleverly placed, and the bait varied, George himself even acting as bait on occasion, but during the entire duration of the long hunt for the man-eaters, no lion ever so much as went near any of the trap-guns. Man-eaters are often wily and as they have to adapt, thinking up clever means to obtain their clever prey, can become fiendishly intelligent. The Njombe lions – the ultimate successful man-eaters – were some of the most adept and seemingly-intelligent lions ever encountered.

A concrete first step would be to estimate the number of lions involved in the outbreak; that would obviously allow for better planning and would indicate how many could still be at large, by monitoring the ongoing attack-rate once some lions had been killed. Lions usually kill by night and rest up nearby in the heat of the day. The Njombe man-eaters did most of their killing in the early evening, but appeared to almost never rest. They would feast and play with their kills throughout the night, but come the dawn would scatter, travelling hard all day in rapidly dispersed groups of two or three, sometimes even singly. Anyone trailing them would have a torrid time in the dry, stony landscape, tracks often impossible to find. They would then hunt apart, sometimes for many nights on end, before once again regrouping for a collective assault on a village. They never hit the same place consecutively and indeed, were never in any area for successive days.

All of these habits are most unusual for lions. It was as if they knew that normal lion behaviour would result in them being caught or shot, and they accordingly took extensive precautions to avoid the possibility. After three weeks George had not even seen a lion and realised that conventional hunting would not bring results. The only advantage he could see was the triangle of roads that covered the area frequented by the man-eaters. Truck and bus drivers could be tasked with gathering information about overnight killings, allowing George to drive to the area as fast as possible, and then follow the tracks until a likely next target could be reasonably discerned. He could then race back to the truck, drive as close to the targeted village as possible and hopefully intercept the lions. It was already a long shot, but was at least some form of strategy. Maddeningly however, before he could exercise this plan he had to return to Mbeya for a week of office administration.

The failure to shoot any lions annoyed George and the locals were already seeing that as further proof of the lions' invincibility. George needed a rapid success; already his scouts were getting nervous and skittish. At least his information service seemed to be working, but each night he sat up in a blind, only to pore over the remains of a kill elsewhere the following morning. These lions at least seemed to eat well, often leaving such tiny scraps of humanity that George didn't even have enough to bait the traps. A feature of their leftovers was a well licked-out brain pan; the Njombe man-eaters seemed to enjoy human brains. As with so many habitual man-eating lions, they scorned their natural prey and domestic livestock. Even the most rickety stock enclosures were left intact, and cattle didn't even seem to fear them. Usually they panic at the very scent of a lion, but so relaxed were they in the presence of the Njombe man-eaters, that the lions would charge into the midst of a herd to snatch the herd boys, sometimes *off the very backs of cattle*, and the herd animals wouldn't even stampede.

What was however clear, was that these lions detested pigs. Very often, George would come across the carcasses of wild pigs while tracking the man-eaters. The stomachs had been ripped open but nothing was ever eaten. To provide some idea as to how brave George Rushby was, it was at this stage that he stopped sitting up in treed *machans* by night – the cold night winds freezing him – and took to sitting in pit shelters. A pit is usually dug to be around three feet deep, three feet wide and four feet long. A tarpaulin is then placed to stand about 18 inches (46cm) high above the ground surface, and pegged down on three sides, allowing a slot to look and shoot out of. Although the night may be dark, the pit is even darker, and one can usually discern objects by even dim starlight.

Hunting from a pit shelter is brave hunting at the best of times, and George was an experienced professional. He knew the risks; he knew what he was up against. With such clever and adept killers afoot, it was almost suicidally brave. To save time and minimise the risk of missing, he took to shooting when he saw or sensed something, then turning on the torch afterward. After three weeks his score was a leopard, a jackal, two hyenas, a wild pig and a goat that had strayed from its enclosure. Its owner was understandably enraged. When George returned to Mbeya, he took two of the scouts with him. Their nerve had gone and the other four weren't in great shape either. Unless George's third attempt was marked by success, they would have to be replaced too. The two replaced scouts were returned to normal duties, their parting comments ringing in George's ears: negotiate with Matamula, end the misery.

When George set off for his third hunt of the Njombe man-eaters, he brought with him two of his most steadfast game scouts, Alfani and Fungamali. Alfani was the same man who had been George's cook on his coffee farm near Mbeya; of distant Somali heritage, he was of fierce countenance and not fazed by lions, were-lions or much anything else. George felt that this time, surely, his luck would change. He stationed these stout hearts at Jumbe Musa's, one of the worst-hit areas. To ease them into patrol hunting, George accompanied them for three days, but there was not hide nor hair of any man-eater, not so much as a track. At last on the fourth day the transport drivers brought news of a bad night at Mambego, some 80km (50 miles) distant. George headed there immediately. The village was visibly devastated; most residents had fled and a goat corral contained the strewn remains of two human bodies.

It looked like a ghost town; tentatively George approached the huts, calling the traditional KiSwahili greeting "*Hodi*?" The only person George could get any sense out of appeared to be a little girl of perhaps eight. "*Karibu*", she replied (literally "Come near" but translated as "Welcome"). The only other folks around were an incoherent and visibly-shocked assortment of elderly, abandoned to the lions when they attacked *en masse* the previous evening. The child told George what had happened, and it was shocking. As usual avoiding naming the lions, she said the insects of the bush had forced their way into two huts, one of which was her family's, using their tried and proven tactic of leaping upon the roofs. These gave way beneath the weight and force of the lions which then found themselves inside. In the melee, some skins hanging from the roof had covered the child, and she lay thus, petrified, until dawn. Luckily the lions too overlooked her; when she emerged, her family was gone and she didn't know if the remains in the paddock were theirs or someone else's. From the pug marks around the outskirts of Mambego, it appeared the cats had literally surrounded the village, until they deemed the time right to attack.

Even though he knew from past experience that the lions were unlikely to return that night, George sat up in his usual pit-blind: there was always that tiniest chance. He had the remaining villagers occupy one hut, well-guarded by the two game scouts. The atmosphere in the village can be imagined, but with so few residents about, there was at least a surplus of food. The little girl brought George some boiled eggs and fresh milk while the villagers and game scouts could be forgiven for delving into the pots of beer that were left. The night however proved fruitless and George, cursing himself for a wasted and exhausting vigil, made for the food hut in the morning. While he was breaking his fast, several of the villagers returned, among them the girl's father. Some of the remains in the paddock, it turned out, were indeed those of the child's mother.

Finishing his meal in haste, George took the two scouts, the girl's father and two other villagers and tried to intercept the lions, based on guessing where they would next attack. The three villagers weren't exactly volunteers, but as Capstick wrote in *Maneaters*, perhaps George managed to convince them by showing the open end of his rifle's muzzle to them; Bulpin wrote that George needed the guides and "wasn't interested in excuses". After three hours they cut the fresh tracks of four lions and in the scorching weather the thorn-scrub seemed even thicker, the going difficult. George weighed the 9.3mm in his hand, feeling the rifle's excellent balance and thanking his stars that it was deadly-accurate, fast and easy to use, and above all, light enough to cart about all day. A heavy old English double would have been a burden in the thick thorn and terrific heat. To boot, the German-made Magnum was hard-hitting and George was sure it would kill when called upon.

Just before midday they came upon the lions, all four together in the shade of a tree and likely having just stood up. They had obviously been surprised by the men as the heavy heat and still air had removed any chance of scenting the hunters, and visibility in the thorn scrub was impossible until the last minute. The closest lion was a young female and George dropped to one knee, firing almost immediately. The sound was shockingly loud in the oppressive heat and silence, the shot smashing the lioness's right upper leg. She spun about, clawing and biting her own wound. Ignoring the scattering lions and his natural reaction to shoot at least one more of them, George shot the young female through the head, and then gave her two more lead pills. He needed this cat dead; the Africans were terrified, eyes bulging, fear and incredulity all over their faces as they clearly thought the man-eater would resurrect herself. George realised with a jolt that this very reason was why he made so sure the lioness had received her quietus. Chuckling at himself, he made his way over to the cat. She was sleek, obviously well-fed and sported no signs of human interference at all. Her coat was glossy and her teeth superb. She was in all-round perfect condition.

The Africans crouched, hunched over for quite a while staring at her, until one offered the only explanation their minds could reconcile with: she was an ordinary lion, not one of the insects of the bush. George shrugged; regardless, the point was that the tribesmen in the area could now be sure that there were real lions in the bush, and killing them was possible. Thus, resistance could be offered with impunity, rather than paralysed apathy. The lion's condition proved she was one of the deadly pride. George felt publicity was in order; a short walk away was a village, and George sent two men to summon the people. They all stared at the carcass, strangely quiet, and when George asked the men to skin it, not even Alfani would touch it. George skinned it himself and once he'd decapitated it, the men seemed satisfied that the creature's magic had gone. The party returned to Mambego with the trophies in tow and the celebration was loud and joyous. The little girl presented George with a full dozen eggs; although eggs actually gave him heartburn, George hadn't the heart to tell the child, who obviously believed that white folks subsisted principally on eggs!

The next day George took the skin and skull to Wangingombe where Jifiki and his court were thrilled at the news. He then made for Jumbe Musa's, from whence word had been sent summoning him with all haste. Dreading what he'd find, George was relieved to find his men raring to go. Although the killings had continued unabated, their biggest problem was with the locals, who not only refused to assist the scouts, but were actually antagonistic toward them, somewhat understandably reasoning that the man-eaters would be further provoked by hunting them. The news of the dead lioness was heartening and George saw the effect it might have on the tribes, if they could anchor a man-eater or two in the area. He had planned to hunt in the area of Jumbe Musa's anyhow, as for some reason, the lions there were becoming regulars in the district. This predictability was exactly what George wanted to exploit. Any pattern at all could be used to definitively hit back. For three days the men tramped about, foot-sore and broiled in the pitiless thorn scrub. It was baffling how, despite such persistence, the man-eaters could avoid them so effectively while kills continued on people throughout the area. George found himself wishing the lions would at least attack the hunters; it was easy to see how terror could spread, with nothing at all to see or hear by night but the wind in the tall grass and the chirping of insects.

But at last – at long, exhausting last – the fourth morning brought relief: the men cut fresh spoor of a large group of lions. They were still trying to discern how many lions were ahead of them when they wandered into the rear-guard of the pride, a large young male. He snarled his displeasure while the rest of the pride decamped and the three men fired almost together. The joyous skinning of the lion was followed by the glorification of the two game scouts to the population of Jumbe Musa's. George wanted the people to see that it could be done, and played up his scouts' efforts. Who had actually killed the lion was academic, and since all three shots hit home nearly simultaneously, it could have been the combination of the three. The doubt helped his plans as any kill by him might be easily explained away as white man's magic. The change in the people was impressive; their joy was almost tangible and George actually had to point out to the headman that only one lion had fallen. The dangers in the area were still very real; the people were running about carelessly after dark, an extremely foolhardy act. They could, however, believe that these lions could be killed like any others.

The following day George had to return to Mbeya to address his mounting heap of administration, but he left the scouts in the area to hunt and decided that on his way back, he would at last drop in to visit - or confront - Matamula. But before George could capitalise on the positive outcomes, he received a signal to make for the Northern Rhodesian (now Zambian) border to relieve a critically-ill supervisor, following which he had to make for the Lake Rukwa area and attend to another severe locust outbreak. A month and a half had slipped by and the hunt's successes had been all but forgotten. It does indeed seem uncanny how anyone trying to hunt the lions was always interrupted in some way, by having to attend to other matters of great urgency. Most of these were official, and legitimate. Capstick wrote about the entire episode that, with the benefit of decades of hindsight, it appears at times as if the

Tanganyika Game Department were even working against Rushby (and the rangers before him) and for the lions.

Corruption in Africa is so rife, and tribal influences run so deeply and so strongly, that it is in every way possible that the influence of Matamula Mangera did indeed reach into the Tanganyika Game Department. It is as well for George Rushby that administration was still largely British, otherwise he may never have brought the Njombe man-eating outbreak to a close. George returned to Jumbe Musa's at the end of March 1946. So disheartened had he been at the loss of impact that the lion killings would have brought, that he was pleasantly surprised to learn that Alfani had tracked a pride *en route* to Kidugala, shooting and killing the rear-guard animal. Unfortunately, all the other five scouts had to report was an ongoing terror from the unabated and ongoing rash of man-eating.

A rumour was circulating that Matamula might call off his lions, if restored to his previous position. The tribespeople were hostile towards George, whom they felt would interfere with the natural (read supernatural) balance of the negotiations, in particular if he intended to relaunch his hunt on the lions. After a fruitless three days hunting around Jumbe Musa's, George and the scouts spent two days at Wangingombe with similar results. Here George had to bolster a faltering Jifiki, who was battling against the superstitions and pleas of his own people on the one hand, and his more enlightened, educated mind on the other. He then made for the Njombe administrative post to touch base with the district commissioner again, making sure to stop off regularly along the route for any news of killings. Around 8am in the morning, as he neared the village of Ihanyawa, he noticed a small hamlet of maybe six huts, and people acting strangely. Women were herding the children inside while the men were armed and watching a cultivated depression.

George heard that one of the men had seen a lion in the depression an hour or so before, perhaps 150 yards distant (135 metres). George left the two men who had muzzle loaders to guard the people while he took the spearman with him; the man had two spears. Just beyond the depression George spotted fresh tracks and following steadily, noted the spearman seeming to grow in confidence the further they tracked. After two hours they glimpsed the animal, a young male with a half-grown, reddish-orange mane, perhaps 50 yards (45 metres) ahead. He offered a clear stern shot but George wanted to make sure and five minutes passed as they trailed the lion. Unfortunately, as they reached a bank of loose gravel, the spearman fell in a shower of stones and a clatter of his spears. Pausing for a second to glance up, the lion came for the men in a full-on, all-out charge, his speed so dauntingly quick that George watched his first shot raise a puff of dust behind the animal as he shot too high.

His tail erect and his mane standing on end, the men saw nothing but hair, teeth and claws as the lion rapidly closed the gap between them, a veritable nightmare of vocal hatred. By the time George could bring his second barrel to bear the lion was only ten yards off and the shot was critical. It went home though, right into the brain, the lion describing the somersault that so many seem to do when dropped at great speed by a frontal shot. George paid the insurance by shooting it in the head again, a wise policy that many have sworn by. It's a careless, stupid and often soon-to-be-dead hunter that doesn't take the time to make certain that the creature can no longer bite. Typical of the Njombe lions, this lion too was young, compact and in superb condition with luxuriant glossy fur. George sought the spearman but that gentleman had fled. George didn't blame him, and after some time was spent shouting and calling, the man returned. George sent him to summon the other dwellers of the hamlet to assist in carrying duties. By the time they returned George had skinned the lion and cut off its head.

The men carried the trophies back to the huts but the people's reaction was a strange one; George was thoroughly peeved to note the listless apathy with which they viewed the skin. He roundly castigated them for their ridiculous belief in black magic, and their response – often the reaction of bush Africans that disagree with someone – was the same apathy that visibly showed that to argue with them was a waste of breath. George stayed in the area for the next three days, sleeping in his truck, but never saw another fresh trace of a lion. The nights were peaceful too. He lectured the townsfolk one last time and headed for Njombe. George was questioning his own sanity by now, hoping the district commissioner would bolster his own resolve to shrug off the superstitions of the Africans. One point worried George; he had initially thought there to be perhaps ten man-eaters, but there was no noticeable drop in attacks on people, despite four of the pride having been shot dead. This was troubling; either some or all of the four dead animals were not man-eaters, or there were far more lions responsible than he'd originally thought…unless of course there was something else about?

Wenban-Smith actually confirmed to George that there was a decline in the predations, but not a decisive one. He was however firmly of the opinion that Matamula should not be reinstated to his position of power, for two good reasons: one, the headman Ulaya – Matamula's replacement in the Iyayi area – had been doing a superb job; and two, the message that would be sent by reinstating him would be tantamount to admitting and acknowledging his magic. The most preferred solution would be the extermination of the lions, be they were-lions or not. George thoroughly agreed on all counts and resolved to continue the hunt. News of the district was that Jumbe Musa's still seemed to be the most under siege, while Mambego was actually quiet. Most of the inhabitants had returned after the mass attack there and George received his customary present of boiled eggs from the ever-friendly little girl. There was also however a message from the game department, that George return to Mbeya post-haste. Eleanor had sent word of an important pending communication. George cursed yet another distraction from the task of killing man-eating lions.

There was however one thing that George relished: finally confronting Matamula. Iyayi was on the Great North Road and right on his way home to Mbeya. After paying his respects to the excellent Ulaya, who seemed pleased that he was officially supported at least, George spoke randomly with the villagers until he came to Matamula's hut on the west side of the road. "*Hodi?*" called George; "*Karibu*", answered Matamula in the traditional KiSwahili greeting. George saw a well-built, medium-sized and clean-shaven man of perhaps forty-five, in the typical *kanzu* (a white shift or gown). The man seemed affable enough but George engaged in the usual small talk, enquiring about the weather, the crops, the stock animals and the like. To wade directly into the subject would be rude and would likely result in the man clamming up. Matamula showed a ready wit and was no fool. At the end of the visit George ventured to mention the lions; casual as you please, he said: "The insects of the bush are not having a very good time. Four of them are dead." Matamula gave an odd little smile, and shrugging almost imperceptibly, he disinterestedly muttered: "Labda" (perhaps).

George drove on to Mbeya where he learned from a delighted Eleanor that Tanganyika civil servants – like George – that had not had leave since the War began, had been granted an immediate 6 months' leave to Britain. George was torn, thrilled to be able to see the two children for the first time in eight years, frustrated at yet another interruption of his hunt of the man-eaters. Handing over his duties to the conscientious *Twiga* Rogers (apparently a tall, rangy man; *twiga* is giraffe in KiSwahili), George suggested he try an organised drive or beat, using large numbers of armed people. The method is commonly used to flush out big cats in many parts of the world and is often successful. Then the Rushbys set sail for Old Blighty on the liner *Mantola,* and after a grand reunion with the children at Jacksdale, and a pleasant time in England, the reunited family returned to a steamy Dar es Salaam in October 1946 on the *Winchester Castle*. The only news George could glean in the New Africa Hotel was that the lion men of the Singida district had been active. There had been a rumoured thirty murders since May that year and witchdoctors were implicated in the confidential investigations.

Twiga Rogers had some interesting news for George when the latter reached Mbeya; one more lion had been shot, and this had been accomplished by three armed tribesmen. Near Mdandu, seat of the Paramount Chief of the Bena tribe, a lion was spotted skulking about. The men stalked the cat and firing together, killed it. This was indeed good news, if for no other reason than the people seeming to lose their fear, sufficient to fight back: the rate of attacks had continued unabated. On the flip side of the coin of news, *Twiga's* organised beat had descended into a farce. Three lions were spotted, again near Mdandu, but although a large number of armed men were involved, the lions escaped. Rogers too escaped unscathed, which was fortunate: the beat descended into a free-for-all, two Africans shot dead and several wounded was the final tally; one of the wounded later succumbed in hospital. George waded back into his range with a will, but needed a fortnight before zeroing in on Njombe again: the northern section of Lake Rukwa was dry and several hippos had to be shot to save them from a lingering death, crushing each other like sardines as the merciless sun dried all beneath it.

Happily, the Njombe district actually showed a slight decrease in the human death rate. Jifiki told George that in his absence, the calls to restore Matamula to power had reached a crescendo, and a delegation had bypassed Jifiki by appealing directly to the Paramount Chief. They were declined a hearing on Government instructions and were naturally most irate as a result. George decided to use Mambego as a base and hunt from there, hoping to bring the pride to book. He even had his pocket full of sweets for the pleasant little girl who always fed him eggs, as he and Alfani made for the village, but reaching it, they saw again the devastation that told of a mass attack. The people wandered about like refugees from a war zone, which I suppose they were. The little girl had been eaten four days previously. Bulpin doesn't elaborate, besides mentioning that George wanted rapid revenge for the death of the child, but there is no need; George would have been deeply saddened and enraged to learn of her untimely demise. He and Alfani launched into the hunt, heading south towards the Mbarali River. On the third day, they cut fresh spoor of an entire pride headed north-west towards Igawa. Pressing the chase, they closed with the cats just before noon and per pre-arrangement, each would take their own lion.

George shot his lion and as it staggered to its feet, he reloaded and dropped it dead with the second shot. Alfani had hit a lioness but his second shot whined off into the bracken. As wounded lions often do, she was clawing and biting a nearby sapling, thinking that it had caused the sudden burning pain. George fed her two more bullets as Alfani snap-shot a third animal. Although there was a blood-trail, it eventually dried and this third animal had to be left. It was keeping pace with the others so appeared to have merely been creased. No mind; two more of the infamous Njombe pride were dead. Both animals were in fine condition and had such glossy, opulent coats that George recalled the supposed reason: these animals were thought to have a human keeper. It was indeed incredible to have such fine skin in the thorn-scrub. As each man skinned his lion, George mentioned the point to Alfani, who was unamused. Somewhat annoyed, George reminded him that the magic hadn't seemed to stop their bullets. Alfani merely shrugged; he supposed so.

Returning to Mambego, eager to share the success with the villagers, the men were instead met by an African policeman from Iringa. Right on schedule, George had been called away on urgent official business. Iringa's township foreman, a man by the name of Bill Marshall, had been trampled to death by an elephant. A ranger was required immediately as the case had another dimension to it. To summarise the Marshall-Cathles affair, three men had been involved in an ivory poaching racket and George dismissed the first man involved, a game scout; then cancelled the hunting license of the second (a local cattle trader named Cathles), and blacklisted the man to boot. Marshall – the third man – had already been punished! Cathles was renowned for his meanness and was prone to taking short-cuts. Shortly after this affair, his car drove over the escarpment, killing him, because he'd declined to keep it properly serviced. Funny thing, karma…

There was a beacon of light in the gloom, however slight; two days prior to the Marshall-Cathles interruption, a herdsman had speared a lion to death when it attacked his cattle. This was unlikely to be one of the man-eaters but it was heartening nonetheless. By February 1947 George was back in Njombe and there was some good news: Jumapili had killed a confirmed man-eater at Mterengani. Two more of doubtful persuasion had been shot at Mawindi, but it was safer to make sure in the current conditions by killing any lions in the area. The total number of confirmed man-eaters was now eight, and there was a definite drop in the predations on humans. For the first time, George could sense victory. The most recent killings had been of three people in the area of Ilembula-Malimzenga. The lions' usual tendency would now be to flee the area on an irregular course, often dog-legging away again at some apparent whim. When they'd venture upon a human settlement they would feed, then repeat the entire process. George picked Halali, ten miles (16km) to the west of the last attacks, hoping he'd strike lucky.

Before dawn, George was up and headed east, but after a fruitless six hours he returned for lunch. Almost unbelievably, a furious George found out that an hour after he'd left, an entire pride of lions entered Halali – the very village he'd left and just returned to – and killed a man in full view of the villagers. They took turns carrying the corpse about and settled to feed a short distance off, consuming the entire body except the skull cap. Normally they would consume the entire victim, bones and all, if it was a young person, but tended to be a bit pickier with the elderly, who were probably a bit tougher. They had obviously been hungry. Hurriedly polishing off a pot of tea, George was pleasantly surprised to find two volunteers to track the pride, a man and a youth of sixteen. Before long George realised the youth was a brilliant tracker, easily following the difficult spoor in the hard, rocky ground. Around 4pm they ventured upon a large field, once cultivated land before the lions started eating the subsistence farmers, and now long-abandoned. It was a nasty hunting area under ideal circumstances, and these were anything but ideal, following the world's most prolific man-eating lions.

The three hunters entered the scrub, the youth leading George and the other tribesman bringing up the rear. After 50 yards (45 metres) they heard the slightest movement and froze, straining to better identify the noise. Another movement was heard, and George waved the two Africans back, crawling forward on his hands and knees for better visibility. After another twenty yards or so (18 metres), George saw a young lioness a mere five yards (4.5 metres) from him and since her surprise froze her, he wasted no time by shooting her through the brain with the .404. Jumping up to reload, George discerned some scurrying in the bushes. To his right front a large lioness took a bound, and at her second bound he snapped off a shot into her guts, too far back to be fatal. She went berserk, tearing about, growling and raging. By the noise in the surrounding bushes there were at least another two lions about. George sat waiting for her to stiffen up or hopefully succumb. For a full fifteen minutes she raised the roof, then for a further ten this became the odd grunt.

To his surprise the youth had stayed by him, although the other tribesman had fled, and George forced himself to stifle his own desired reaction to return to camp until the following day. To overcome his fear, George smoked a pipe. When he was done, he whispered to the youth to stay put and crawled in the direction of the wounded lioness, concentrating intently on the spot. In the lives of great people, or of people who have achieved great things, there is usually one or more defining moment, with which or without which they would never had reached their goal. When hunting man-eating lions, these moments are common and are often decisive. George Rushby was about to experience his defining moment, certainly of this extended and historic hunt.

From his left rear, a mighty roar froze George in mid-step, the impossible sound reverberating in his guts. He whirled about and stared into the face of death itself just five feet from him, nothing between the man and a huge brown-maned male lion but a thin bush. George knew it was too close, regardless how fast or well he might shoot. Capstick wrote often and well about proximity and seemingly-fatal wounds to big game, some running 200 yards (180 metres) with hearts shot to ribbons. Even fatally wounded, a lion just needs to reach a human to kill it, and this one was right here. For a split second they locked eyes before the lion bolted away through the thorn bushes. It was an impossible escape, a fluke, a fate-lined moment that was not lost on George Rushby. The shock to his heart was a cold, physical pressure, and George sat down to work through another pipe. Before he'd finished it, George resolved to kill that lion; it had missed its chance. Next time, he would not. When he was able to speak again he summoned the youth who came directly; the wounded lioness still had to be followed up. With the youth brandishing his spear and George leading, they reached the spot where the lioness had torn up the earth. A large pool of blood showed where she had been lying.

Forty yards (36 metres) down the blood spoor they found her in a half crouch, and George had no intention of waiting for her to charge. He shot her twice and she fell on her side, kicking spasmodically. The youth tapped George on the shoulder and asked if the lioness was dead; George asked why and was told that the villager killed the day before was the boy's father. Understanding, George told the youth to stab her quickly, as she was still alive. The boy did, and when they returned to the first lioness George had shot, the youngster speared her, too. George watched the youth with much sympathy; the nervous tension of the day was dropping off and he now knew the boy had been harbouring grief as well. They returned to the village, retrieving the other tribesman from his treetop refuge *en route*. For the rest of the month George hunted from the village but never saw any sign of the big male or the second lion. The skins of man-eaters have to be kept for display to the locals and George was not in the habit of collecting hunting trophies, but the head of that male lion that had nearly given him heart failure was a prize he dearly wanted. Returning to Mbeya for a bout of paperwork, George was just considering dropping by Iyayi when he saw Matamula outside his hut.

"Two more insects of the bush have died," said George, "Ten of them are now finished." On the surface, Matamula seemed faintly amused as before, but who knew what he really felt deep down. Again, his almost imperceptible shrug, then he said "You have hunted very well. It will be interesting to see the end of this matter." George nodded and drove on, musing on the absurd stories about Matamula. He was annoyed with himself but the man had gotten under his skin. The lions George had shot showed no signs of human interference at all, and their lustrous pelts could be attributed to the diet of soft human protein, but they were lions and nothing more. How they had learned such advanced attack and avoidance strategies was indeed worrying, and not like normal lions, but he supposed the specialised methodologies came from hunting humans, that devise better defences than prey animals. George got to thinking about the Singida lion-men, where he'd heard a massive police investigation was in full swing. He planned to go there and compare events with those at Njombe. Perhaps that might clarify some peculiarities.

For the next two months, George was occupied with crop-raiding elephants. They had trampled vast areas and eaten their share, but the real problem came when they went for the harvested crops as well. An entire village could lose a full year's supply of food in one night, and many did. The only effective prevention method was to shoot the culprits, preferably in view of the rest, then drive the rest back into the wilderness. This must have been a strange case of *Déjà vu* for George, who had spent a period as a successful ivory hunter. There was no profit of any sort in this case though; it was an unpleasant job and George was happy when it ended. He then had to wrap up the anti-*rinderpest* operations on the Northern Rhodesian (now Zambian) border. The danger of the disease spreading was thought to have receded. This was good news, aside from the freeing up of staff and directing of resources elsewhere; much of the operation had involved butchering thousands of animals merely because they had wandered to within five miles (8km) of the border. George then had to escort Captain Keith Caldwell and his wife on an impromptu safari, which wasn't unpleasant, but George had the man-eaters on his mind.

By June 1947 he at last made it to Singida for the extensive court case. The saga occupies some time and space in *The Hunter is Death*, and is a study in the levels of depravity to which human beings can sink. George didn't stay for the high court sessions; he felt he'd learned enough to establish that there were no real similarities between the Singida lion-men, people obsessed with supposed supernatural influences on human beings, and the Njombe man-eaters, a lethal collection of lions. Lions were not an essential to killings by black magic, as he recalled the hyenas in the Mbugwe country. The witchdoctors in the Poroto Mountains had used leopards to the same ends. George concluded that if one accepted the lions' strange behaviour as a feature of eating humans, then Matamula's supposed control could be dismissed as a public fancy or an ingenious fraud. It was likely both. The one thing common to the Singida and Njombe sagas, however, was the all-pervading terror of black magic that gripped the superstitious and ignorant populace.

When George reached Wangingombe, Jifiki had good news for him. The redoubtable Alfani had killed another confirmed man-eater some ten days before, and the death rate had dropped to such an extent that no more than two or three man-eaters could still be at large. These remnants, oddly, also seemed to have lost much of their mystique, their movements more predictable and more like lions. The only place still suffering seemed to be within a fifteen-mile radius around Jumbe Musa's, which had always been the worst-affected area. George concentrated his scouts there, and the welcome was an uneasy one; the villagers had always regarded hunters as merely a provocation to the lions. George assured them the continued attacks were the result of the area being the last stronghold. The people were frightened by the number of scouts, and George's explanation that it was because the man-eaters now seemed concentrated there unsurprisingly comforted no-one.

For a full week the men hunted without success before George dispersed them into pairs from the eighth morning. George and Jumapili cut fresh spoor of two lions almost immediately, the tracks over the dew. To strengthen the men's resolve, they appeared to be of a male and a female, and the male's closely resembled those of the lion that had scared George so severely in the scrub. George told Jumapili about that narrow escape, and they resolved that Jumapili would shoot the lioness, leaving the prize male to George. The confrontation after three hours' tracking was anti-climactic. The lions were in the shade and engaged in affectionate attentions. Hearing the men, the male walked into the sunshine, where George immediately recognised the beast that had haunted his dreams. His romantic spell may have mellowed him, George thought, but he looked like a lion now, not a demon from hell. George shot him through the heart while Jumapili shot the lioness through the lungs, reloading to finish her off. The male looked deflated and strangely innocent, George thought, and would've felt sorry for him had he not known of the animal's grisly habits; he looked like a tom-cat killed in a road accident.

Both men skinned their lions and cleaned the skulls, then carried the trophies to Jumbe Musa's where they were met by the usual infuriating animosity. George however most looked forward to wiring Wenban-Smith of the end of the outbreak. The district commissioner was to be transferred at the end of that month to Dar es Salaam, and George wanted him to hand the district over well-purged of the trouble. His message was answered with a relieved "*Allah hu Akbar!*" ("God is great" in Arabic, or in this context, "Praise be to God!") A few days later, he was still trying to update his administrative backlog when Wenban-Smith sent him another telegram, early in June 1947. It wasn't good news: "You're wrong George. Regret. Woman eaten yesterday at Matipu village."

Somewhat understandably, George Rushby vented his anger long, loudly, and likely in some choice foul language. He had so wanted Wenban-Smith to finish with a clean slate, and was only able to get back to the Njombe district on 16 July. To his surprise, his welcome was cheerful; people were brewing beer, slaughtering livestock in obvious preparation of a feast. Just the previous day, the scouts had killed two lionesses, numbers 14 and 15 of the confirmed man-eaters. With five other doubtful man-eaters also killed, and two wounded but never seen again – so likely dead – the total for the entire episode was a maximum of twenty-two lions, collectively responsible for the greatest concentrated outbreak of man-eating by a single group of lions ever recorded.

George was thrilled and heartily congratulated the scouts and made for Wangingombe the following day. Sitting with Jifiki beneath the jacaranda trees was a pleasant way to enjoy some beer and reminisce about the entire disaster. The headman was not as happy as he should be and seemed preoccupied. Only when George rose to leave did Jifiki awkwardly broach what had been on his mind. He told George that the people would never forget his efforts to save them, but warned against him expecting the populace to believe that the lions George shot were the ones that were killing them. George was incredulous; "Why not?" he blurted out. A clearly-embarrassed and distressed Jifiki told George that the people had heard Wenban-Smith was leaving, so they sent a large deputation to the Paramount Chief at Mdandu, begging that Matamula be reinstated. They argued this could be done before the new district commissioner was in place, and the Paramount Chief relented. Ulaya was deposed at the end of June and Matamula was rumoured to have called off his lions. The people were very happy and that was that. George Rushby looked at Jifiki in silence for a while, lit his pipe and drove off along the Great North Road, back to Mbeya, back to Eleanor and the children.

Most accounts of the Njombe man-eaters end by stating that there have been no further recorded killings by man-eating lions in the district. For decades that was true; perhaps - and disturbingly - it lasted as long as Matamula lived. That would be difficult to establish; but there was indeed another outbreak, in the late 1990s. It was however nothing as large as the 1932-47 episode and fitted right in with the spate of new attacks that resulted from Tanzania's population explosion. Regardless, a nagging doubt or two remain; were the Njombe lions in any way trained or controlled by people? Their unbelievable ability to evade hunters was uncanny, and their habits were most unlike those of normal lions. As for Matamula, was there something to him and his control? Was the Singida lion sect really totally separate from the goings-on in Njombe? Why the hiatus in killings in 1940 at Wangingombe? Mere chance, or had Matamula demonstrated his control over the lions to Jifiki by temporarily halting the killing there? Try convincing the locals that Rushby was the reason the killing stopped. Africa is a big place, with a lot of maybes.

*　*　*

I tracked George Rushby Jnr down in 2003 over the internet, where he was a grazier (beef cattle farmer) in New South Wales, Australia. When we moved to Brisbane late in 2006, I decided to try and find him again. In 2008 we met up, my family and I driving down to Ballina just inside the New South Wales border and some 2-3 hours' drive south from Brisbane. George and his wife Jeanette were retired and at 75, he was still fit and strong, a volunteer reserve fireman. In the catastrophic fires that tore through the State of Victoria in 2009, George went south to help. His stories and photos were humbling, awe-inspiring. The fires wreaked such havoc and destruction that entire communities were simply razed, the 100km/h-plus blazes sweeping areas clean. It spoke volumes about George the man; at the age when most are reclining in armchairs, he was ably assisting young professionals in one of the most hazardous and physically-taxing occupations on earth.

George and Jeanette were wonderfully welcoming and friendly towards us, but perhaps by 2008 it was again a novelty to have strangers speak to George about his famous father. The story runs deeper though. When the Rushbys were struggling in the late 1930s, George Jnr contracted malaria, along with Janey, the nursemaid. George Snr's mother was to sail out to Cape Town to meet Eleanor and take Ann and George Jnr back to England until their parents had found their feet, and to nurse the children back to health in a temperate climate. Eleanor would stay in Cape Town with Kate at her family. So, on 10 February 1937, the little family – minus George Snr – flew out from Mbeya headed for Cape Town.

Although Eleanor and Kate would be back, it was the last George Snr would see of Ann and George Jnr for eight years. George Jnr was not yet four years old, and that separation – coupled with an eternal reaction of gushing celebrity to him introducing himself as George Rushby – resulted in him taking his nickname of Mike, earned while on a stint with the Army in Burma. By June 1937

Eleanor returned to Mbeya with Kate, while Mike and Ann would stay with Eleanor's parents – where all the children had recovered well – until George's mother took them to England at the end of the year.

Mike seemed to have a reconciling of sorts with his father in later years, but it's plain that the time away cut him very deeply, as did the reaction of people to the name of George Rushby. His father was rightly world-famous and Mike knew the real George Snr: just a man, trying his best to provide for his family, at times dragged down by bad luck and downhearted by hardship, and whom a little boy may have felt had perhaps not wanted him. The years in England included the Second World War, remember, with all the risks and fears that went along with that from the child's point of view. It is a tough subject to broach, and I only managed to skirt around it, there as friends and not as interviewing researchers. Mike is a steadfast, calm, deep personality, with the tough stock of his father running though his veins, coupled of course with that of his equally-steadfast mother.

He and Jeanette warmed to my family and have been very kind to us, especially to my children. Mike gave my daughter a magazine article that features in *The Hunter is Death*, a time on the farm in Mbeya where Eleanor was harassed for several nights in George's absence by a leopard. The family dog Paddy is also a source of good fun for the children. Watching their reaction at having the company of children is a pleasure; although they have grandchildren of their own, most are grown now. When we met up with Mike in 2008, the rest of the Rushby children were spread out across the globe: Ann, the eldest, was in Virginia, USA. Kate was in England. John was in Ottawa in Canada, while both Jim and Henry were in Fish Hoek, near Cape Town, South Africa.

The baleful yellow stare of lions; the lioness is disdainful but alert, the male curious and probing for a weakness. **The images are in the public domain.**

A lion as close to you as this in the bush that starts a real charge will leave you with no more than three seconds to stop it – dead – before it reaches you. **The image is in the public domain.**

Renowned lion conservationist Craig Packer; his work has been instrumental in helping people to avoid being eaten by lions throughout East Africa, and in saving lion populations as well. **The image is in the public domain.**

Picture: National Geographic

You are stirring the cast-iron pot full of *posho* (maize meal porridge); your baby is secured to your back with a blanket. There is a garden hoe against the reed wall of your hut, but it's some metres away. You look up at a slight sound and see this; you have fewer than ten seconds left to live. What do you do?

The two Tsavo man-eaters as they are mounted in the Field Museum in Chicago today. In real life they weren't this scrawny; the skins served as rugs for 25 years before the taxidermists had to make do. The jury is still out on their final tally of victims, but it may well have far exceeded a hundred people. The image is in the public domain.

The bridge over the River Tsavo today. The image is in the public domain.

The two Tsavo lions again, as displayed today at the Field Museum. Photo by Jeffrey Lung, licensed under Creative Commons Attribution-Share Alike 3.0 Unported, 2.5 Generic, 2.0 Generic and 1.0 Generic license.

The first-killed of the two Tsavo lions, with Colonel John Henry Patterson, author of the Man-eaters of Tsavo (no direct relation to Bruce D. Patterson, author of The Lions of Tsavo). This picture gives better indication of the actual size and condition of the lions. **The image is in the public domain.**

A carriage of the Uganda Railways in the Nairobi Railway Museum, Kenya. It was from a carriage such as this that Superintendent Charles Ryall was taken by a lion in 1900 at Kima Station. The big cat took the body through a window. **The image is in the public domain.**

Ryall's gravestone in Nairobi. **The image is in the public domain.**

The huge Mfuwe lion, as he is mounted today in the Chicago Field Museum, near the Tsavo lions. He is the biggest man-eating lion ever reliably measured and stands five feet tall (150cm) at the ear tips, while on all-fours. Like the Tsavo man-eaters, he is maneless. **The image is in the public domain.**

The same Mfuwe lion, replete with a replica of the laundry bag that he took from the dwelling of his sixth and final known victim. The massive size of his body and depth of his chest are obvious in this picture.
The image is in the public domain.

The Kasungu man-eater, shot in 2003 in central Malawi after killing and eating at least seven people. He was huge and eight men couldn't lift him.
The image is in the public domain.

The American hunter, adventurer, cropping officer and superb author, Peter Hathaway Capstick (1940-1996). He accounted for several man-eating cats during his career, killing the Chabunkwa lion with a spear as it mauled his tracker in the Luangwa River Valley. His books are deservedly lauded as some of the finest of the hunting genre ever written.
Photo by Ken Wilson, Sportsmen on Film.

The eccentric Colonel Ludwig von Steinacker, commandant of Steinacker's Horse during the Boer War. This photo appears to be pre-war or post-war; during the War the Colonel was almost comically scrawny, which - amazingly - accentuated his massive moustache.
Photo by Stevenson-Hamilton Library, Skukuza, Kruger National Park, South Africa.

A massive male lion in South Africa's Kruger National Park. The tourist is oblivious to its presence and with his car window down, could easily be pulled out of his car. Lions in Kruger have killed innumerable people and are particularly large; the biggest recorded wild lion ever shot was a member of the Kruger sub-species.
Photo courtesy of the Kruger National Park website, warning against careless behaviour.

Assyrian ivory panel from Nimrud, around the 8th century BC. The panel is in the British Museum. **The image is in the public domain.**

A billboard warning residents of the Rufiji man-eater while it was still at large in Rufiji, southern Tanzania, between 2002 and 2004. The sign says that the man-eater has killed 40 and injured a further seven people.
The image is in the public domain.

The Rufiji man-eater when he was captured in 2004; he had already been active for two years and was still a youngster. Although he may be subjected to severe torment in this picture, his feelings toward people are obvious. This was a dangerous animal that killed and ate around fifty people.
The image is in the public domain.

The Rufiji lion after he was shot. The image is in the public domain.

Legendary Kruger ranger, Harry Wolhuter, raw-boned, wiry and tough as nails. In 1903 he stabbed a lion to death with a small sheath knife as it dragged him off to consume him, then survived the wounds and infection for nearly a week before treatment could be administered.
Photo by Stevenson-Hamilton Library, Skukuza, Kruger National Park, South Africa.

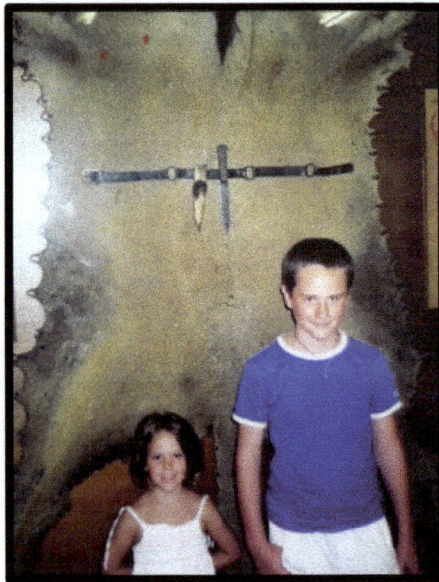

The author's children with the skin of the lion that Wolhuter killed, in the Stephenson-Hamilton Library in Skukuza, Kruger National Park, South Africa, in December 2005. The sheath knife is clearly visible as are the two stab wounds to the heart, to the top left of the photograph with red felt backing.

Maneless male Tsavo lion, photographed in Tsavo East National Park, Kenya, 2007, by Mgiganteus. Licensed under the Creative Commons Attribution-Share Alike 3.0 Unported license.

Harold Trollope; this remarkable man was instrumental in the formation of both Kruger and Addo National Parks in South Africa, but it was his lion-hunting exploits that brought him much of his fame.
Photo by Stevenson-Hamilton Library, Skukuza, Kruger National Park, South Africa.

George and Eleanor Rushby; George was larger than life, a remarkably successful man and was instrumental in killing the Njombe pride in what is now Tanzania, the most prolific man-eating lions in a single area in recorded history. **The image is in the public domain.**

The fabled writer TV Bulpin, whose works are much sought-after Africana today. His superb book *The Hunter is Death*, largely a George Rushby biography, recounted the story of the Njombe lions and the strange African black magic of lycanthropy. **The image is in the public domain.**

American writer Robert Frump, whose excellent book *The Man-eaters of Eden* highlights the extent of the man-eating problem in South Africa's Kruger National Park. **Photograph by Getty images.**

The well-known Tanzanian lion hunter Musa Manga. Man-eating in Tanzania is more rife than anywhere else, and is at least as rife today as it was in centuries past. **Picture courtesy of National Geographic.**

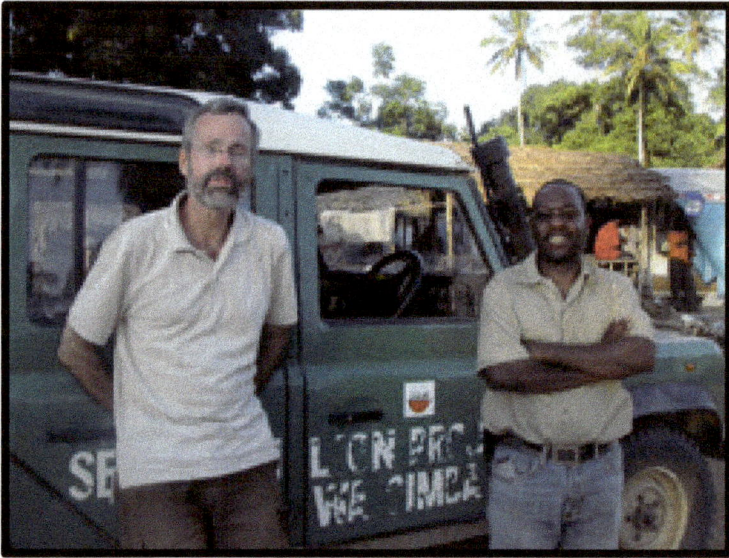

On the right, Tanzanian lion researcher Dennis Ikanda, an erstwhile protégé of Craig Packer (left). Ikanda theorises that humans have always formed part of the diet of lions. Records and statistics show that he's likely correct. **The image is in the public domain.**

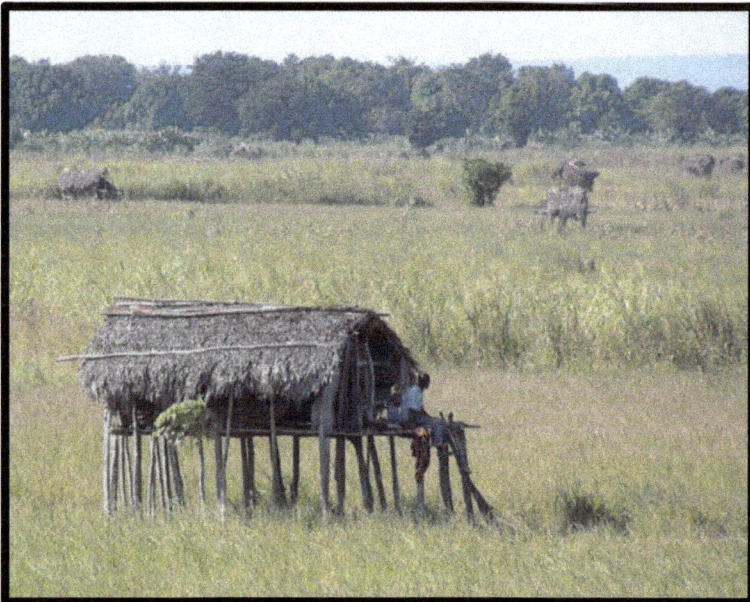

A *dungu* in a Tanzanian *shamba* or small crop holding. Lions have learned to associate these *dungus* with people and as can be imagined, are often successful when breaking into them. **The image is in the public domain.**

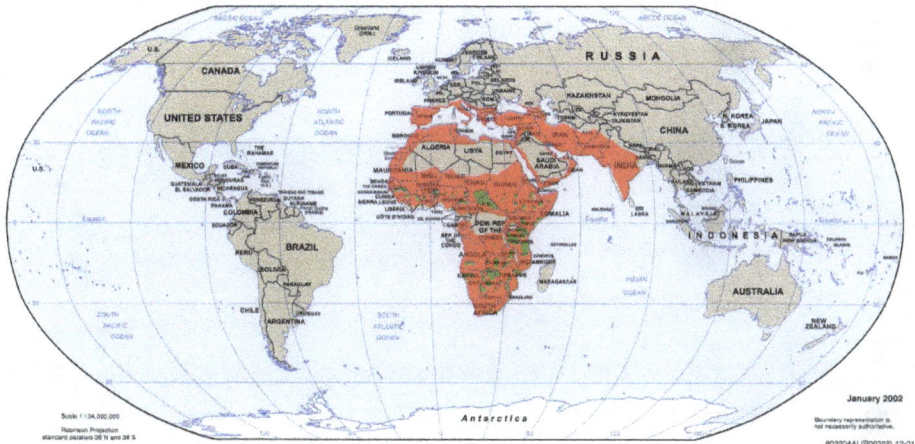

A 2002 image indicating where lions once reigned (red), and where they remain (green); a visibly catastrophic regression. Of interest is their erstwhile presence in Europe, and all along the coast of the Arabian Gulf.
The image is in the public domain.

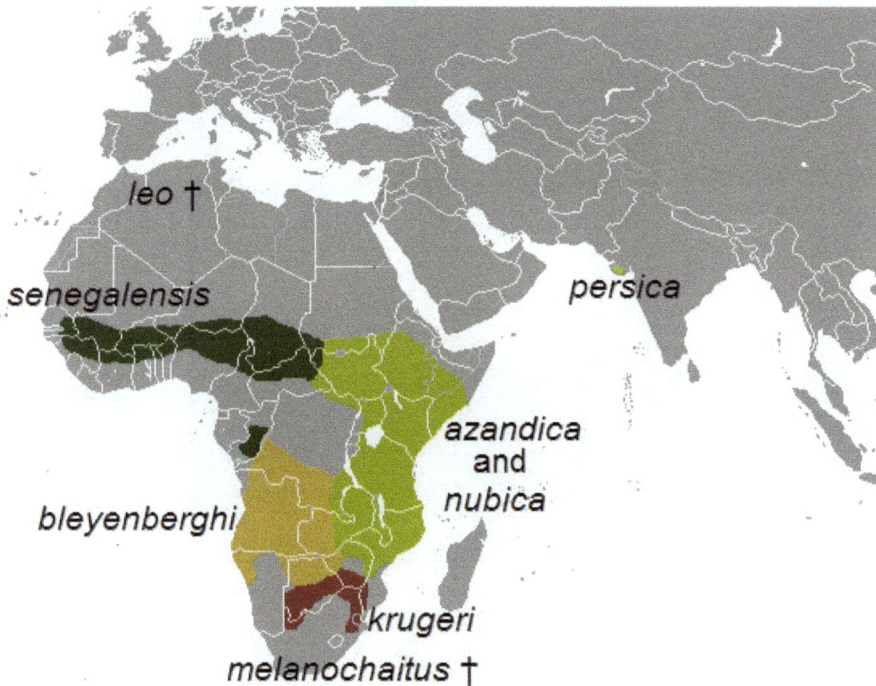

A map showing the approximate distribution of the various lion sub-species.
Image courtesy of Wikipedia.

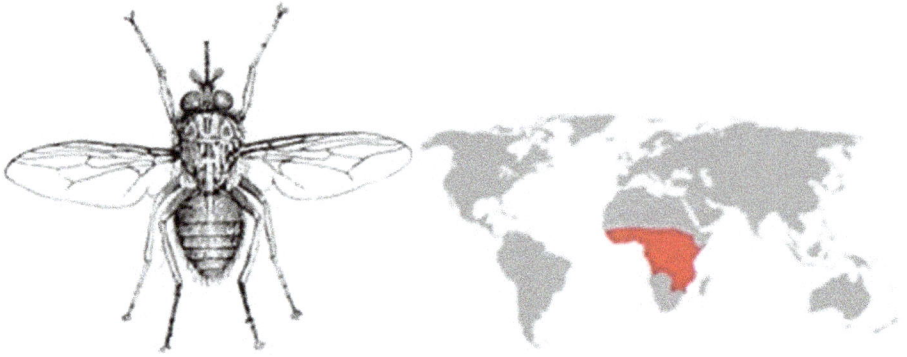

The saviour of Africa's wildlife: the legendary Tsetse fly (genus *Glossina*) and its distribution. Cattle ranching and other stock farming is not possible where this fly is found as it carries sleeping sickness to people and *nagana* among other infections to animals.

The first image is in the public domain, the distribution image courtesy of Wikipedia.

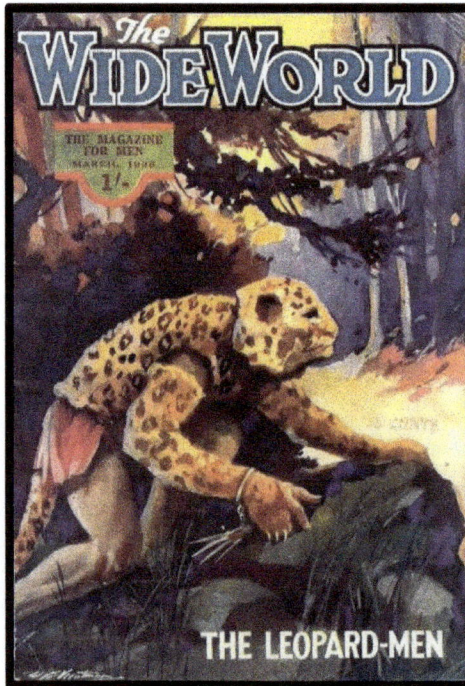

The cover of Wide World magazine for March 1936, featuring an article on the Leopard Society of central Africa. Lycanthropy – the black magic of animals changing into people and back again – has long featured in African mythology; and indeed, in reality. The image is in the public domain.

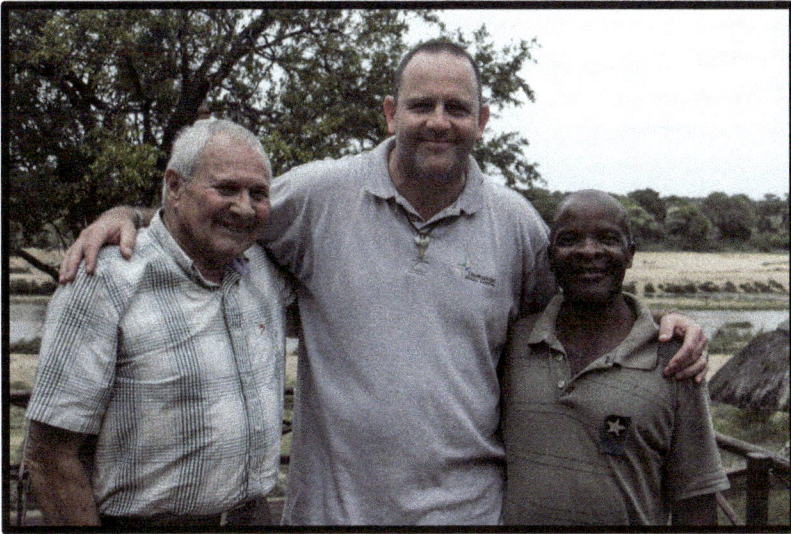

The author (centre) with Paddy Buckmaster (left) and John Khoza (right) at Izinyoni Lodge, Marloth Park, South Africa, in December 2014. John's escape from a war-torn Mozambique through the Kruger Park, running the gauntlet of man-eating lions, is a harrowing tale of survival.

The author with two legends of Africa: Fiona Claire Capstick, and her husband, Adelino Serras Pires at their home in Pretoria, South Africa, in January 2015. Fiona is a phenomenally successful author, and was previously married to Peter Hathaway Capstick. Adelino was a pioneering safari operator, his client list featuring royalty, European aristocracy and famous dignitaries. He passed away in August 2015.

7   Mfuwe – the biggest man-eater

The story of the Mfuwe lion is one of those that illustrates perfectly the mind-numbing fear created by a man-eating cat; compared to many lions, leopards, tigers and bears that have developed a taste for people, he was hardly very prolific at all, his final known tally a mere six people. Compared with some of the protagonists in this book - not to mention the Indian killers - he was almost irrelevant. But three things mark him out as unusual. One, he is the biggest recorded man-eating lion ever reliably measured. Secondly, he was maneless, still a novelty for the majority of people around the globe that haven't studied lions; and third, this was *now*, modern times, the 1990s, nearly a century after the Tsavo lions first gained notoriety. This reminded people that man-eating by lions is not just an interesting feature of colonial times. As do many man-eaters, he had an element of the supernatural to him, a black magic that paralysed the area of Mfuwe (Pronounced Mm-Foo-Weh, not Muh-Fuh-Way or Mu-Fu-Way as often seen), in eastern Zambia's Luangwa River Valley.

In September 1991, Wayne Hosek arrived in the area on a hunting safari. Hosek, a native of Chicago, had spent many long hours as a child in the Field Museum developing an interest in foreign lands, cultures and animals. In the same hall where the awe-inspiring elephant mounts stand – Hosek wrote "in long silenced power" – stood a bronze casting of human warriors facing lions across the hall from them, and the young Hosek would stand before the lions and wonder what it might be like to have nothing between himself and them, for years pondering the circumstances that would lead to such a confrontation. One day, little did he then know, he would find out.

Of all the cultural centres, the African exhibits spoke loudest to Hosek, a feeling often replicated by Westerners. We seem to have an ancient urge to go to that continent, to experience wilderness, wildness and freedom. He led an active, healthy childhood until a trip to Yellowstone in 1954 resulted in him contracting polio. His biggest dread was that he'd not be able to experience his desired adventurous life in Africa. It was, incidentally, the year the Salk vaccine brought relief from polio, but it only arrived just after this incident. Hosek noted that although the vaccine arrived too late for his purposes, he at least was to survive; many of his ward mates weren't so lucky.

Surviving polio means having to re-learn motor skills and basically start from scratch. Hosek determined to live fully, healthily and to keep himself fit. His interest in target shooting blossomed and when he moved to California in 1967 his path crossed with that of Robert Majares, a target-shooting world record holder. He and other crack-shot friends had been on hunting trips to Africa, and the large-scale poaching that was then sweeping the continent had sickened them all. This gave rise to many hunting concessions, determined to conserve the wildlife for future generations and improve local communities at the same time using controlled hunting. It was to one of these that Hosek went, when in 1991 a window of opportunity at last opened for him to go to Africa, his soul's tonic.

The successes of the Luangwa Integrated Resources Development Project have been noted already. It was into this much-improved scene that he stepped, noting on his first night in Kamana Camp that he met a Japanese lion expert, who was leaving the following morning, dejected at having been unable to hunt down a man-eating lion. Hosek's ears pricked up, the discussion proving most intriguing to him. Six lionesses had been shot over the previous three months, the latest earlier that very week; but the Japanese's dejection was soon explained. Despite these measures, the sixth victim had been taken just the night before. The lion was still at large. This is a depressing scenario for any hunter or game control officer; lives are still being lost, and you appear to be shooting innocent lions. Or worse, the deaths are being caused by several lions, perhaps a pride, and the problem is thus bigger than originally thought.

The feeling grew that these lionesses were part of a man-eating male's pride. Accompanying Hosek were Charl Beukes, a Zambian hunter and lodge operator, and Willie Cloete, Beukes's trainee. Beukes felt that the male may have witnessed some or all of the lionesses being shot, which would serve to make him more wary. In addition to the Japanese, a hunter named Carr had tried to kill the man-eater as well but the lion had always managed to evade him, often uncannily, before striking elsewhere. This tendency was first noticed in the Tsavo lions and just further illustrates the clever thinking displayed by an animal that hunts clever prey. The situation was growing increasingly desperate, until the local officials approached Beukes for assistance. So far, his available time had been limited though, due to commitments to hunting clients.

Hosek slept like a log that first night, a legacy of the 35-hour flight from Los Angeles. How soundly he slept is reflected by the story

99

he was told the following morning by Beukes. Not long after everyone else turned in, a clan of hyenas set up an awful shrieking near the skinning area and were only driven away after repeated attempts, an hour or two later. Then a baboon made its way into the kitchen tent and wreaked havoc, imagining the pots were drums. This is a common problem in Africa and between baboons and vervet monkeys, immeasurable quantities of food have been stolen in this way, and people bitten into the bargain. These two were merely the prelude to the main event: around midnight a herd of elephants moseyed into camp and set to the camp flower beds for a full hour, not ten metres (33feet) from the tents.

Eventually Beukes, implored by the camp manager, fired a shotgun over the elephants to scare them off. Through all this, Hosek slept on, blissfully unaware of any of it, although when told, he mentally stored this information about how bold these animals were. It was to be his last decent sleep until he left two whole weeks later. For three days the men combed their concession area for signs of a mature male lion, but although they saw several lions, no mature male or even sign of one was so much as seen. An interesting aside was that they saw no Cape buffalo, a species usually abundant in the area. The two years previous had seen a severe drought and the herds stayed in the parks to utilise the water there. Did this affect the lion behaviour in the area? Almost certainly, it would seem.

Despite the pervading haunting atmosphere, Hosek was as happy as a pig in the proverbial; he was in Africa, listening to the night sounds and breathing the clean air. His biggest annoyance was the absence of buffalo, and he despaired of seeing a lion. Whether or not to cut his trip short at Kamana and head South to Victoria Falls, the Kfuwe flats and the myriad exotic antelope species was running through his head. But as he lay, dozing one day in the afternoon heat while the cicadas rent the air asunder with razor-blasts that seemed impossibly loud, a strange feeling began to come over him. He became acutely aware that everyone in camp, not to mention the villages in the area, was dependant on his decision, on his very movements. For some inexplicable reason he began to feel an escalating guilt that he was not assisting to eradicate the area of the man-eater. I reckon he was just a good guy, and felt that he should step in.

His jet lag had well and truly set in and after his comatose first night, he'd not slept much at all. Despite this his shooting was of its usual high standard. Although he had his mental reservations, Hosek marched up to the camp professional hunters and told them he wanted to try and kill the lion. Beukes and Cloete then told Hosek their interesting theory: they had doubted for some time that the lion was a lioness at all, and that he may be a maneless male. The next step was to determine whether or not killing the lion would still generate revenue for the Development Project, since they were actually outside the designated concession area. Happily, it would. But the biggest advantage was the relief to the local population from the fear of a most horrendous fate. Hosek and the two hunters set their teeth and headed into one of the most daunting prospects in the world: hunting a known, accomplished man-eater in the animal's back yard.

The first task was to try piece together the killer's *modus operandi* by speaking to survivors and eye-witnesses. The team's trackers combed the area, scanning minutely at every place they stopped. The idea is to try and decipher a pattern, a tendency, a habit, anything that will help predict his next move, much like the psychological profiling carried out on human serial killers. It can also identify weaknesses, shortcomings, anything to gain even the tiniest edge over the quarry, and it is an interesting human equivalent of what the lion is doing at the same time, as it probes for a weakness, something to exploit. That part of it is chilling to contemplate. The villagers that spoke with them were clearly petrified, their stories horrific, draining just to listen to. And it was then that, somewhat unexpectedly, Wayne Hosek started to feel another emotion: anger.

The village of Ngozo was the scene of the lion's sixth and most recent victim and it was here that its reputation took on a strange dimension that launched it in the minds of the community to the status of a supernatural being, a demon-lion or an animal clearly controlled by *mbojo* – black magic. The day after eating the elderly woman, the lion was clearly seen to enter her house, and exited with her white carry bag or laundry bag, full of her possessions. This was creepy enough to the haunted thoughts of a hunted community, but he then marched through the village in plain view, pausing to roar loudly, pick the bag up again and repeat the process. The villagers shouted and beat pots until he departed. He was seen to play with the bag a few more times and the next day it was found about a mile (1,6km) from her house, in the riverbed of the Lupande, dry due to the drought. Although it was visible, no-one would venture near it and Hosek wrote that even the hornbills seemed to avoid going near it.

From the safety and comfort of my table at home, the lion's behaviour is merely the same as a housecat would do. It's actually endearing, if admittedly a trifle macabre, but the circumstances whereby he acquired the bag were definitely not: he had killed the bag's owner the day before, and no-one was likely to appreciate any playfulness on his part, especially not in rural Africa, where only the supernaturally evil could brazenly walk into a village and touch the possessions of the dead, never mind play with them. The next morning the bag was found several hundred yards upriver, the lion's tracks showing that he'd again played with the bag overnight.

That did it; the local elders gathered to discuss things and they decided that the lion was a sorcerer, or at least demon-possessed. The bag, they said, was undoubtedly bewitched. Hosek noted that the lion did indeed seem to revel in the discomfort he was causing, although again his writings are so reminiscent of a playful cat that it's difficult not to smile, albeit momentarily. The lion was spotted by an adult male villager but made no move to attack. This person finally verified the villagers' reports that the lion was a very large light-coloured male, and that he was definitely maneless.

One curious phenomenon regarding the terror of a community is that the fear and negative energy do seem to exacerbate matters, and affect other people. In days gone, the (educated, white) hunter / writer would bravely save the superstitious, uneducated and helpless masses from the ravages of a foul man-eating beast, his own beliefs and moral backbone shaken, but ultimately victorious. Stiff upper lip and all that, his neatly clipped and very British moustache evident on the referred-to lip…but every so often, Africa throws a curve ball. And even the hardiest, most mentally- and emotionally-stable educated Westerner realises with a bump that there may just be something to African black magic after all. The Njombe lions, for instance, featured a dose unlike any other before and probably none since. Wayne Hosek realised that he too was susceptible to the atmosphere of dread.

A certain game scout had been particularly frightened for his family's safety ever since the lion started his reign of terror, and had several times seen the lion melting out of the tall, golden grass surrounding his village and back. Lion tracks around the perimeter verified his account. While Hosek and the hunters spoke with the game scout, his terrified children huddled around, wordlessly staring at the white men in the way that African children have. As the villagers were all too terrified to go near the bag, the scout took the men into the middle of the riverbed and pointed it out from some 40 yards away (36 metres), flatly refusing to go any nearer.

Hosek recounts the experience as being the most eerie sight, following the massive lion's tracks in the dry Lupande riverbed, guns in hand, and seeing the bag. He notes the blood draining from his face and indeed, his entire body, to seemingly settle in his feet, and despite the overpowering heat, he felt what he could only describe as his blood going cold, a feeling so awful that he hoped never to experience it again. The sudden realisation of the reality of where they were, and what was happening, hit Hosek with a shock. The tension was palpable, the trackers refusing to make eye contact, everyone terse and on full mental alert. As have hundreds of hunters in similar situations, Hosek's whole being told him that he most definitely did *not* want to be there, at that moment. But at the same time, he knew he would not turn back until the task had been completed.

Realising that they might track indefinitely while the lion killed again, the men decided to bait the cat to shorten their odds. A spot was chosen 60 yards upriver at the foot of a fever tree, and the team left for the night, Hosek noting a feeling of disbelief at the predicament he was in. He slept poorly, despite being sufficiently bush-conditioned already that his mind had filed the usual African nocturnal orchestra as background noise. They were up before dawn to build a blind, placing a large piece of deceased hippo at the foot of the smooth, yellow-green thorn tree before settling into the blind in the mid-afternoon. Once in a blind when hunting a man-eater, you are there until the next morning: leaving in the dark is sheer folly.

Nothing appeared that night besides a genet, punching way above its weight by sampling the hippo remains, and a live hippo that actually bumped into the blind before the man-scent reached his nostrils, and he bounced off in that way that hippos have when startled. It's comical to see such a large animal galvanised into surprised action, but understandably, no-one laughed. When the trackers came for the team in the morning, however, the man-eater's tracks were near the bait and the blind. He had come prowling about, and the men, despite being alert and actively hunting him, had been none the wiser. More fresh tracks surrounded the white bag, which had been moved again.

That day the hunters decided to collect all the baits from their various placements since the hunt had commenced, and add them all to the hippo portion near the blind. This was a huge and revolting undertaking but was a good idea, as many of the baits were large and would have to be dragged, leaving various trails which the lion was bound to scent. They made sure to drag one right by the white bag. Hosek noted the tension climbing as each minute slipped by, and felt a strange, surreal feeling of detachment. This is often felt by combat soldiers but is also a feature of jet lag exhaustion, when you wade straight into a very tense task and aren't able to relax until time corrects your body clock. Hosek likely had a combination of both.

Entering the blind again around 3:30pm, the heat and tension put Hosek into a strange semi-sleep, a condition again common under combat or hunting conditions. The brain rests but is alert; in itself is it disturbing but wonderful, and I have often marvelled at it when it has reacted on my behalf, even though I know I had been asleep. Nothing happened until the middle of the night when a branch cracked not two meters from the blind. In a millisecond no-one was even semi-asleep, but it wasn't the lion. If anything, it was something even more dangerous; totally oblivious to their presence, an elephant was right next to the blind, feeding off a tree. If he sensed the men and panicked, or just stepped the wrong way, they would not be completing their lion hunt, nor doing much anything else, ever again.

Beukes slowly angled his .458 upward and everyone held their collective breath. After a few minutes the pachyderm sauntered on, blissfully unaware of the men or the near-cardio failure he'd just caused. When they could get their hearts started again, it took another while to get them back to normal speed, then the men settled back into their half-slumber. At dawn the trackers arrived and told the hunters how the man-eater had drifted through the village before catching and eating a bush pig on the outskirts, the entire village being treated to the soundtrack. Beukes glanced at Hosek and verbalised the gloom and frustration they were all feeling at their failure to make any sort of contact with the lion: "He knows what we are doing."

It was at this point that Hosek notes the conflict taking a new turn, the battle now mental as well as physical and maybe even deeper than that, to a spiritual level. They met the chief of Ngozo Village, Kakumbi, who told some of the terror that his people were living under. What struck Hosek most was the children's part in all this, and almost without him realising it, the anger he'd already been harbouring for a while began to boil over inside him. It may sound dramatic and like a justification to shoot an animal; but I have seen little kids in Kenya with limbs lost to lions, and the most pitiful stories to boot. It takes a while for the gob-smacked feeling of surprised disbelief to leave one, but I'm sure if you hear enough of them, it will make you angry.

Hosek ventured to tell Beukes of his feelings, and Beukes bounced them right back; he too had felt slowly-mounting rage at the lion. Hosek mentions that he was by now on such an adrenalin buzz that he made a mental note to concentrate. They still had a job to do and one that required focus and lightning reactions, with very little margin for error. He knew the adrenalin was a good thing as his system charged his body for the task ahead, but how much was being placed there by fear and how much by rage, he knew not. As their spirits were low, they went off to hunt for the rest of the day with the trackers. They needed the mental break and this also allowed Beukes to refine their strategy.

The men built a new blind some 60 yards from the first one and hung new bait. Hosek photographed some children who watched as they built it, the eldest another lion victim with one arm. They then found out that the lion had attacked a 14-year-old boy just the day before, the youth slamming his hut's door in its face after it had stalked him. Although the entire area seemed to be in a blue funk of terror, Hosek noted that old African fatalism: the 5pm curfew was in place, yet some people still milled about the roads beyond the curfew, in the belief that the lion would grab someone other than them.

After another sleepless night the men saw to their intense satisfaction that the lion had fed in the night from the new bait. He'd even lain brazenly on a footpath to finish his meal before having a snooze, still on the path. Hosek took a photo of the lion's pug mark but his camera froze, broken. There was no need to share thoughts as the men exchanged uneasy glances. In the world of hunting dangerous game, never mind confirmed man-eating lions, the slightest thing can go wrong at the most inopportune time. This often adds up to a death, and it can be the hunter's. Capstick wrote often about the presence of Murphy's Law while hunting. The camera breaking seemed to be an omen, and no-one liked the idea.

That afternoon, 9 September 1991 (a real humdinger for the numerologists), the team once again settled into the new blind. The local people had been instructed to stay indoors. Not only might there be bullets flying around, but a wounded man-eating lion may soon be on the loose, and nobody wanted that to happen. He'd already proven adept while healthy; a bullet wound or two was unlikely to improve his demeanour. An hour hadn't even passed when Beukes indicated silence; he'd caught a glimpse of the lion circling them in the grass not 15 metres (17 yards) off to the one side of the blind. Time passed slowly. After hours of straining tension, Hosek felt himself wanting to doze off around dusk, a natural reaction to a sustained state of hyper-adrenalin. Any "high" has a downside, even a natural one such as adrenalin. Suddenly Beukes actually stood up, urgently motioning Hosek to do the same!

Cloete pointed the lion out to Hosek, the beast cleverly using the bait tree as cover, and coming towards the men in a straight line, almost unseen with the tree directly between him and the blind. Eventually Hosek saw him, coming along in a fast trot. When he got to the tree, he came around it and the men saw him clearly for the first time. Hosek's first reaction was that the cat was huge. The animal ignored the bait, trotted on past the blind and snarled at them, fully aware of the men's presence. Why he did this is a mystery; he clearly knew the men were there. He also clearly wasn't coming to feed as he ignored the bait completely. Perhaps he was coming to the bait and just before getting to the bait tree, he scented the men and kept on running. But surely then he'd veer off and not continue merrily on by them? He was young and not that experienced; maybe a year later he'd have reacted differently. Whatever his motivation, it was fortunate for the men as, although he was trotting and starting to pick up speed, in passing the blind he offered a full broadside shot.

Hosek took it, the .375H&H round audibly thumping home as the shot raked the lion's lungs. Beukes' .458 fired in a blur of orange beside Hosek as the professional triggered the follow-up shot, Hosek hearing no report in his heightened sensory state. The lion opened the taps and disappeared into the tall grass. Presently the gurgling death rattle of a hard-hit animal reached their ears and it was followed by a bout of beautiful silence. Hosek stood savouring the surreal moment as the professionals went to check on the lion, despite his relief still strangely feeling the fear that had stayed with them for weeks now. The trackers had heard the shots and were bringing the Land Rover. Hosek exchanged greetings with them as they drove by him, and stopped where the two hunters had found the dead lion; it had travelled some 40 yards (36 metres) before expiring.

Then Hosek experienced another side of Africa, hauntingly beautiful and deep with meaning as Gilbert - the chief tracker - gave a soul-stirring rendition of The Kunda Lion Song, which can only be sung when a lion has been killed. Indeed, so seriously do the Kunda take the singing of that song, that they believe to sing it if no lion has first been killed will soon result in the singer themselves being killed by a lion. It is thus rarely heard. The trackers were overjoyed, hugging and even kissing Hosek in their relief and gratitude. The horizon glowed orange as the local community lit large fires in celebration, shouts and singing ringing out as the news spread. In the darkening evening, the three white men and three trackers stood, with a background of orange and the voices of the community, with the dead man-eater at their feet. Hosek stood imprinting the surreal scene on his mind.

When the community arrived, a crowd of children took turns spitting on and beating the lion, the fear and anger pouring out after months of anguish. An ancient crone, a respected elder, squeezed Hosek's hand and thanked him profusely, which prompted the entire village to do the same. When Hosek eventually approached the lion, he was indeed a massive beast, the biggest man-eater ever reliably measured. He was 10 feet, 6 inches long (315cm) and when on all-fours, was a staggering five feet (150cm) at the ear tips, suggesting over four feet at the shoulder. When the men weighed him, he displaced 500lb (227kg), but this was after losing a good deal of blood and other fluids. He is a full mount today in the Chicago Field Museum where Hosek spent so much time as a boy, in the same hall as the Tsavo lions. The depth of his chest is incredible, suggesting a weight while alive of around 550lb (250kg). His body is massive. Indeed, author Philip Caputo estimated his weight at 249kg. Part of the display - fittingly - is a white laundry bag on the ground beside the lion.

Strangely enough, in death the Man-eater of Mfuwe still got a little dig in at Wayne Hosek, Charl Beukes and Willie Cloete: during the evening celebrations with the villagers, Beukes brought his camera, remembering how Hosek's had broken as they tried to photograph a pug mark. It had been an unsettling moment for the men. But on that night, when they tried to get a snap for posterity's sake, Beukes's camera also refused to work!

8   Kruger – the terrible secret behind the jewel of Africa

Let's be clear right from the off: it is impossible to determine exactly how many people have been killed and eaten by lions in the Kruger National Park, but between 1960 and 2005, when the Park effectively served as a border between South Africa and Mozambique, even the most ridiculously, laughably-conservative estimate of victims far outstrips the other protagonists in this book, probably by many times over. It is just as well that an accurate number cannot be determined, as it actually constitutes one of the greatest ongoing tragedies on a large scale in all of modern recorded time. The death rate is one of pandemic proportions. It would be wrong to say that, compared with the Kruger lions, even the Njombe lions are a mere litter of kittens. This is principally because the Njombe lions were lethal, efficient killers and over a concentrated period, are unequalled in recorded history as prolific man-eaters. But over an extended time, and over the entire area of the Park, the number of human deaths attributable to the Kruger lions far, far exceeds the total of the Njombe lions.

There are a variety of reasons as to why this fact is not widely advertised, but it has been alluded to and attempts have even been made to quantify the number of victims. The figures are shocking, and yet it continues to be ignored or given short shrift when an effort is made to bring it to light. The knee-jerk reason is well-known. Potential bad publicity in a tourist-rich area drives much of the image portrayed of any destination. Throw in the fact that most of that period, 1960-2005, coincided with the Apartheid government's tenure (the first democratic South African election was held in 1994); this meant that the country was effectively under siege from terrorist insurgence and had an active military border to patrol from South-West Africa (now Namibia) in the west, Botswana and Zimbabwe – for much of this time, still Rhodesia – to the north, and Mozambique to the east. The influx of refugees from a war-torn Mozambique was even a bad thing to South Africa's non-white residents, as these people competed with them for work.

So, everyone conveniently ignored the fact that people crossing the Park were occasionally eaten. To admit that people regularly crossed the Park would have been a political problem; by the very nature of the secretive crossings, no-one has any idea how many people crossed or how often. The only tangible evidence is the record of the people caught by the police, military and game department personnel and many of these, after being deported back to Mozambique, promptly turned around and crossed the Park again. Naturally, anyone that successfully made the journey was never going to admit the fact, never mind brazenly advertise it. The intention would have been to disappear into South Africa, perhaps assume a new identity and find employment, the more casual the better. Data analytics is a probability science; it can hardly ever be 100 percent accurate. So, using the already-shaky numbers of refugees intercepted, no tally so devised will ever be reliable. But it may help to paint the picture and shock people out of their reverie. In short, the warnings to stay in your vehicle in Kruger are among the most vital to obey in the world. Many, if not most, of the Kruger lions have eaten humans and many have done so with monotonous regularity.

The Kruger National Park - often just referred to as Kruger - was officially formed and named thus in 1926, from the merging of the Sabi and Shingwedzi Game Reserves. It had originally been conceptually envisaged by one Jakob Louis van Wyk in 1895 and President Paul Kruger endorsed the idea. In 1898, the South African Republic first protected the area that was to become the Park. It now forms part of the Great Limpopo Transfrontier Park, in conjunction with the Gonarezhou National Park in Zimbabwe and Mozambique's Limpopo National park. For decades it was acknowledged as the world's best-run and best-managed national reserve, certainly the best in Africa. The park's initial intention was to control the rampant hunting of the time, and in so doing, to protect the rapidly-diminishing wildlife species. The man that was to have the greatest impact on the institution that is Kruger became the reserve's first warden in 1902: Major James Stevenson-Hamilton, a Scot that is rightly viewed as the father of the park and a Lowveld legend. The Park over time became part of the very fabric of our being as South Africans, a national treasure and escape from civilisation to which people would flow, a great source of pride. The rest of this chapter notwithstanding, it is still a phenomenal reserve, a place of wonderment, a uniquely brilliant example of how a national park should be run. Little did we know the terrible secret that lurked just below the glossy surface; like anything tied to the really wild places, it has a dark underbelly.

The signs were there; it was common knowledge, and rightly so in any large and wild reserve, that to alight from one's vehicle was exceptionally risky. In later years, rumours started to swirl about refugees from Mozambique traversing the Park at night and being eaten. The reaction was almost universally that Kruger was an effective border. In that regard, I am as guilty as anyone, except perhaps those that knew the stark truth in detail and still did nothing about it. In post-Apartheid South Africa, the rampant crime rate and the number of road-accident deaths each year rendered the number of deaths by lion as almost irrelevant. Coupled with the propensity to cover the truth for tourist reasons, the extent of the problem was never pandered about.

More on Kruger's rampant man-eating problem later; for now, I want to introduce you to Harold Trollope, probably the most lethally-effective lion hunter in modern recorded history. Born in 1881, the man who would eventually earn the name "Vukani" (a Zulu and Xhosa name meaning "Wake Up"; the Shangaan people called him "Mavukane", which means he who rises early) is not widely known today, although during his life he was a legend in South African game reserve circles. He gained the tribal nickname based on his metronomic ability to rise early (4am), day-in, day-out, regardless how rigorous the previous day's activities had been, and loudly rouse his companions. He was instrumental in the forming of the Addo Elephant National Park in South Africa's Eastern Cape Province, but it is for his time in Kruger that Trollope is best-known. There is a hut named after him in the Malelane Restcamp, where he plied much of his deadly trade. He was actually one of the original owners of the Camelthorn Reserve that was incorporated into Kruger and his family reside in the area to this day, in Thabazimbi, while they operate Camelthorn Hunting Safaris. Barbara Matthews wrote a book on his exploits, *The man they called Vukani, the life and times of Harold Trollope* (Bluecliff, 2005).

Lions were declared vermin in the 1920s to protect the stock when large-scale cattle farming was introduced into the area. Lions being the energy-efficient opportunists that they are, large meat-rich animals all nicely lined up such as cattle are much more tempting than a fast hardy antelope or buffalo. Enter men such as Trollope, tasked with thinning out local lion populations and following up 'problem animals' (these last-mentioned translate as crop-raiders, stock-raiders and man-eaters in game reserve-speak). When Trollope was allocated the Malelane area, along the Park's southern border, he was so effective that he shot over 400 lions there alone. That sounds like mass slaughter, but it was the way that he did it, the man himself, that was noteworthy. The other rangers actually considered Trollope to have been slightly touched.

Trollope was a force of nature, a man whose mighty will and unshakeable self-belief were backed up by the most mind-blowing shooting ability seen anywhere. He was even castigated for inviting lion charges, allowing chased-down ones to recover, tormenting them and waiting until they were within a lethal distance before snapping off a shot through the brain, the cat often falling dead at his feet. His undoubted ability notwithstanding, this – if I may blight the aura of a Park legend – is foolish in the extreme. The numbers of things that can go even slightly wrong while hunting big game are many and when something does, it's usually critical. To deliberately and unnecessarily place oneself in harm's way with no margin for error is suicidal, not to mention dangerous to companions.

In 1926 Trollope for once let his guard down, or more precisely, his luck appeared at last to have run out. A wounded lion charged him and would have killed him, but for the interventions of Ranger-Corporal Nombolo Mdluli. Mdluli shot the cat, and it fell dead across Trollope's legs. The great man never forgot this, and for years after he'd left the employ of the Park, Trollope would still send Mdluli an annual gift of £2, a considerable sum back then. As an interesting aside, Mdluli served the Park for nearly 40 years – from 1919 to 1958 – and it was a fitting tribute when he was recognised in 2011 by the official opening of the Nombolo Mdluli Conference Centre at Skukuza, Kruger's capital. Trollope was never tagged by a lion; this one time that he'd dropped his guard, Mdluli kept his record unbroken. The overarching impression left by Harold Trollope was a lion population in Kruger that learned to bolt at the very scent of a human. Harry Wolhuter considered man-eating by lions to be most unusual in Kruger. This was obviously due to the lessons dealt them by rangers and hunters such as Trollope. As the Park built better fencing, the predators needed just as much protection from poachers as the herd animals. Lions were no longer shot *en masse* in Kruger.

To understand the mindset of the time, we need to go back to the appointment of Stevenson-Hamilton in 1902. The first task he set his mind to once he had appointed Harry Wolhuter, the first ranger, was to arrest and convict some policemen of the South African Constabulary that were running a fine poaching racket. Today, this is an easy sum: acknowledged crime, arrest and convict. Back then, a conservation area was still a novelty, white policemen were as above the law as one could get, and carnivores were classified as vermin. It was while engaged in pursuing these poachers that

Wolhuter was attacked by a lion which he managed to stab to death with a small sheath knife. That incident is recounted later in this chapter. When the men in question were eventually arrested, Stevenson-Hamilton was so convinced they would be freed that he recorded in his log how nauseating it was to think they would likely not be convicted.

There was a pleasant surprise in store: in a precedent-setting case the men received stiff fines. Stevenson-Hamilton – and the Park – had arrived, and it was clear that he was not a man that would blame the indigenous Africans while allowing the powers that were to abuse that power. The message was out: poachers would be hunted themselves, regardless of their status or ethnicity. Stevenson-Hamilton was a gifted natural conservationist, and unlike so many hunters that later turned to conservation (Robert Frump used the term "repentant butchers" in his excellent book, *The Man-eaters of Eden*, The Lyons Press, 2006), he realised instinctively that the carnivores needed saving too, or the entire ecological area would suffer. He was however no hypocrite and no saint, and remained a lion hunter throughout his active life. Cleverly though, he tempered it to the Park's advantage.

Initial feeling against the establishment of the Park and the conservation efforts was literally hateful. At a 1905 meeting of the Transvaal Game Protection Society, the (then-Sabi) Reserve was roundly castigated for breeding lions, not protecting game. A full twenty years later, little had changed; in a 1925 letter to Farmers Weekly, the Sabi Game Reserve was accused of scandalously breeding lions for twenty years. It was the one thing that all three main population groups – Boers, Brits and indigenous Africans – agreed on; lions should be exterminated. Calls to eliminate the lions would have been successful if actioned; Stevenson-Hamilton considered there to be only 600 in the entire Park in 1925. But his sleight of hand was what saved the lions; he killed lions when necessary to appease ranchers and political interests, making a great show of displaying the skulls and outwardly showing the public that lions were not allowed free rein. Meanwhile though, he made sure that the species would not be eliminated. There is no question that this action saved the species from extinction in South Africa. Even the environmentalists of the time thought it wise to remove lions with a view to saving the game animals!

There was another landmark reason to save lions: the government was growing restless subsidising the Reserve. Stevenson-Hamilton realised that hunting and tourist money would have to help finance the running of it, and persuaded the railways to schedule a stop near what is now Skukuza, the Park capital. The railway company already ran railroad tours of South Africa so Stevenson-Hamilton asked them to add a few hours in Kruger. It became clear almost immediately that the attraction was not defined "game" – antelope and other herbivores – but lions. The trip was considered a failure if no lions were seen. It was against this backdrop that Stevenson-Hamilton had to juggle his control of the lion population to appease the political powers and ranchers, while providing tourist viewing that was deemed worthwhile. So in 1926, when Kruger was formally chartered as a national park, the killing of lions was officially halted: it had been noted how the lions confined their activity to the night hours when hunted, and this meant they would not be seen by tourists, who were day visitors.

Tourism flourished once people were allowed into the Park in their own cars; the lions worked out pretty quickly that vehicles weren't edible and didn't attack the cats either, so they ignored them. This worked out well for everyone. It's an odd phenomenon that the cats seem to see people inside cars as part of that car, unless one breaks the outline by getting out, standing up above the roofline or some similar act. I think they're more intelligent than that, and even the most rampant man-eaters among them realise the investment in effort, danger and risk of injury that could come from attacking a vehicle, and deem that risk too high. It does however result in the closest viewing of wild lions on earth, one being able to literally drive to within a metre (2-3 feet) of the cats before they deign to move.

People have tested the theory of breaking the outline as safely as possible, on the far side of the vehicle from a pride of lions, Frump himself even trying it once. The lions are instantly up and growling, or run off. The theory is that we humans appear hostile on foot, a harking back to the primal days for lions, obviously. So, the lion war had been won; the rangers had saved the lions from extinction, the lions saved the Park by providing a stream of tourists. But there was a proviso: a new breed of lion with no reason to fear humans. Bob Frump, by the way, is a brilliant writer-editor out of New York, and has a professional history in wealth management and consulting services, mostly as editor-in-chief for some of the world's foremost financial organisations. Throngs of his ex-colleagues revere his personable, human approach and consider his mentorship to be invaluable, often life-directing. His research is excellent and he likes the aspect of practical experience as well.

The Man-eaters of Eden reveals much of the guarded reality of Kruger.

When the Park was finally made official in 1926, the local inhabitants (mainly the Shangaan tribe) were forcibly moved west into South Africa, or east into Mozambique. As they had for decades, people continued to travel through Kruger, mostly into South Africa, with its powerful farming and mining economies. This increased once the Portuguese colonial government upped sticks and abandoned its colony in 1974 (following which the civil war really shifted into top gear), but by then the ruling National Party in South Africa had written Apartheid into law and gradually the borders were fenced off, electrified with a lethal voltage and patrolled. Nearly a hundred refugees are said to have died on the fence, so the flow of immigrants hardly can be said to have stopped as a result of closing the borders. Frump likens the border's effectiveness to that of the border between the US and Mexico: not very high. What did happen, however, was the change in behaviour on the part of the Mozambicans; since the patrols and helicopters could spot them by day, they started to travel at night.

The net result was a huge and constant flow of immigrants through the Park at night, which was met by a lion population with no fear of people, and in its gleeful and grateful element of darkness. Yet still the people kept making the journey; the conditions in Mozambique can only be imagined if running that gauntlet of death was preferable to enduring them, and once in Apartheid South Africa, things were hardly likely to be rosy for any successful immigrant. But the pull of family and tribe were strong enough for people to keep making the journey, that and the likelihood of work – however lowly – and a meal or two a day. The reality is that before Apartheid, there were few recorded instances of man-eating in Kruger, aside from the odd occurrence or two. Some of these are noted in another chapter of this book. The exception was a bout in 1898 when the Boer War broke out. The mines shut down and the Mozambican workers were simply offloaded. Forced to march home through Kruger, many were exhausted or ill and the lions picked several of them off, adding a British sentry or two for good measure. Stevenson-Hamilton logged this but felt it easily explained as lions exploiting the weak.

In the 1970s the immigrants were joined by refugees fleeing the civil war in Mozambique. The country suffered the added misfortune of alternating floods and famine, not just once or twice, but for many years on end. The result was a huge flow of humanity into the Park, and the consumption of people by lions ramped up to pandemic proportions. Frump interviewed John Khoza, currently of Izinyoni Lodge in Marloth Park, which is owned and operated by Paddy and Pauline Buckmaster. As a fifteen-year-old in 1972, the death of both his parents had left him destitute. He needed to cross the Park to get to Johannesburg and a better life. So, John chose the wisest option, paying a guide to cross the Park, and set off as one of a group one July morning at 2am. Many crossed with no guide, just heading west, and many of these people especially were captured by the security forces, or killed and eaten by lions. Resting up in the shade by day and avoiding patrols, helicopters and tourists was difficult enough; but the nights featured the real dangers. Elephants, hyenas, buffalo, rhinoceros; all these animals could and did present very real mortal danger to people, and many were indeed killed by these creatures. Elephants especially can be lethal and surprising them on foot in the dark often ends badly for the people involved.

John Khoza's group were found on the second night by the lions. The guide had stressed what they all knew anyway: never run. In the wilds of Africa there are three hard-and-fast rules: 1) elephants have right of way; 2) never get between a hippo and the water; 3) never run from a lion. To run from a lion, even a mildly curious one, is a death sentence. It triggers an age-old chase reaction in the cats and that is generally that. The group stood stock-still for fifteen minutes and more, frozen to the spot. After a while the lions left them, there being no visible weak point to the group and no instinct was triggered by someone running. This was repeated several times a night, for the many nights it took to cross the Park. At length, the group came to the Crocodile River – as Frump says, it is aptly named – and swam it. To safety; to work and thus food, survival.

John was at the bottom of the South African resident food chain, even though he wasn't even a legitimate resident. It speaks volumes that he was happy as these conditions far outstripped those in Mozambique. Apartheid South Africa was no haven or utopia for anyone of colour. And so, life continued for John until one day in 1985 when a uniformed official picked him out of a group and sought his papers. Naturally John had none and was merely driven right back across the Park to a holding area on the Mozambique border with Kruger. The fencing here was weak; it didn't need to be good. The lions were as effective a deterrent to crossing the Park as could be imagined. But again, it speaks volumes about Mozambique in 1985 that John Khoza waited until the guards' attention was elsewhere, and dashed into Kruger, toward the west, toward the lions.

He ran like a madman, two other refugees seeing him and following. He knew it was risky but it was daylight and he needed to place as much distance between himself and the border as he could, as fast as possible. Khoza headed west for a time then cut south, knowing he had to get over the Crocodile River to lose himself among the plantation workers. The men reached the river but the other two couldn't swim; Khoza would probably have to get a length of rope to help them if he wasn't caught. He surrendered himself to fate and dived in, making the 100-foot swim (30 metres) without incident. He had just made it to the road when an armoured Land Rover appeared. Before he could run John Khoza was staring at the open end of a South African assault rifle. The two young white men bundled him into the vehicle and one smoked relaxedly while the other contacted base about their capture.

He had been so close; he was still close. John Khoza gazed out over the corn fields and made a dash for freedom. Surrendering himself to fate much as he had in the Crocodile River, Khoza made it through several fields, his pursuers gaining. Ahead were a group of farm workers, and Khoza's luck was in. They were Mozambicans and told him where to hide. The soldiers thundered by and John Khoza was safe, at least temporarily. He worked in construction for a time before running into Paddy Buckmaster and helping to build Izinyoni Lodge. He is now settled and Paddy was instrumental in obtaining South African citizenship for John. John Khoza is a happy man with a wife and six children. His story is epic, but more amazing is that he is merely one of many thousands.

For a full understanding of this constant refugee flow, a bit of background on Mozambique is needed. In September 1964 the indigenous people commenced with their drive for independence as the Mozambican Liberation Front (or Frelimo), their part in the casting off of the colonial yoke that swept the continent at the time. This resulted in a bitter war that only ramped up in 1974 when the Portuguese withdrew and Frelimo established a Marxist government. Other factors then worsened, not improved, the plight of Mozambique's citizens. South Africa had a strong functioning Apartheid government and Rhodesia (now Zimbabwe) largely embraced the practice as well, if not officially written into its legislation. Mozambique now posed a threat to these countries' eastern borders from a viewpoint of cross-border insurgence raids. Border security was increased and an anti-Marxist guerrilla force was established within Mozambique (the Mozambican National Resistance or Renamo). The war was savage, bitter and long. Human rights violations by both sides were constant. The country to this day features an AK-47 assault rifle on its flag and coat of arms.

The inevitable result was an increased stream of people across the Park towards South Africa, but no longer merely pulled by the economic promise of a job and regular meals, but rather pushed by the slaughter in Mozambique as well. Frump wrote of the two sides of the coin; the refugees were starving; they were willing to risk the lions. The lions saw weakened easy prey. They would risk attacking people. So, how many? How many people fled Mozambique? How many risked death in Kruger? The numbers in the 1970s were considerable, and grew exponentially in the 1980s and 1990s, driven by poverty, then war, then natural disasters. The capture rate provides a starting point but actual traffic was far larger. In 1982 the annual capture figure was 2,000 people (largely between 1960 and 1980). By 1985 this had ballooned to 1,500 a month, a massive 18 thousand a year. These are the captured refugees, remember.

By 1984, a total of 45 thousand refugees had been driven out of Mozambique; by 1985 this rose to a total of nearly 220 thousand, to a total of 350 thousand by 1986 and to a mind-blowing total of 900 thousand during the plague year, 1987. By 1990 the figure had climbed to 1.4 million refugees and by 1993, it reached 1.7 million. So, a total of 1.7 million people - refugees - had fled Mozambique between the 1970s and the 1990s. Many, if not most of these went through the Kruger National Park. By then, Nelson Mandela was free and the 1994 elections in South Africa promised relief and opportunity, hence the ramping up of the numbers. The *de facto* policy of the South African government is that the refugees have no legal standing in the Park, no rights. They 'steal' jobs from South Africans. This has continued to be the case in the new South Africa. If anything, it's an even greater problem as the borders are far less-stringently policed, the free haven of the miracle country that will provide for the entire region proving an irresistible lure to millions. The problem boiled over in massive xenophobic riots in 2008 as South Africans revolted in the poorer townships against the influx of people from all over the region, that were supposedly taking their jobs.

The northern region of the Park is dry, desolate and much less-frequented by tourists. It is in this region that many refugees

117

crossed and where a staggering number have been killed and eaten. Initially, as alluded to before, lions scattered at the sight of people in the daytime. When they were no longer hunted, they stopped fleeing. Then the refugee supply grew, and started traveling by dark. Again, the lions' behaviour changed. Eventually, to navigate, the refugees – many weak, starving, wounded or sick – would stagger along using the Cahorra Bassa power lines overhead; these are fed power by the Cahorra Bassa dam. And again, the lions adjusted their behaviour accordingly. They learned to gravitate toward the power lines, as these usually resulted in a steady flow of refugees. From there it was normal carnivore behaviour: select a weak target – someone small, overweight, injured, sick – and eat it.

Absurdly, man-eating can even be a drawcard: at a private game camp elsewhere in Africa a few years back, a tourist was lost to a lion and the rangers feared a slump in business. But business boomed; the tourists wanted to know the place was authentic, the dangers real, and they saw that it was. Some private game lodges in South Africa have climbed 2,500% in value over the past twenty years. But back to the refugees in Kruger; by the mid-1990s the army considered 100 thousand people a year were moving through the Park, 50,000 having been caught in 1995 alone. The rangers and the army considered themselves to have apprehended 25% of the people that crossed. As Bob Frump suggested, one would suspect that the lions could have done at least as well, considering their detection equipment and incentive to find the people.

Frump himself however admits that it's not that straightforward. There are further factors to consider; some of the refugees were bush smart, had better survival skills, didn't run to trigger being chased, had better means to evade harm. The many people apprehended by the officialdom means that effectively they were gotten to before the lions could get to them. So, the chance is probably greater that the lions would not catch as many as the army and rangers. Frump tabled the refugee traffic and possible deaths as follows, using the almost absurdly-conservative guess that the lions would only kill one percent of the refugees that crossed Kruger, in other words perform twenty-five times worse than the human patrols; he has kindly allowed me to reproduce the table:

Estimates of Refugee traffic and lion kills in Kruger at 1 percent

Years	Refugees per year	Total crossing	Arrested by rangers, police and army	Fatalities if 1 percent killed by lions
1960-1980	8,000 per year	160,000	40,000	1,600
1980-1990	35,000 per year	350,000	85,000	3,500
1990-1997	100,000 per year	700,000	175,000	7,000
1997-2005	16,000 per year	128,000	70,000	1,280
Total		1,338,000		
Total fatalities				**13,380**

Many scientists feel this top-down approach is too inaccurate, but many others, and I must agree with these latter, consider the estimate to be way too conservative, regardless. For reasons stressed throughout this book, such as the very nature of consumption of humans by animals resulting in the evidence being removed, I think they could be at least ten times the above estimate. So that would equate to more than 130,000 people. These figures remind me of the Holocaust in that they are too large for proper comprehension. One cannot grasp them in terms of human suffering and death, and the figures seem to lose the impact they deserve. But they could well be this extensive. The saddest thing is that, as Frump mentions, these figures pale by comparison with other pandemics, diseases and genocide on the continent of Africa, and since Mozambicans don't have great public relations, their plight was never going to result in any meaningful action. That was of course assuming that one could establish conclusively that a problem existed in the first place, and that it could be quantified. And as we have seen, it cannot, certainly not reliably.

Bob Frump interestingly observes that although the Kruger lions are some of the most dangerous in modern history, they are some of the easiest to kill, as they have no fear of people at all. It's one distinct difference between them and other deadly man-killers like the Njombe or Tsavo cats. These latter lions avoided being hunted and knew when they were being pursued. The Kruger lions are almost blasé. There is surely no need to run from people, or a Land Rover full of rangers with dart guns? This is what the rangers were confronted with when they had to cull the Punda Milia pride in the Park's north. It's a sad experience for the rangers, who effectively have to euthanise the charges they have sworn to protect, especially when these lethal man-killers confusedly watch and mill about after the darts hit them. But the families of the refugees that have died quite rightly wouldn't care. It seemed hopeless, no winner, no great white hunter to save the day. The great monster that was the system had created this situation. But as so often when a situation is desperate, help will unexpectedly arrive.

Around the turn of the century, Albert Machaba was chief ranger for the Satara district of Kruger, the central region. One cold sunny morning in July 2000 he got to bend the rules, in the best tradition of the park founder and lion saviour, Stephenson-Hamilton. He drove east to the Park border with Mozambique and through the gates to a village just inside the border. Officially, of course, he wasn't there. Unofficially, he met with a group of Mozambican rangers and villagers, and told them they need to avoid being eaten by lions when crossing the Park. They all knew the people would continue to cross forever more; they all knew the Park needs the lions. So, Albert Machaba instructed the people to cross in groups of thirty, with a guide. He told them they would then be safer. And best of all, he told them that if his staff apprehended them in groups of thirty and accompanied by a guide, he would let them go. They were also warned not to light fires at night as those often run wild and cause immense damage to the Park.

The results have been excellent; no deaths reported in the Satara region between 2000 and 2005. Somehow, Machaba appears to have slain the monster, the system that provided a steady supply of people to be eaten by the lions of Kruger, while maintaining it. So, there was a great hunter after all, but he wasn't white. Machaba now, incidentally, is the Regional Ranger for the Far North section, the Nxanatseni Region. This is the region where the most killing occurred, so once his Central Region successes became known, one imagines his methods have been applied to the Far North too. Things appear to have greatly improved, but overall in Kruger, the killing has continued.

* * *

The Kruger National Park has a wealth of stories from its century-old history, some of that covered above, but another legendary figure rises up from Kruger mists to claim a definitive spot here: Harry Wolhuter. His excellent book, *Memories of a Game Ranger,* a compilation of his memoirs and field notes from 44 years as a Game Ranger in what became the Kruger National Park, was published upon his retirement in 1948 and has become a classic. It was extra-special to me as it was one of the three works mentioned in the introduction to this book. The work features a foreword by James Stevenson-Hamilton, the Kruger Park's long-time warden and a real legend of the Lowveld, as well as several truly brilliant illustrations by C.T. Astley-Maberly, who also edited the book. The illustrations capture the animals' habits and mannerisms with uncanny accuracy, a legacy of the long days Astley-Maberly spent traversing the park, alone and on his bicycle! Considering the number of people consumed by lions over time in Kruger, Astley-Maberly was a lucky man to survive these regular and lengthy excursions, although during most of his tenure the Kruger lions were terrified of people, for reasons already discussed.

Harry Wolhuter was born in the small town of Beaufort West in the Cape Province's Karoo area, in South Africa, on 14 February 1877. At the age of 14 he moved to the Transvaal and took his first job at a trading store in Maraisburg. After some hunting and farm management, he served on the British side when the Anglo-Boer War broke out, as a member of Steinacker's Horse; by 1901 the British had occupied the *Lowveld* and reaffirmed the status of the Sabi Game Reserve. The unit spent the war harassing parties of Boers along the road to Delagoa Bay (now Maputo Bay). Steinacker, replete with large handlebar moustache, often threatened his unruly men with courts-martial and the firing squad, but it didn't seem to have had much effect: the men fondly referred to their leader as "Old Stinky"!

To call Colonel Ludwig von Steinacker eccentric just doesn't capture the essence of the man; Wolhuter regretted there being no photograph of the "pompous little cock-sparrow", all five feet, three inches of him in his boots. He was small and wiry and Wolhuter thought him to weigh perhaps 120lb (55kg). Astley-Maberly's illustration of him is hilarious, and considering the brilliance of his other illustrations, doubtless accurate. There is actually a surviving photograph of him, from peace-time when he's better-fed, from the Stevenson-Hamilton Library in the Kruger and which I have included in the photo pages. Discipline fell far short of most other units in the army; indeed, Steinacker's Horse was at times known as The 40 Thieves. They also provided fully-mounted hunting trophies to other units, which could be taken back to England! Eventually the War ended and the unit was demobilised.

Wolhuter's life was about to change: having been informed that the Sabi Game Reserve, later the Kruger National Park, was about to be revived, he met the newly-appointed Warden, Major James Stevenson-Hamilton. Hamilton offered Wolhuter a position as Game Ranger (incidentally, the new Park's first), and he accepted, noting that he never regretted his decision. His first encounter with man-eating lions mentioned in his book is touching, heart-rending and indicative of how much it affected Wolhuter, who obviously harboured a sensitive soul beneath his leathery, tough-as-nails exterior. Wolhuter was patrolling the Reserve's western boundary when he happened upon the remains of a native resident. After studying the tracks for some time Wolhuter pieced together the pitiful scene.

A mother and her toddler were travelling along the path, likely *en route* to family or friends at another village, and had paused to rest in the heat of the afternoon. The mother sat beneath a tree in the shade, cracking *marula* tree nuts to eat the kernels while the child scratched peaceably in the dirt. The fruit of the *marula* tree's pip or nut contains two or three small kernels which are pleasant to eat. A large male lion suddenly launched from the grass behind the mother and ripped into her, the terrified toddler following its natural reaction and running *towards* her mother. Just as naturally, the lion smashed the little mite with a huge paw while he executed the mother in a crush of giant fangs, feeding off both corpses until the scraps of humanity that Wolhuter chanced upon were all that was left. This enraged Wolhuter, and he stayed for several days in the area to eliminate the lion, but failed despite some close calls.

Later in the season Wolhuter happened to shoot a very old lion in that area and believed that to be the culprit: no further reports of man-eating were forthcoming. But the event that was to define

Harry Wolhuter, indeed to understandably bring him wide-spread fame, occurred in August of 1903, as he returned from a patrol on the Olifants River (Afrikaans for elephant). He intended to overnight at a watering hole but it was dry when he got there, around 4pm. The next water-hole was 12 miles (19km) distant and although that would mean travelling in the dark, they - 3 native policemen driving pack donkeys and 3 powerful Boer dogs were accompanying Wolhuter - had no choice but to continue on.

Instructing the men to follow as they were on foot, Wolhuter rode on ahead with one of the dogs, the largest, a tough, ragged lion-dog called Bull. Never having seen lions in that area before, Wolhuter heard animals jump up in the long grass ahead, thinking them to be reedbuck. His error became apparent when the sound came closer, and he at last saw two large male lions leaving him in no doubt as to their intentions. He wrenched the reins around to turn his horse but the lions were too close, and with a thump one of the cats landed on the horse behind Wolhuter. It promptly fell off the wildly-bucking mount but knocked Wolhuter from the saddle in the process, the man falling right onto the second lion, which at that point was trying to head the horse off. This second lion grabbed Wolhuter by the right shoulder and dragged him off, the man hearing the departure of his horse, the first lion and Bull, following each other in that order.

The lion headed towards the Metsimetsi *Spruit* (stream), Wolhuter dragged on his back beneath the animal's body. The pain and fear hit him like a thunderbolt as he realised in clear thought that he was about to land up inside this creature. Every so often his spurs would snag in the ground, causing the lion to wrench him free with an irritated jerk of its great maned head. Wolhuter recounts the pain as "great physical agony." There is much debate over the pain caused by a lion bite or mauling, a statement by the famous explorer David Livingstone declaring the pain to be numbed by shock. Wolhuter actually mentioned that statement and categorically disagreed. What is clear is that there are many differing experiences and many differing reasons why the extent of the pain can fluctuate so much. Survivors often speak of a dream-like state, numbing the pain. I can only deduce that on these occasions, your mind is convinced that you are about to die, and anaesthetises you. People that experience severe pain during a lion mauling perhaps haven't reached that mental point yet.

Different people have differing pain thresholds and the mental perception makes a massive difference too. For instance, if you're stalking a lion and for hours your tension levels are as sky-high as they are under those conditions, you may have a numbed nervous system should a lion grab you. Then again, the drawn-out nervous tension may make you more susceptible rather than less. Your brain could have built up such a state of terror - which is understandable and forgivable when tracking a lion - that it has your nervous system convinced of great pain, for the slightest scratch. What you may have eaten over the previous 24 hours, or not eaten, or how well you slept, or didn't, may have an influence too. No-one knows for sure, but there is no hard-and-fast rule. Suffice it to say that a lion bite *can* be hell on earth. That is, of course, provided you survive to recount it in the first place…

A glimmer of hope sparked in Wolhuter as he remembered his sheath knife, attached to the right of his belt. His hope dimmed when he remembered taking a fall from his horse three times during the Anglo-Boer War, the knife falling out on all three occasions. Using his left hand – the right one unusable with that shoulder in the lion's mouth – he felt carefully beneath his back and with the joy of desperation closed his fingers around the knife's handle. Realising that he needed to hit the animal's heart to do any real damage and hopefully save himself, Wolhuter then moved his left hand across the lion's chest to shank it just behind the left shoulder in a backhanded motion. His two quick strokes caused a furious roar to emanate from the punctured cat, yet still it held the man, and in desperation Wolhuter slashed a third stroke at its throat. He must have slit the jugular as he recounts a stream of blood soaking him. The lion dropped him and slunk away, its long moans audible.

Wolhuter staggered to his feet, likely ably abetted by adrenalin, and thinking that his shouts would drive the big cat off, swore long and loudly after it. With no rifle and armed with a sheath knife, he suddenly remembered the second lion, considering it likely that once it got going, the horse would prove impossible to catch. That meant the lion would likely return, and find a rather exposed and bleeding Wolhuter instead of its companion. The man tried to light fires in the grass but it wouldn't take. Wolhuter was now in a serious predicament, as his right arm was useless. The lion's dew claws had raked it, cutting the tendons as it dragged him off, and his shoulder had been mangled by the cat's teeth in any case. He needed to climb a tree, and a decent-sized one, but effectively had the use of only one arm. Eventually a small tree with sufficient branches was found but once he was settled, fainting and in shock from blood-loss and pain, Wolhuter knew he wasn't high enough to be safe. Meanwhile, the stabbed lion expired in a death-rattle, to Wolhuter's extreme satisfaction.

Were these lions even man-eaters? Wolhuter is definite is stating without doubt that they were attacking his horse. He also fell, perchance it appears, into the very jaws of the one lion. What is certain, is that the lion was about to eat him; this supports the theory that lions, like most carnivores, are opportunists and blood and meat, once tasted, are much like blood and meat, if you catch my meaning. It just illustrates another possible way for a lion to develop a taste for people, really. The horse running triggered their predator response to chase and by the time Wolhuter fell, their blood was up. This seems the far more likely scenario than the possibility that they may have been accomplished man-killers that recognised a horse as usually being associated with people. Regardless whether or not they were man-eaters before, they were definitely in the process of becoming such.

Teetering in his precarious perch, Wolhuter had no time to enjoy his victory over the lion that had grabbed him; he heard rustling in the grass and the other lion had indeed returned. Cold from sweat and the wet blood – both his and the lion's – which had soaked his bush jacket, and obviously in shock, Wolhuter had used his belt to strap himself to the tree, his dizziness likely too severe, he thought, to trust his strength. He was also suffering the acute thirst that accompanies an extensive blood-loss trauma, but sitting a mere twelve feet off the ground, he knew to his horror that his number was up; the lion was clearly about to make the short climb that would allow him to grab the man. Shouting loudly at it, Wolhuter bought himself a second or two when the cat paused, startled momentarily at this turn of events. He saw its eyes reflected in the starlight as it looked up at him.

The second or two turned out to be invaluable: salvation arrived in the shape of Bull, the big Boer dog. He had realised at some stage that Wolhuter was no longer on the horse and had returned to find him. The treed man's relief can be imagined and he remarks, somewhat understandably, that never was he happier to see any living thing. The dog needed no urging - even though Wolhuter provided it - to sic the big cat, tormenting the lion for an hour or more until it alternatively charged him or spent some time skulking in the undergrowth. At length he heard his men arriving and after briefly shouting to them what had happened, instructed them to fire some shots to scare the lion. This they did and then built a large fire. Almost frantic with thirst by now, Wolhuter discovered the calabash empty which meant making for the next waterhole, still 6 miles (10km) ahead.

Throwing firebrands in the direction of the lion and with the dogs keeping up a crescendo, they eventually came across some huts from Wolhuter's military days, and at least had that protection. Wolhuter's ordeal was however still far from over. To his intense disappointment, the water pool was dry. In sheer desperation of death, Wolhuter sent two of his men to find water, however and wherever they could. He commends them for doing just that, venturing out with a lion about, and eventually returning with a muddy concoction that Wolhuter gratefully almost drained, keeping a bit so his men might dress his wounds. He was in too much pain however and they had to stop. By the next morning Wolhuter had a fever, the infection caused by septicaemia setting in. He lay up all that day while he sent his men to skin the lion he had stabbed. They still harboured doubts that he had killed it as he recounted, but they changed that train of thought when they found it where he said, and skinned it. They brought the skin, skull and perforated heart which verified Wolhuter's account. The next day they set off.

Eventually reaching some native kraals, Wolhuter had relays of four men at a time carry him in a *machila* - poles suspending a blanket - to Komatipoort. They arrived four days after the attack where a Dr Greeves set about putting the torn ranger together, with no morphine! Wolhuter recounts the pain as crushing, acute. The following day he went to Barberton by train and was at last booked into a proper hospital. Invalided for many weeks, the doctors fearing for his life, Wolhuter eventually recovered, a testimony to the toughness of the man: the septicaemia from a lion-mauling has been known to kill people inside twelve hours, treated or not. He never recovered full use of his right arm; indeed, it plagued him for the rest of his life. In his article to the *Journal of the Society for the Protection of the Fauna of the Empire*, Wolhuter noted that the lion that dragged him was old, with a grey-streaked mane and worn teeth, and that its stomach was quite empty. The one which treed him was much younger. He concluded that hunger had driven them to attack him, or rather, willingly switch from his horse to him for food.

The lion's skin – complete with clearly visible stab-wounds – adorned Wolhuter's wall at home for decades and was eventually donated to the Kruger National Park where it hangs to this day in the James Stevenson-Hamilton library in Skukuza, mounted beside the knife that ended its life. I photographed my children beside it upon one of our visits to the Park in late 2005. As a footnote, the heroic dog Bull that undoubtedly saved Wolhuter's life, died in mortal combat with a baboon. In this way he sadly went the way of many dogs in the *Lowveld* over the years, but at least his toughness was proven even in death: the baboon too died as a result of the fight.

In subsequent years Wolhuter had more brushes with man-eating lions in the Kruger, but oddly considered it extremely rare that they even attacked people, much less devoured them. This may have been the case during the majority of Wolhuter's tenure, and due to the livestock-protecting mindset of exterminating them as vermin. It just bolsters my argument that conditioning works. Wolhuter considered old age and injury to be the initial causes of man-eating, eventually forcing the animal through hunger to overcome its instinctive fear. He does however concede that once the lion discovers how easy we are to catch, you have a real problem animal. A young animal that has never learnt to fear man is a danger as its youthful curiosity can lead it to experiment. Once the deed is done, he noted, the animal becomes deadly-dangerous.

Other Kruger rangers have experienced man-eating by lions as well. Hannes Kloppers' excellent book *Game-Ranger* (the English version of the Afrikaans original, *Veldwagter!*, Juta, 1972), a biography on the life of the ranger Harry Kirkman, contains the following heart-stopping story: in 1938 Kirkman was suffering a severe bout of malaria and the huge, raw quinine tablets of the time required a fierce will just to ingest. Kirkman was delirious and suffered greatly, his wife Ruby tending him day and night for weeks, when one morning he seemed to turn a corner and could actually converse again. Gradually Harry gained back sufficient strength to take in a little sun beside the house. Suddenly the gardener appeared, accompanied by a strange African not known to the Kirkmans. The people of Sokis's village, just outside the Kruger boundaries, had sent him to Harry for help. He apologised profusely for troubling the ranger, as news of Harry's severe bout of illness had spread throughout the area, but the stranger's despair when noting that the village had nowhere else to turn, made Harry study the man's face more closely. Something was dreadfully wrong.

The man told Harry that a lion had dragged a child off the night before, and that the youngster was dead. Ruby involuntarily put her hand to her mouth. Weak as a kitten, Harry staggered to his feet, leaning on his wife merely to stand. He had to sort the situation out, and Ruby understood. She made Harry comfortable in the back of the car and accompanied him, as there was no way he could drive. All the African rangers were out and otherwise occupied. Eleven miles (18 km) outside the Park boundary they reached the village, just after sunset. Kloppers recounts Harry as noting the piteous wailings of the mourning women, which is indeed a heart-rending sound. The gathering twilight seemed to exacerbate the realisation of the transience of all things; it is an odd melancholy time in the bush. Waves of hot pain engulfed the dreadfully ill Harry as he merely climbed out of the car. A group of eight men greeted him soberly with the greeting reserved for royalty: *"Bayete!"* (Hail). Harry was embarrassed and humbled by this, and greeted the men. He asked which of them was the boy's father and learned from him that the youth was fourteen or fifteen. The youth had been the man's only son, a dire loss in a community that measures wealth in cattle and descendants.

Despite his condition, Harry felt the fire of fury at the injustice suffered by the man, and leaning on a tearful Ruby - who had followed the conversation which had been held in Shangaan - Harry avowed to bring the lion's skin to the father before the sun set on the following night. The men spontaneously blurted out *"Bayete!"* again, as they knew Harry Kirkman well; he was a deadly shot and not a boastful man. It appeared that the youth had been sleeping on a reed mat just inside the door of the family hut, and had opened the door for relief from the oppressive heat, against his parents' warnings: the lion had been prowling around the village for several nights before. Around midnight the mortal shrieks of the youth mingled with the snarls of the lion had roused the entire village but by the time anyone could light a grass bushel for a torch, the youth was nowhere to be found and all was again silent. Harry examined the crumpled reed mat and its single large bloodstain, and the group followed the tracks out past some large boulders. Just 50 yards (45 metres) from the village the lion had eaten the youth.

The scene was horrific, and sent shivers up and down the spines of the watching people. Amid the large dark puddles of dried blood and flattened grass lay the pathetic remains of the youth. The only thing that identified the pile of matter as human was a left hand. Fighting down the urge to retch, Ruby helped Harry hobble back to the car, the ranger having warned the villagers to secure all livestock and stay indoors themselves until his signal sounded, and to return the gruesome scraps of humanity to the family hut in accordance with tradition. An exhausted Harry sank back in the rear car seat and before he sank into oblivion again, had to swallow another quinine dose, the effects of the previous one still making his ears ring. Armed with a flashlight, Ruby intended on keeping her lonely vigil so Harry might rest, but he had no real choice. The night was pitch-black and overcast, the distant rumble of thunder sounding from beyond the distant mountains in the west. An hour passed, then another. The oppressive heat was too much and to stop herself nodding off, Ruby opened the front car door a bit and rested her feet on the running board. There was a peculiar stench, as of putrefying meat, that seemed to be getting ever-stronger so Ruby alit from the car and stood outside.

A faltering gabbling came from Harry, still visibly prostrate on the back seat: "Ruby…get…in! Into…the…car…quickly!" He was delirious again, she guessed, switching on the light in the car's ceiling. "Close…the…door!" "He…is…right…here…very…near!" "Close…the…door…Ruby!" A wave of anxiety washed over her in her concern for her husband; what was Harry on about? She closed the door though. With a superhuman effort, Harry forced himself into a sitting position and rubbed his eyes open.

When Ruby tried to push him back against the seat, she could not. He seemed to have regained some strength. Sipping some water, he was able to speak more lucidly: "Switch off the roof light, Ruby. He is very near!" Ruby was confused but obeyed. Telling her to wind down the window and aim the flashlight, Harry readied the Mauser. "Light, please, Ruby. Quickly!" Ruby wound down the rear car window and switched on the light. Did Harry really think the lion was trying to get through the fence, twenty yards distant, where the torchlight flickered? "Nearer, Ruby, nearer! He is right here!" Ruby lowered the beam and nearly dropped the flashlight in terror. Eight yards from the car a pair of yellow orbs glowed in the torchlight, black ears flattened as the tawny beast crouched.

The report from the rifle was thunderous, the enclosed space inside the car multiplying the sound and shocking Ruby again. With a vicious grunt the lion leapt straight up and bounded away into the night. Harry sank back, utterly exhausted again. "Never mind, Ruby, I have got him. He won't get far. I'll track him down tomorrow morning. Let us get some sleep now." And with that the ranger sank back into unconsciousness, leaving his severely shocked wife to drive them home, and contemplate just how close she had come to becoming the lion's next victim. Somehow Harry's psyche had dragged him back from the depths of his malaria-induced delirium, and not before time. The smell likely resonated in his sub-conscious as indicating the presence of a lion. After five hours' sleep and another quinine dose, Harry was able to walk unaided, although he attributed that to the cup of coffee he'd drank! He took a tracking dog with him at sunrise when he and Ruby returned. Harry smiled when he noted not a soul astir in the village. They had followed his instructions well.

Within a few minutes, a group of villagers accompanied the ranger to the scene of the shot, the pugs showing the lion had passed within two feet of the car and moved off a few yards as Ruby opened the door. He then began to creep toward her until she closed the door, Harry's warning coming not five seconds too soon. Following the blood trail, the dog bristled after some 50 yards (45 metres) but there was no need for further caution. The lion lay on its side, quite dead. Headman Sokis verbalised in revered terms what the watching men all felt; Harry had done as he'd promised, and almost a day early.

One last task remained; the revolting one of proving that the lion had consumed the youth. None of the Africans would dream of opening the beast's stomach to determine the fact, so Harry gritted his teeth and slashed the lion open with his bush knife. The sad remnants of the youth were found. The other remains were added to it, as to Harry's surprise the lion became the youth's tomb, and it was sewn closed then burned on a pyre. A song recounting the youth's potential, his tragic but honourable death, and the heroic role of Harry, rang out as thunderclouds gathered symbolically in the west. A real Viking funeral, Harry Kirkman remembered thinking.

An interesting result of the extreme weather – Kruger experienced the same crushing drought that accompanied the Great Depression as did the rest of South Africa – was that while the herd animals suffered in the heat, the lions, understandably, enjoyed their times of plenty. When the rains finally returned, and the Park had restored itself, it became the lions' turn to experience hardship. The worst drought in the history of the National Park (1928-34) was followed by a period of unequalled peak rainfall (1935-9). In February of 1937, a short time before the story above, ranger Harry Kirkman was sliding his battered and worn Chevrolet along the muddy road when an elderly African appeared ahead on a ramshackle bicycle. When he spotted Harry, the old-timer dropped the old bike skeleton and blurted out his story, so fast and disjointedly that the white man had to stop him and try calm the man down. This seemed to further increase the old man's agitation but at last the ranger was able to decipher that the man's wife had just been attacked by a lion.

They loaded the old bike in the car and Harry used the old Chev in a way that would have thrilled its manufacturer's marketing department, had they known. On the stretches of road that allowed for communication, the old villager told the ranger his tale; his wife had left their hut to fetch water and had been set upon by a lion. She shrieked with gusto and the entire hamlet's population rallied to her aid, brandishing every implement imaginable. The old man, named Mangauan (pronounced Mun-gao-wahn), told the ranger that the lion just held onto the woman by her shoulder and clearly conveyed that he was not going to relinquish this meal. The people shouted, threw stones and pretty much everything else until finally, the lion relented and was scared off. Better news was that the woman was alive. After half an hour of Kirkman's budding rally-driver work they pulled up at a small circle of mud huts. The victim had been made as comfortable as possible on a reed mat in front of one of the huts – a risky move, I thought, with a still-hungry man-eater about – and Harry examined her wounds.

She was incredibly lucky, as despite two gaping wounds in her shoulder, and several claw marks in her head and left leg, no bones were broken. All of this told Kirkman that the lion must have been in a decidedly weakened condition. Normally, a human being has no chance at all of surviving an attack by an adult man-eating lion, especially in Kruger, where they tend to be so large. With no first-aid kit at his disposal, Harry decided to get the victim over the Sabi River, and then by lorry to the doctor at Komatipoort. To the joy of old Mangauan, his wife recovered completely, but for some large and unsightly scars. Just two days later, another ranger shot the lion, and it was in an advanced state of starvation. The lions' seven years of plenty during the drought was definitely at an end. From three or four decades later and onward, however, the mass shootings of lions had long-ceased, they were accustomed to people, and the refugees had begun to cross the Park.

9   Mozambique – the strife-torn south-east

Mozambique (formerly Portuguese East Africa) in the south-east corner of the African continent has endured a tumultuous past; never a wealthy country, when the "wind of change" swept through Africa in the late 1950s and early 1960s, Mozambique was inevitably swept up as well. As I've recounted in the previous chapter, the indigenous people launched the Mozambican Liberation Front (or Frelimo) in September 1964. The first phase of the bitter war ended in 1974 when the Portuguese withdrew and Frelimo established a Marxist government. An anti-Marxist guerrilla force was established within Mozambique (the Mozambican National Resistance or Renamo). The subsequent war was an even worse one, with constant human rights violations committed by both sides. On the heels of the war came more poverty and a string of natural disasters that must have had the population wondering whether or not they were cursed.

One of the most colourful characters in an industry and a profession noted for the unconventional, the eccentric, the brash and, occasionally, the downright offensive was John Taylor, an Anglo-Irishman known by his Chinyungwe moniker of *Pondoro* (lion). Taylor was born into a very well-off and successful family in 1904, his father a wealthy and highly-regarded surgeon, who was knighted in the wake of World War One, and his mother a Louisiana heiress. Expelled from Ireland as a religious and politically-undesirable, Taylor ended up in Africa aged just eighteen. He was to become as African as any white person born overseas ever did, living there for most of his life in basic conditions, converting to Islam and assuming a firm belief in African witchcraft. Some of the tales he recounted really give one the chills, but I'll leave those for another time.

Taylor spent many years in Northern Mozambique (then still Portuguese East Africa), largely poaching for a living. His sorties were many and noteworthy, not least of all for the quality of his shooting. He seldom needed many shots to anchor any animal, and spent most of his time after "problem animals", these being man-eating lions and crop-consuming buffalo and elephants, his income in the shape of the ivory gathered. As often happens when the human victims try to fight back against crop-raiding elephants, they'd wound a few, with disastrous consequences. The elephants often then developed a disturbing habit of graunching the humans into the African soil. Taylor probably spent the majority of his time on elephant and buffalo (to use the old hunters' plurals for big game, such as lion instead of lions, which Taylor tended to do. I've noted Gordon Cundill do likewise), but man-eating lions consumed much of his time as well.

John Taylor was without doubt an extremely controversial character, and much has been written about this by several people, but his bravery was absolutely unquestioned. At several junctures while reading Taylor's *Maneaters and Marauders* (1959) I would literally stop reading, gob-smacked, at the matter-of-fact way he'd use to recount his pursuits of the various groups of man-eating lions, *alone and at night*. With each subsequent read of that work I am no less astounded. Even the bravest hunters rightly consider the hunting of man-eating cats at night to be akin to suicide. The animal's vastly superior night-vision renders such a contest very uneven. Throw in the fact that the occasional African night is overcast and blacker than anyone who hasn't experienced it can imagine, and the human being that pursues confirmed man-killing felines in the dark is one very exposed creature indeed.

In some of these instances, Taylor writes that certain prides or groups of man-eaters were not at all accustomed to being hunted, and this made his job easier. On the surface this theory appeared to make sense, at least initially. Taylor made use of a shooting lamp, which was far from the modern equivalent. The light it would project – which in hindsight seemed sufficient, it must be said – would have been nothing like the magnesium-white beam projected by modern devices. The lions were usually transfixed by this rather than exploding to all points of the compass, as would lions accustomed to being hunted. Naturally, to avoid warning the lions, Taylor would walk along in the dark until his inner warning system would tell him the man-eaters were near! Yes, it wasn't "sporting" in the true hunting sense, but these were man-eaters and had to be exterminated. Normally, hunting at night using lights is a strict no-no, and rightly so.

The Tsavo or Njombe lions, for instance, would likely have been on Taylor in a flash, were he to pursue them at night, alone and in pitch darkness, his undoubtedly advanced sense of danger notwithstanding. The better lions get at man-killing, the more careful they become and the less likely to offer any shooting chance to hunters at all. The mere chance of stumbling upon a 'conventional' lion, elephant, rhino or buffalo in the pitch dark would make Taylor's methods extremely risky and he could have counted himself very fortunate, regardless how well his system worked for him. There was one instance in the area of Mandimba, near the border with Nyasaland (now Malawi) where he came close to being nabbed, but again his advanced inner warning system alerted him precisely to the danger. Taylor's senses started to scream at him that the lions he was after were very close. He had come around a bend and seeing a straight section of path ahead, put his lamp on, the lions - three of them - starkly illuminated in the glow.

Taylor instantly shot the nearest lion, the other two decamping forthwith. Knowing they would not reappear for a while, he retreated a half-mile (some 800 metres) back the way he'd come, propped himself against a tree and smoked a pipe. His intention was to go back to the dead lion in a short while, knowing that lions usually come back to a dead companion, either to see what had happened to them or to feed off the carcase, or both. But to his surprise, his inner warning sense started going crazy, indicating in no uncertain terms that the surviving lions had crept up on him, not returned to their dead companion. My surprise when reading this was that he was surprised; he does quite correctly remark that this just served to illustrate the unpredictability of wild animals. There is no hard-and-fast rule for how any species will react. Just incidentally, at the last minute Taylor turned his lamp on and shot both lions stone dead. Both had indeed been right there, about to pounce on him. Quite effective, the John Taylor Inner Warning System, patent regrettably not pending!

Taylor made interesting observations to the effect that man-killing cats and crop-raiding elephants seem to know they are doing something wrong. This has been stated by other hunters and writers as well. After making a kill, man-eating lions often scatter to the winds, putting as much distance between themselves and the "crime scene" as possible. It was behaviour just such as this by the Njombe lions, for example, that invoked people to make that common observation that the lions were "not like lions". Elephants too seem to get as far away as possible after raiding crops or harvested stocks. Over eons of interaction with humans, they likely know that there will be retribution in some form, but it seems to be more than that, and Taylor opines that they appear to feel guilt, or know that what they have done is wrong in some way.

On one occasion, also in the Mandimba area, Taylor bemoaned the fact that his new cells for the lamp (flashlight batteries) appeared to be contraband or of very dubious quality indeed. He was in pursuit of a bunch of man-eating lions again, on a night that was darker than the inside of any proverbial you can think of, and found that his lamp's power died in short order, the light fading as he watched it. The batteries were obviously rubbish but this left Taylor in a rather worse predicament than being merely annoyed. The lions he was after were no rookies, having already built up a good score and proving difficult to even find. There was no choice but to return the 3 miles (4.8km) to camp, which Taylor did; but his brilliant sense of danger told him the lions were following him, and he considered that to be the longest three miles of his life. The following day he traced his tracks to the point where his lamp had given up the ghost and he had turned around. Just beyond that point, the tracks of several lions joined the path, and followed those of the man, almost all the way back to his camp.

Taylor owned a trading store at Benga, in Mozambique's north-west, near where Zambia, Zimbabwe and Mozambique meet on the Zambezi River. A trio of lions were just starting their careers as man-eaters, and Taylor's first sortie after them was at a nearby hamlet, at ten o'clock in the morning. This is most unusual timing for any lions, man-eaters or not. After making an unsuccessful attack on a woman, the obviously starving lions set upon a hog and were that occupied with it that Taylor could approach to within 6 metres or so (20 feet). He dropped the male where it lay, the two lionesses making off. Taylor managed a good hit on one of the females before she made off to his right. Sadly, a local hero with a shotgun interfered and peppered the other lioness with buckshot. Taylor blew a whistle, a trick he often employed to get game to halt and look back, and the buckshot lioness stopped to look around. As Taylor was about to settle its hash, the shotgun wizard loosed off again, and the lioness disappeared.

A furious Taylor passed his rifle to the nearest man lest he commit murder, and dealt the intrusive shot-gunner a swift kick in the trousers. The man was turning already dangerous animals into lethal killers, and Taylor was fully justified in this reaction. He found the first lioness, dead as he thought she would be. His shot had destroyed the large arteries above the heart, yet she'd still been able to get to her feet immediately and run off. Taylor marvelled at the cat's tenacity and vitality, as have countless hunters before and since. He felt sure the peppered lioness would return to find the male that night, and left the skinned carcases of the first two lions together. Using his tried-and-trusted method of approaching in the dark with the intention of turning on his lamp to shoot, Taylor ventured to the carcases throughout the night, and just before the dawn was rewarded: the third lion stood gazing down at her erstwhile companions and Taylor killed her with no trouble. The Benga Man-eaters - at least that batch - were no more.

One of Taylor's earliest jaunts against man-eating lions came in the Maccua area, in Mozambique's hinterland, which is characterised by the thorn scrub referred to earlier. Indeed, it is the area David Livingstone singled out as having particularly high numbers of man-eating lions. He wasn't wrong, and not much has changed since. As they often do in Tanzania and Mozambique to this day, man-eaters here seem to operate in groups of 1 to 5, with three the common average. The thick scrub makes smaller groups more sensible, one would imagine. Taylor recounts maneless males being the norm here, and directly attributes this to the dense thorn scrub. It is so impassable in places that shooting is nigh-impossible, a deflected bullet almost always the outcome. Although recent studies in the Tsavo area have proven the phenomenon of maneless males to be an adaptation to the crushing heat, the thorn-scrub theory must hold some water, especially since some of the lion sub-species in the north of the continent live in even hotter climes, yet have full manes.

John Taylor learned a great deal about hunting man-eating lions in the Maccua area, mainly learning that rushing off after reported kills was fruitless. The tendency of lions, once an attack has been successfully carried out against people, is to leave the area and put as much distance between themselves and the scene as possible. Following them is most unproductive. The best reaction is to double-guess the beasts, waiting for them in a village where they are likely to strike next. This can be gleaned to some extent over an extended area by picking a spot that hasn't been attacked for a time, and a map is helpful here, but is pure chance even so and usually costs the lives of several people before the hunter strikes lucky, if ever he does.

Taylor selected a village and had his men shut him into a trap as human bait, in the compartment normally reserved for a goat, the intention being that the lion would trip a wire and shut itself into the other compartment. The trap was actually an upsized version of the common traps used to catch stock-raiding leopards, and is a much smaller version of the "contraption" made famous by JH Paterson with the Tsavo lions. Just like Paterson's, this trap too was to work, although unlike at Tsavo, Taylor managed to make it stick. His men had been gone a mere half-hour when Taylor likely aged a few years in a few seconds; he was sitting by design facing the other compartment, so he could shoot the intended lion that would venture into it, and thus could see nothing that might approach from behind him. With no warning, a deep sigh sounded right beside him. Turning his head, Taylor saw a maneless male lion, looking in at him a mere 18 inches away.

Beyond it he discerned a lioness. The male presented such a gilt-edged target that Taylor was about to withdraw his rifle from its position and pop the creature, but just then a third lion – also a lioness – rushed into the trap. She was sure she had an easy kill before her but the door closed and Taylor noted she could not reach him through the bars separating the two compartments. While she vented her fury on the bars the second lioness appeared beyond the now-closed rear trap door. The maneless male stood stock-still, doubtless wondering what the lioness was doing in the trap so Taylor withdrew the rifle and shot him where he stood. At the shot the lioness in the trap nearly burst Taylor's eardrums with a terrific roar. He was less than a yard away from her, remember. Backing up, she came up against the rear door and in her fury launched herself at the bars between them again.

Luckily, she had not sufficient momentum, otherwise Taylor felt sure she'd smash the poles. Nothing stopped her nearly blowing his head off with another roar though, and he shot her in the chest a mere foot away. The second lioness moved into cover and Taylor couldn't get a clear shot through the bars. He decided to sit up for her, but learned another valuable lesson; although she prowled around visibly all night, she remained in the background and in the shadows, never offering a clear shot, as she now associated the trap with guns and death. For the next few days there was no sign or word of her, but then, as so often happens, the people dropped their guard. A group of women went as usual to fetch water from the river and wash themselves.

Foolishly, one lingered, her daughter walking some short distance ahead of her after the rest of the group had gone. The group suddenly heard a single shrill scream, followed by several as the child raced up the path toward them. Looking around a bend in the path the women saw the lioness crouched over the body of the child's mother. The younger and fitter individuals among the group ran toward the village, ululating loudly. Taylor guessed the reason and grabbing his rifle, raced down the path. He remembered being grateful that the area was away from the infernal thorn scrub.

Rounding the bend, the Anglo-Irishman had a clear view and shot the third Maccua man-eater, dead as a doornail.

Another man-eating hotspot was at a place called Nsungu, at Lupata Gorge on the Zambezi. Between Nsungu and Kasanya upriver, and again from Nsungu to Chimbidzi in the north, the lions had the entire area in a blue funk, as man-eating lions tend to do. The local headman told Taylor that three lions had often been seen together, and sometimes five, but whether these same five sometimes split into a pair and a trio, or that there were two or three separate groups, he knew not. The lions had reigned for nine months when Taylor started to hunt them and they not only feasted on the locals, but on passing travellers from Tete with equal relish. They started hunting people by day, which was unusual to Taylor, and often would select a village for the night, lying there all night if need be until a human exited a hut to relieve him or herself. They'd occasionally jab a paw under a reed door or even through the wall, Taylor felt almost as if trying to get someone to awaken and hopefully come outside. They never smashed through a door, roof or wall as has often happened in Tanzania.

Taylor was nonplussed that these lions turned to man-eating in the first place; game was common and varied in the area. This just underlines two things to me: one, lions are sensible opportunistic carnivores, so why expend energy with a far easier food source available; and two, this is just more proof of the theory that lions have always eaten human beings. Taylor chose Nsungu as the most central juncture and the headman instructed his people to inform the hunter of lion activity as fast as possible. The sun-baked ground made tracking nigh-impossible and the locals took to burning the long grass off to lessen the animals' hiding places. The people made sure they were indoors by nightfall, leaving Taylor and his three men to ponder how the lions had denied the local populace their only pleasure, that of talking and laughing around the evening fire. Behind the men was a clump of as-yet unfired grass and scrub, ample cover for stalking lions, so the men turned in rather than remain so exposed to attack.

Taylor awoke sometime during the night; he was sure he'd heard one of the village drums, warning everyone within earshot of lions. There it came again, a series of rolls and taps strangely reminiscent of a lion's roars. Instantly he and his gunbearer, Saduko, made for the village whence the drum was sounding, descending the hill in the dark. Taylor later learned that a lion had sniffed at the reed door of one of the huts and loosed a deep sigh, often a sign of hunger.

That had the owner shouting to the village drummer - also safe inside his own hut, drum and all - to beat out a signal summoning Taylor. As the two hunters came to the open space between the huts, Taylor put his lamp on, the beam showing a growling lioness standing full broadside and another lioness with a maneless male just behind. Taylor shot the closest lioness and she dropped like a stone. At the shot the second lioness described a complete circle and stopped, also offering a full broadside shot. She too never knew what hit her while the male, who hadn't so much as flinched at the first shot, leapt over the second lioness as Taylor killed her.

He didn't go far though, turning almost immediately to look back at the men. Taylor shot him just behind the left shoulder and although the cat dashed off, he dropped dead after forty yards or so (36 metres), shot through the heart. For two or three days there was peace in the area, then word came from Chimbidzi; the remaining lions had killed again. As tends to happen in areas exposed to man-eating, the people seem to revert to their normal routines when a mere few days pass without incident, the fatalism I've already alluded to well-ingrained. An elderly man had left his hut at dawn to relieve himself and was immediately grabbed, his cries cut off suddenly by a lion's deep growl. The people knew it was pointless to go to his aid and after a short time, crept from their huts. Two lions were busy consuming the old man, and two runners had immediately made off to fetch Taylor. It was ten or twelve miles (16 or 19 km) one way, so by the time the hunters returned to Chimbidzi, the old man's remains would only have filled a large handkerchief.

The men tracked the lions for two hours, covering perhaps a mile (1,6km), when they reached a place where the pugs were clear. The two lions were joined by three others. Soon however the ground became stony and the men had no alternative but to return to Chimbidzi. That evening, the sound of drums emanated from a small hamlet between Chimbidzi and Nsungu, which was only a mile or so distant; the lions had returned. Immediately Taylor and Saduko set out, and as they approached the sounds of people shouting and lions growling and snarling were clearly audible. Taylor switched on his ever-present lamp and all five lions were clustered outside the door of one of the huts. The hut's occupants were jabbing a spear through the reeds of the door, and judging by the snarling lions, were hitting home more often than not.

Taylor dropped a lioness and her almost-grown cub with his two barrels at "fifteen or sixteen feet" (5 metres), then swapped rifles with Saduko and dropped the male with the first shot from his second rifle. Before he could loose off the second barrel, the other lioness disappeared between the huts with her own almost-grown cub in tow. Taylor wisely resisted the urge to snap-shoot the youngster, which would likely have hit the hindquarters. Most decent professionals only shoot when they're certain to kill. A wounded animal – and especially a man-eating lion – nobody needs. The people emerged and were jubilant, but the Anglo-Irishman reminded them that two man-eaters were still at large, and bade them return to their huts until his all-clear had been sounded. The hunters occupied a hut, leaving the lights off and the door ajar (told you Taylor was brave). The white man sat up while his men dozed off (and how brave were his men!), and he spotted the lions beyond some huts on the far side of the compound. He wanted them close to be certain of killing them but this time he waited too long; presently he saw them about to disappear into the bush again.

Presuming the adult to be in front, Taylor thought it best to kill her despite the long shot. Switching on his lamp and pulling the trigger, he was disappointed to see the lioness bound over her dead youngster and lose herself in the tawny, lion-coloured grass. She would now definitely stay gone and the men returned to Chimbidzi to catch up on some sleep while it was still dark. Early the following morning they made their way towards Nsungu. After a few miles' walk, Taylor suddenly felt that danger was very close. It was here in *Maneaters and Marauders* that he wrote it was imperative that one heed these inner warning feelings. They are unerringly accurate and trying to use reason in their stead can be fatal. His senses even drew his eyes to his right, zeroing in on the danger. The scrub was more dense that side of the path which supported his premonition. Taylor and his men actually moved off the path to the left, onto the more open ground, to buy the white man some shooting time. He was totally convinced the lioness or another man-eater was close by.

Despite his heightened senses Taylor only saw the lioness when she flicked her tail, so well did she blend into the bush. It is indeed uncanny how small they can make themselves when viewed from the front. He sank to one knee to maximise the raking effect of the bullet as the cat exploded out of the bush after him. His first shot broke her lower jaw on the way down into her chest, and as she staggered to her feet, choking and retching, he popped another lead pill in through the top of her head. Yet again the man's bush-honed sense of danger had proven absolutely accurate. The furious cat had sought the men, and had very nearly been successful. Taylor stayed in the area for ten more days but there were no further lion problems.

At Lifumba, where Taylor often had annually to thin out the herds of buffalo when they'd make raids on local crops upon returning to the area, a *chefe de posto* - a Portuguese East Africa government official - had decided to get a good close-up photograph of a wild lion. Hearing of one that had killed a hog on the island in the lagoon, the idiot made for the area, bringing with him a heavy steel lion trap weighing perhaps 80 pounds (36 kg). He had another hog tied up near the trap as bait and sure enough, that evening pandemonium broke loose and the sounds of a thoroughly enraged lion emanated from the direction of the trap. The men approached the following morning and after making several attempts to get near enough for a photograph with real impact, they were sufficiently scared out of their wits by the lion's concerted and violent efforts to free itself and end their lives.

On their last approach the official urged his assistant to retrieve the camera, which was quite close to the lion, while he would cover the man with the rifle. The lion again vented its fury so vehemently that the enraged creature lifted the trap as if it were a feather, causing the severely frightened gunman to shoot, which was most unfortunate: he merely wounded the big cat. Decamping to rethink their strategy, the *chefe* decided to shoot the lion and then take a picture. Approaching yet again, they discovered a severed paw in the trap…and no lion. This meant that a lion was now at large - on a densely-populated island - that was seriously and most painfully injured, but nowhere near fatally, and his general disposition towards people can only be imagined. Taylor was understandably furious with the government official, as the lion would be a holy terror to the locals as soon as it became hungry enough. This was to be a case where human carelessness and stupidity had directly spawned a man-eating lion.

For five days the lion lay licking his wounds but then his hunger forced him out of cover. The locals were first alerted to his presence when he killed a small hog, and his ear-splitting roar as he made the kill indicated that he'd inadvertently placed some weight on his raw stump. Following this the people shut their hogs away at night, as they always had secured their goats. The lion then commenced consuming people, but what is interesting here was that even after he'd become a man-eater, he'd still occasionally take a pig whenever one was available. This is unusual, as man-eating lions tend to convert to human flesh and forego all other. Leopards, those ultimate survivors and perfect carnivores, merely include people among their many protein sources once they become man-eaters, continuing to catch the wide range of prey to which they are partial. Taylor felt this lion would happily have lived on pork even after his debilitating injuries, but once the people locked them away he had to eat something.

His first victim was an old woman wandering along the water's edge in search of driftwood for her fire. She hadn't even time to make a peep before she was dragged into the thick *matete* reeds, but some women nearby heard a savage snarl, indicating the lion had again stood on his injured leg by accident. The Maiembi man-eater (pronounced My-yembi) was born. His next kill was far more brazen; in the pitch dark he merely sauntered into a hut, pushing the reed door open and snatched a man where he lay, so silently that no-one would have been any the wiser, except for the fact that he again trod on his leg that had once ended in a paw. The resultant snarl woke the victim's wife, who looked up to see a large male lion exiting the hut with her dead husband in its jaws. Her screams alerted the villagers but the lion had once again disappeared into the impassable *matete*.

After an emergency meeting, the villagers decided to gather all the noise-making articles they possessed and drive the lion off the island in a noisy beat. The intention was to drive the cat towards the part of the island that ran to a point with the river in front of anyone or anything headed that way. This all went to plan until the lion reached the point. Taylor thought the idea would have worked had the drive taken place at sundown, and that the cat would have taken to the water, but it was noon and the lion decided otherwise. He turned about-face and mauled the first man he saw, thus breaking through the vanguard of the drive, the line of men. The lion was now faced with the backup line, the women. When confronted by the lion, the two women directly before him turned and ran. The lion sprang on both, crushing one's skull with his paw and luckily for the other, delivering a mere glancing blow with his injured stump.

The surviving woman's piercing screams silenced the beaters, and they arrived upon the scene where he'd attacked the women as the second of the two was struggling to her feet. The first woman wasn't moving. The villagers realised the lion was now between them and the village, so to avoid it and to make the return easier, they decided to walk along the shore. *En route* they discovered the injured man; his shoulder and chest were badly clawed and one ear hung down in strips. His shouts when attacked hadn't been noticed as everyone was shouting anyway. That all ended the beat but it was successful after all; the lion himself left the island either that night or the one following. The islanders had no idea until word came from the opposite shore that the man-eater was now beyond the water; naturally their relief was considerable and they hoped he'd stay away.

Taylor arrived in Lifumba for his annual sortie against the buffalo, and no sooner had he set up his base camp than some men arrived by canoe, bringing news of the man-eater. He appeared to have set up operations over a 6-mile (10km) stretch along the river, eating people and their pigs at a steady rate. At that time, he seemed to be concentrating on the area of the chief's *kraal*, and Taylor learned of a woman who'd had a narrow escape. Due to the crop-raiding buffalo at that time of year, the people took to sleeping in stilted *dungu* huts, some two metres (six to seven feet) off the ground. The woman had just climbed her ladder when the man-eater appeared below, about to spring. She dashed her basket down on top of him and he attacked it, which bought her time sufficient to get inside the flimsy dwelling and secure the door. These shelters are no protection at all against a healthy lion, but with no room to balance once atop the platform and no way to climb a ladder with a front paw missing, the woman was relatively safe from the crippled Maiembi man-eater.

He came prowling around the same *dungu* the following night and when Taylor and Saduko came to intervene, the animal had cleared off, leaving a plethora of pugs and no indication as to which direction he'd taken. There was no word of the lion for three or four days and all indications were that he'd likely killed a pig or some other small game animal. A pig seems more likely as the small antelope species are all extremely fleet-footed. Lions normally don't bother with them, as much for the fact that the reward in meat quantity is just not worth the effort, as for the fact that they often literally can't catch them. That niche is nicely covered by leopards and caracals. Taylor's young help, an excellent lad named Friday, asked to be allowed to hunt with Taylor's old rifle, as he sometimes did, for the pot. Taylor consented, provided the boy stay in the open *mopane* forest to Lifumba's western side.

Taylor ventured the other way and after a short time headed for the landing where his large canoe was berthed, awaiting the men with the load of buffalo meat from the animals Taylor had shot. Walking down the pathway that led to the landing, Taylor saw the prints of a child walking ahead of him, and just as his old feeling of impending danger started to flutter his guts, the tracks of a large lion with one front paw missing appeared out of the bush and joined the path, over those of the child. His growing horror hurried him along and because the path twisted and turned to follow the topography of the landscape, one couldn't see for any great distance along it. At last though, Taylor rounded a bend with the lake visible some 50 yards (45 metres) ahead. About halfway to the landing was Friday, staggering under the load of a dead impala, and closing him down was the Maiembi lion, limping heavily on his three remaining paws. To avoid hitting the child, Taylor dropped to one knee and shouted. The lion turned side-on to look behind him and the rifle crashed.

The look on Friday's face can be imagined; it turned out the boy had shot an impala, the bullet carrying on through the buck and wounding another. The conscientious little hunter followed the fleet-footed creature, and when he eventually caught up with it, the antelope had succumbed to its wound. Finding himself far nearer the landing than the base camp, Friday decided to drop the carcase off there before returning to collect the other impala. In his sensible diligence though, he'd forgotten all about the lion. The spoor showed the lion had been lying some ten yards off the path when the boy ventured by, and had Friday stopped just once to rearrange his heavy burden, he would have been done for. As it was, the plucky little hunter hadn't stopped.

*   *   *

One of the most famous, successful and capable hunting safari operators was Adelino Serras Pires. His story is epic, tragic and fraught with injustice. He has suffered immeasurable loss, been unjustly imprisoned and had his rights abused several times over, in different African countries. And yet he has still won; Adelino was one of the most positive people you could ever hope to meet and his spirit was irrepressible. He was a true warrior in every sense of the word. In his latter years, Adelino was married to Fiona Capstick, and lived in Pretoria, South Africa, my hometown. I am honoured to have met him. Adelino's story is told in *The Winds of Havoc* (St Martin's Press, 2001), a joint work between him and Fiona Claire Capstick, Peter's widow, who wrote the foreword to this book. It was recently updated to include new information and is an enlightening read indeed.

144

Adelino arrived from Portugal in Tete, Mozambique on Christmas Eve 1936 and his first memories were of the roars of the Benga man-eating lions over the river. As his father said, Adelino would become a hunter. By early 1937, there was a confluence of malaria, sleeping sickness and leprosy which was exacerbated by the fierce heat. Right on schedule the lions turned to man-eating on a large scale, the sick, dying and slow-moving locals proving impossible to resist. Adelino's uncle was *chefe de posto*, a Portuguese colonial government role with many duties, basically a head of station. He gathered his tribal officers, known as *sipaios*, and alerted as many of the able and capable people in the area that could bring firearms or medical supplies, or both. The men were gathered for a night-time assault on the lions, using the battery-powered lamps that attach to one's head, such as those used by John Taylor.

Adelino was to accompany them and considering his age – a mere 8 years – it was doubtless a terrifying night for the youngster. I'm struck by how something of this nature could never happen today; the outcry at this endangering of a child would be so excessive that no-one would ever consider it worth the trouble. How times have changed. Adelino had to carry the water bottle and stick close to his father; he recalls feeling like a very big boy indeed, bursting with pride. As the party neared the pride that was their target, Adelino's father tightened his grip on the child's shoulder and the urgency of the situation was conveyed through that grip. The night was heavy with pregnant silence until an ominous low noise emanated from the gully before the men. Suddenly everything exploded in a cacophony of noise and cordite. Then Adelino's father shouted to the men to cease firing.

Thus ended Adelino's introduction to hunting. Although he was not to have much direct exposure to man-eating lions in his career, he did hunt lions many times with various clients, in several African countries. One day back in Tete, at the end of the 1940 school year where Adelino boarded in Salisbury, Southern Rhodesia (now Harare, Zimbabwe), a rather-intoxicated man summoned him as he strode by one of the town's notorious bars. The man turned out to be John Taylor, who was curious as to why a Mozambican youth would be afoot wearing the uniform of a posh English private school. Taylor hated colonial authority, just by the way. The two soon discovered they had common ground, and spent some time reminiscing over the man-eating lions that plagued Benga. Adelino never forgot his meeting with Taylor and many years later, it was Adelino that had to collect Taylor upon the latter's arrival from

Nyasaland (now Malawi), and take him to his ship, bound for Italy. It was 1953 and Taylor was about to head for Australia, via Italy, where he wrote the last two books he completed.

Speaking of Taylor, and just to underline what a small world it is, it was Adelino's uncle that transacted on behalf of the authorities when Taylor opened his trading store at Benga. Incidentally, Adelino considered his father to have shot perhaps a hundred lions during his career as honorary game warden of Tete, in the two decades between 1933 and 1953. Most of these were "problem animals" (read man-eaters and stock raiders), and this was no small achievement: Sir Alfred Pease actually wrote that he felt sure no man could shoot a hundred lions and live. Adelino's father was a careful man and a good shot, and his luck held. Adelino passed away on 10 August 2015 after suffering a massive heart attack; the great free spirit is now truly free.

*   *   *

A contemporary in Mozambique of both John Taylor and Adelino Serras Pires was the celebrated Wally Johnson. Peter Capstick told his story in *The Last Ivory Hunter* (St. Martin's Press, 1988). Wally was likely the very last of that incomparable breed of men, the ivory hunters. To this day there are cropping officers and game wardens that have racked up far higher totals of elephants shot, but these can't compare with the ivory hunters, whose income and survival depended on the mass and quality of the ivory gathered. Cropping officers receive a salary regardless how many jumbo they terminate, and have to eliminate entire family groups, so it's about quantity. Wally poached and hunted elephant until the civil war finally drove him out of Mozambique in 1975, whereupon he became a Botswana citizen and continued hunting there.

Wally recounted an interesting instance from 1952, where a man-eating lion put in an appearance at a small native settlement while Wally and his party were present. The animal, obviously suspecting a trap, declined to enter the hut by its open side, preferring to break through an intact hut wall and remove a man. The screams of the poor wretch awoke the men around 4am and Wally fired in the general direction of the sounds, which could clearly be heard, of the lion consuming his victim. He wanted to follow the lion right then and there but his gunbearer, Luis, wisely convinced him to wait the short while until it was light. The man was clearly beyond help and the lion might escape, or more likely add to its tally in the dark. The men retired to get outside some coffee and when the light allowed it, set off following the drag marks of the body.

They first came upon the man's lower legs, bitten off clean as a whistle at the knee. A bit further on the remainder of the corpse was found. It was a nauseating sight, the head and arms perfectly intact, and the ribcage largely too. Everything else was gone; organs, torso and upper legs, all eaten. Suddenly the lion flashed away from nearby cover in powerful bounds. The tracking was easy in the dew of the morning but every time the men closed in, the lion would bolt off again. Realising the folly in this, the party decided to return to the remains and sit up over them, shooting the lion when it returned. Returning to the scene, however, the body had disappeared. The lion had doubled back and reclaimed his meal. Tracking again, the scene was repeated as the party found the remains, but again the lion growled and ran off from nearby cover.

Taking the half-corpse with them, the men had just selected a tree and were planning the *machan* shooting platform, when a car arrived with six black policemen in it. They had been sent to shoot the lion and an incensed Wally told them to clear off; he was well-known to the Administrator. Orders were however orders, so Wally relented. The policemen planned a line-beat, where the locals were to herd the lion towards the end of the plain. There, of course, the policemen were all ensconced in trees, rifles at the ready. Wally shook his head in disbelief as the beat turned into a farce; many people walked in single-file instead of abreast. The lion merely bypassed them and was thus never even seen, much less shot. The policemen now changed plans and since they'd not shot the lion, informed Wally that they had to bury the body. No-go, Wally said; he needed it to bait the lion. But again, orders were orders, and Wally had to relent.

Eventually the poor man was interred sufficiently deep so that the hyenas wouldn't dig him up. The men secured a goat instead and sat up for the lion, with no success. Most of the party had to then return to Rhodesia (now Zimbabwe), and then Wally made for Gorongosa Mountain to shoot some ivory. When he returned, village after village was deserted, dead-quiet. At length, one man poked his head out and divulged the reason: the lion had since taken another five people. Just then, another local man rushed in, pleading with Wally to shoot some buffalo that were raiding his crops as they spoke. They dashed off, seeing five big bulls all together in the man's field. Wally shot the first, then another. As this second animal got up, Wally shot it again, and what should appear, attached to the buffalo's throat, but the man-eater!

Wally snapped off a shot and the lion came in a full-blooded charge. That made four shots from his magazine, one left. But Wally saw to his dismay that the rifle was empty. The rest of the party was already high in the trees so Wally – with no chance to reload a magazine rifle in that time – was truly alone. Beside him was a *mopane* sapling, and with literally nothing else between him and a charging man-eating lion, Wally determined to try to climb it, or keep it between them. He was about a metre off the ground when the lion arrived. Wally clearly recalled thinking, this is it: the demise of Wally Johnson. The animal crouched to spring but never made it into second gear; instead it started to stagger, retch and roll over. Wally's snap-shot had hit home, and although he shinnied a few feet higher, he knew the lion could reach up to nail him with no trouble whatsoever. And there they all stayed for a few minutes, until Wally's men shouted to him from the trees!

They asked if the beast was dead, and Wally, seeing no sign that the creature was still breathing, answered in the affirmative. His men then asked him why he was still aloft, since the cat was dead! Quite cheeky, thought Wally, so to save face he tentatively descended, making sure to stay well away from the lion, until one of his men threw a spear into its chest. There was no movement; the lion was dead. Why there was no fifth round in his magazine, Wally never found out. Lucky man, Wally…

In September 2004 a lion was finally killed in a hail of bullets and arrows by policemen and villagers, in Mocimboa da Praia, a town in Mozambique's north. The hunt was long and costly and despite being peppered with bullets and arrows, the animal seriously injured two of its attackers before its hash was finally settled. It had operated in the area since the January of that year and racked up a tally of fourteen known victims. That same August, the south of Mozambique was beset by the attacks of escaped Kruger lions. In the 1990s, there were around forty attacks a year in northern Mozambique and southern Tanzania, but by 2006 there were around a hundred a year, and seventy percent of these were fatal. As Mozambique's poor population has had to endure decades of bloody violence in one form or another, they could be forgiven for feeling hard done-by when lions feast on them. Sadly, this doesn't look like stopping any time soon. Indeed, since many of the Tanzanian lions have been subjected to poisoning *en masse* in recent years, many others moved south over the Mozambique border to join lions that were already there. Add the comings and goings of the odd Kruger lion, and Mozambique is probably the country worst afflicted by man-eating lions as at 2014.

10   Zambia and more

Lions have been eating people since long before any of the recorded instances in this book, in fact since lions and people started sharing space. There are many carvings, motifs and reliefs throughout recorded history of the royalty of the day hunting lions, shooting lions and in mortal combat with lions, to bear this out. Several involved lavish ceremonies with droves of assistants to ensure the safety of the royal derriere. The Assyrians seem to have recorded many of these, several of which survive today. The British Museum features one from Nimrud, around the 8th century BC. The panel is in ivory and a feature is a lion holding a man by the throat.

The Tsavo man-eaters are well-documented and have been discussed earlier. One of the reasons for this wide-spread notoriety was simply that it was one of the earliest such instances to be properly documented. This was partly because those two cats did indeed warm to their task, and – assisted on occasion by the most mind-numbing luck, so often a feature in big-game hunting and man-eating – eventually became quite proficient; but also partly because this affront was against the most powerful empire of the day, no less than Victorian England. Communications were vastly superior to those around even 50 years previously, so the result was that the Tsavo lions were some of the first truly world-famous living beings.

Similar occurrences may and probably did happen several times before. Why these never came to light can be explained by the fact that by its very nature, and as already alluded to several times, a victim of man-eating is often devoured. Remains are often found by the deceased's family or tribe members who have seen or heard the attack, or when a missing person is sought and has been tracked. Sometimes the lion or lions are interrupted while still feeding. But there are many occasions where there are no witnesses. If left alone, a lion can consume an entire human, often eating shoes and clothing too, and although many seem to leave the very hardest bits – the heel bone or skull plate – they just as often leave nothing. In any case, what they do leave tends to disappear down the gullets of Africa's garbage disposal units: hyenas, jackals, the lugubrious marabou storks, vultures, maggots and even ants. As an old professional hunter friend of mine used to say, *vleis lê nie lank hier nie!* Meat of any sort doesn't lie around for long in Africa.

Of course, there's more to that than initially strikes one; people with grudges or criminal intent may easily have someone disappear, safe in the knowledge that a widely-accepted reason is that they were taken by lions, or a leopard, or hyenas. Murdered people are often dumped in the bushes, where the afore-mentioned garbage disposal units go to work. For the victim, it's academic at best. But there are remote areas in Africa today, where people disappear and it will never be reported. There are entire communities ignorant of what we Westerners would consider basic communication methods, and modern standards of community responsibility just don't apply to the average bush African.

All of this adds up to some hair-raising conditions, at least by modern standards, and the adaptable opportunist that is the average lion will be able to exploit them, if he so chooses. During 1925, two lions devoured a reputed 124 souls in Ankole, in Uganda. By then of course, the Tsavo lions had rendered such an extensive reign as old news and since this occasion didn't stop the British Empire, it has gone largely unnoticed, except of course for the poor community that were subjected to it. Fast-forward ten years and a group of five sub-adult lions made a name for themselves in the Lindi district of Tanzania; they notched up 20 victims but this paled by comparison with the 140 people killed in the same area, over a mere few months around the same time. South Tanzania is the world's man-eater hotspot, and many deaths and outbreaks of man-eating go unreported there in addition to the recorded ones.

The Tsavo lions weren't the only man-eaters to which John Henry Patterson was exposed during his escapades in British East Africa. In 1900, Patterson dined one evening with Superintendent Charles Ryall in a railway carriage. Little did the men know that a few months on, Ryall would suffer a terrible fate in that very carriage. A disturbingly capable man-eater had started operations around the Kima station. At one time he even climbed onto the roof of the station, and in his fervour to reach the people inside, started to pull up the metal sheeting that formed the roof. He was unsuccessful but so concerted were his efforts that he lacerated his paws in the process. Blood on the metal bore witness to his intent. One night an engine driver sat up in an empty water tank to shoot the lion but the beast tipped the tank and the man became the hunted. Luckily for the man, the animal couldn't reach him and he at least scared it off when he fired, although he didn't hit it. In an attempt to destroy the lion, Ryall travelled up by rail from Makindu to Nairobi, with two colleagues, Parenti and Huebner. They halted when they reached

Kima, some 400km (250 miles) from the coastal city of Mombasa. Their carriage was detached and shunted into a siding close to the station, but as the line was unfinished and not level, the carriage stood at a pronounced list to one side.

The three men went out to see if they could find signs of the lion but were unsuccessful. After dinner, all three again sat up and eventually Ryall convinced the others to rest while he took first watch. The carriage featured two berths, one a high berth over the table at one side, the other at the opposite end and lower down. Huebner occupied the high berth and Ryall offered Parenti the lower one, but the Italian declined and reclined on the floor instead, his feet toward the sliding door. It is thought that Ryall, growing weary and likely nodding off, decided that the lion would not show itself and lay down in the lower berth. The lion however was at large and indeed stalking the men. He silently made his way up the two high steps to the carriage and slid a paw into the small space left open for air between the door and the side of the carriage. Once he was inside, the door snapped shut, as the carriage was tilted to one side. A man-eating lion was now shut inside a railway carriage with three sleeping men.

Just to fuel the curiosity and further bolster the beliefs of the superstitious, the lion selected Ryall, which task he could only achieve by actually standing on the sleeping form of Parenti (why not just take Parenti?). Huebner awoke to a cry, and his eyes were greeted by a sight he was likely to remember forever more; a large lion was standing on his one colleague while it was engaged in grabbing the other. His only way to safety was through the connecting door to the servants' quarters, opposite the door through which the lion had entered. To reach it, however, Huebner would have to scale a considerable obstacle: the lion. Astonishingly, Huebner did just that, actually climbing over the cat; but when he reached the inter-leading door, the terrified Indian workers had - understandably - grabbed the handle and held it fast. The frantic Huebner managed to somehow prise it open enough to slip out of the carriage, following which the Indians bound the door shut with their turbans.

There was a huge crash and the entire carriage lurched with the impact as the lion took Ryall through the window. Parenti immediately leapt through the opposite side's windows and took refuge in the station buildings. Ryall's remains were found the following day a quarter-mile away (400m / 440 yards) and sent to Nairobi for burial. Happily, one of the railway staff managed to trap the lion sometime afterward with what Patterson called "an ingenious device". After being displayed for a few days, the animal was shot, a not-unreasonable pattern that seems to be the custom in East Africa.

The story above brings to light an interesting phenomenon regarding man-eating lions; they often seem to select a victim when it would have been far easier or more convenient to take another. John Taylor was a famous hunter of lions, buffalo and elephants, and wrote four popular books on his exploits. He is perhaps best-known for his knowledge of calibres, rifles and ammunition, and until the appearance in 2013 of *Great African Calibers* by the legendary Tony Sanchez-Ariňo, Taylor's writings on the subject were considered definitive. He was a controversial character but if there were two subjects he knew about, elephants and lions were those subjects. Taylor wrote in *Maneaters and Marauders* of the strange tendency of a man-eater to single out a victim.

In one instance, Taylor mentions a lion taking a man, a stranger who had joined their party for the night. The cat walked past thirty of Taylor's staff, stepped over one of the men sharing the sleeping mat with the eventual victim, and actually stood on another to collect the man! As Taylor wrote: why? It seems on the surface to make no sense at all, but perhaps a little delving would be worthwhile. It could be that the cat had followed the man before he joined the party, but even so, surely there were easier meals to collect once the men had settled down to sleep. Wally Johnson, who was Taylor's contemporary in Mozambique, recounted an episode where a man-eater ignored the easy access offered by a hut with one open side, preferring to break through an intact wall to gain access to one of the men inside! Johnson and Capstick, who wrote of the episode, theorised that the lion was an experienced man-eater, and was naturally suspicious of the open door representing a likely trap.

So why else could a man-eating cat select a certain individual when it would be far easier, quieter and more energy-efficient to take someone else? After reading of many such instances – such as with Ryall and Parenti above – I posed the conundrum to my (then) wife. She had a possible answer which makes as much sense as any other. Lions often zero in on a specific zebra in a herd, and experience often teaches them to stick to a choice rather than deviate mid-charge. I have several times seen where an easier catch was possible had they not been so single-minded. But could it be they are following other senses, senses that people don't yet

153

understand too well? In an earlier chapter I mentioned the Jouberts' famous 1992 documentary *Eternal Enemies: Lions and Hyenas*. They wrote a book which covered the time in the film and then some, titled *Hunting with the Moon* (National Geographic, 1997). At a photograph of a large pride male, Dereck Joubert wrote that the animal was "ever alert to a range of sensations beyond human perception."

There have been documentaries on dogs that have identified cancer in their owners, repeatedly sniffing and whining at their stomach, for instance, until the person has a check-up that identifies a growth or tumour. Can animals smell a problem such as this? It is well-known how predators seek out a weakness and remove those creatures from the system. Is the reason they lock onto a specific herd animal driven by a perception as yet unknown to people? Perhaps a man-eating lion selects a human victim based on some unseen defect. My ex-wife's theory holds as much water as any other; at times the way lions seek out specific people is otherwise inexplicable. To the superstitious mind, the theory of black magic, that someone is cursed, can seem a very valid argument in these cases.

In 2003 in Kasungu, in central Malawi, a lion killed and ate at least seven people after escaping from a game park before hunters managed to kill it. It was a large male, thought to be eight-to-ten years old, and was so big and heavy that eight men couldn't lift it onto the pickup truck once it had been killed. Four hunters were involved and their first two shots went through the cat's guts. This was unfortunate as it enraged the lion, and it attacked the hunters, smashing the arm of one and raking the leg of another. Two more shots did for the lion before he could add to his tally. The local people were themselves largely to blame, according to the Assistant Director of Parks and Wildlife, Hackswell Jamusana. They had vandalised some 110km (70 miles) of electrified fencing, and poached so much game that the lions unquestionably had fewer prey animals than before the fence was damaged.

Zambia has a plethora of man-eating lions in its past. A feature of many Zambian man-eaters is their large size, a characteristic of the Katanga sub-species that lives there. They also tend to be prolific. In Barotseland, on Zambia's western plateau, a huge wounded lion killed and ate around 50 people until a European hunter shot and killed him. He was named the Kazangula Killer and his *modus operandi* was marked by stealth. He would sneak into a village and remove a sleeping resident in near-silence. The favoured method for these silent executions by a man-eater that knows his job is to immediately bite the victim through the soft bone of the temples, the 3-inch fangs often meeting inside the skull. Death is instant, a mere shudder usually being the only reaction. Capstick noted at least one instance of this exact method, when he was hunting the Chabunkwa lion, also in Zambia.

In 1909 a legendary Zambian man-eater was eventually shot after killing and devouring around 90 souls. The lion was pale in colour and was named Chiengi Chali (pronounced "Chee-yengi Charlie"). The British knew him as The White Lion, Chiengi being a British border post, and Chali eventually teamed up with two other males to terrorise an area covering several villages. He was adept at avoiding traps and poisoning. Among his victims was the servant of the hunter that was sent to kill him. One survivor was recorded, a woman that stuck a firebrand in Chali's face as he ripped her mud wall open to get at her. Although some accounts record Chali as eventually succumbing to a trap-gun, there is another version.

Chiengi Chali's story was also recounted by Thomas Alexander in the journal "East Africa" of 4 April 1929 and was relayed in the Northern Rhodesia Journal. It is brilliantly written and so I have reproduced it here in Alexander's own words:

In the district in which he carried on his nefarious practices Charlie had become a celebrity, almost an institution. He was alluded to with the almost affectionate familiarity with which some people speak of the devil. A man-eater with a very black record, the natives without exception implicitly believed that he was in fact a devil, and his peculiar appearance – he was almost white and had lost half his tail – seemed to them further proof that he was no common beast.

That the uneasy spirits of the dead sometimes took the form of lions they all knew, and that some living men could change at will into the form of an animal was also common knowledge. Chiengi Charlie was without doubt one of these, for had not a white man once wounded him, and, following the blood spoor, been led straight to a native hut, where spoor and lion had alike disappeared? Perhaps a very powerful witchdoctor might conquer the spirit, but witchdoctors did not care to interfere in such matters. It might be that in the form of the lion they suspected one of themselves. Like old age or a drought, this terror that walked among their villages must be endured, till time or the greater spirits brought about its end.

Even the Europeans had begun to credit Charlie with the possession of a charmed life. His cunning and elusiveness were extraordinary, and he seemed to have an uncanny premonition of poison and traps. He had been known to kill within a hundred yards of a watcher patiently sitting up for him; or again he would take victims at places fifty miles apart within twenty-four hours. Almost every white man in the district had been out after him, and one visiting big game hunter of great renown had promised to make short work of him, but had fared no better. It was simply a waste of time to go after him, people had begun to say. No doubt he would walk into it one of these days. And with that pious hope they changed their subject.

Along the track – for it was long before the days of motor roads in Northern Rhodesia – Galatea, the mail carrier, was making his way, followed at a respectful distance by his wife with the mail bag on her back – for Galatea, an ex-askari, believed, as befitted an old soldier, in taking things easy when possible. The track was burning and dusty, but the journey was almost done, and already the flag over the boma was in sight. Galatea walked with his eyes half shut, pleasant visions of repose in his mind, and of beer in plenty. Suddenly there was a rustling in the bush, and out onto the track not twenty yards away there walked a lion.

Galatea knew instantly that it was Chiengi Charlie. The lion sat down on his haunches like a great dog, and for a space, man and beast stared at one another motionless. With an effort, as if breaking a spell, Galatea turned to his wife. "Woman" he said, "put down the bag and climb a tree!" Then with curious deliberation he began to load his old muzzle-loading rifle. He had come to regard it more as a badge of office than as a weapon, for never before had he had to use it. Now he poured the powder in recklessly. What matter if it should burst? It was useless against this devil. He knew that he must die, but he came of fighting stock, and the idea of flight or of abandoning his mail bag never entered his head.

If this must be the end, so be it. But he would fight first. He rammed the powder down and poured in a handful of buckshot, and in with it went a pebble or two, a few odd nails, all the contents of his pouch. Never for an instant did his eyes leave the lion, who remained, as he had first sat down, motionless, except for a slight movement of his mutilated tail. A little breeze rustled in the bamboos and stirred the feathery leaves of the mimosa; and a pair of ring doves fluttered down on to the track for a sandbath. Galatea took a pinch of snuff, and looked for a moment at the bush and sky; he would take one good-bye glance at these old friends.

Then, fixing his eyes again on the lion, he went slowly forward, Charlie's tail moved a little, a very little, faster, but he sat as if carved in stone until the man was within a few yards. Then his lips curling back in a snarl, he crouched. As he did so Galatea fired, and staggered back from the shock, bracing himself to meet his deathblow from those deadly claws.

And so, half-blinded by the smoke he waited. Gradually it cleared away and he saw the lion. Chiengi Charlie was lying dead on the track with half his head blown off. Galatea turned about, "Woman", he shouted, "come down from the tree and pick up the bag"!

The Kasama district featured a prolific and very dangerous lion that had been wounded by a missionary from Kapatu. This was an instance which clearly illustrates the value of following up wounded lions and finishing the job. He was already a man-eater but continued unswayed and was eventually clocked out in 1922, having killed and eaten an estimated 80 people.

An interesting man-eater was Msoro Monty, who operated around Msoro Mission in Zambia's Luangwa River Valley between 1926 and 1929. Rumoured to have racked up an impressive 100 victims on his own, he developed a knack of avoiding traps. Some accounts say he was eventually poisoned, but others record that he suddenly just disappeared, no trace of him ever being found. This would actually be consistent with a death by poison, the body devoured by hyenas and vultures, themselves likely further victims of the poison. Since this was not noted, it is a creepy possibility that Monty merely changed location one day, to likely take up his grisly habits elsewhere.

In 1943 a remarkably bold lion around Kasawa in Zambia developed a habit of sauntering into villages in broad daylight, and removing his victims' limbs. He then walked off with only the torso, to feed on that in peace. How he was named *Namvelieza* - the Cunning One - is baffling, as the Blatant One would have been far more appropriate. His eventual tally was 43 people. In 1954, a lion ate an African girl inside the school dormitory at Mpika.

Regions such as this and Mporokoso have long histories of man-eating, the average in Mpika suggesting at least a person a month being taken over an extended period. Rather, these are the figures known about and reported, and are likely to be even higher. Indeed,

Mporokoso alone had a death-rate of two a month for an entire decade, a tally for this single pride from that and other villages in the area topping a thousand souls at the rate of around a hundred a year. This is approaching Njombe levels and yet is relatively unknown.

Zambia was also the principal haunt of a true doyen of the adventure writing genre, and man-eating lions consumed much of his time there. Peter Hathaway Capstick had a long and successful career as a hunter and game control officer before going on to write of his exploits, becoming the world's top selling hunting and adventure author. He was a born raconteur, the spiritual successor to Hemingway and Ruark. Anyone who remembers the Luangwa valley in Southern Zambia where most of his African exploits took place will understand just how accurately he described it. One of his most hair-raising exploits involved the Chabunkwa man-eater, a lion that was already an accomplished people-processor when Capstick was tasked with cancelling his career.

Readers Digest featured an article on the story and the illustration that accompanied it gives stark perspective on the reality of a conflict in thick bush with a lion. The size of the animal is the first shock, the reality that it's *there*, with no spare time and no space, is the next impression. It is an impressive picture, and Fiona, Peter's widow and an accomplished author in her own right, has an enlarged print of it on a wall in her house in Pretoria, South Africa. I have seen it myself, a reminder and nod to the memory of a man that inspired thousands to go to Africa, and largely inspired me to pen this manuscript. Capstick recounted the story in *Death in the Long Grass* as only he could, but the gist of it is as follows:

As the safari season was winding down, the district commissioner sent a runner to Capstick, the man's folded note in a cleft stick instructing Capstick to contact the commissioner on the short-wave radio, but urgently. A lion had just taken his ninth victim at the hamlet of Kampisi in the Eastern Province of Zambia. As the *modus operandi* appeared to be the same, the lion was thought to be the very one that had killed and eaten eight other people at Chabunkwa, some 8km (5 miles) distant. The tribal council demanded action, and as game control officer in the region, Capstick had to step in and save the local populace, in this case from being consumed by an animal that obviously was no mere trifle threat.

When Capstick and Silent - his legendary tracker / gunbearer - made their way to Kampisi and heard what had happened from the village headman, that old African fatalism showed itself again. Three men had been sleeping off a session of indulging in the locally-brewed millet beer. It is potent stuff, and although not by any means unpleasant, it is a heavy brew and large doses overpower one to the point where the sleep which inevitably takes over one's senses, more closely resembles a state of suspended animation. Capstick aptly wrote "comatose." The net result was that the three men were outside overnight, for all intents and purposes passed out, with an active man-eating lion in the area.

Capstick, a master storyteller, described the lion's latest attack in spine-tingling real detail, as he and Silent pieced together what had happened from the headman's account and the tracks in the village. It was a deliberate, chillingly-efficient attack by an animal well-versed in the ways of its human prey. The lion actually passed over the first two men, pausing to sniff at their heads before selecting the third and executing him in the way most likely to ensure complete silence and instant death: a bite through the skull at the temples. He then gently pulled the corpse between the other two men and the hut alongside and carried it off, walking nearly 5km (3 miles), all the while carrying the body. Only twice did he stop for a mere second to change his hold. Try carrying a third of your weight for 5km, and see how many times you need to stop to change your grip. Getting the picture?

The big cat stopped in a maze of undergrowth and ate most of the man before making for the Munyamadzi River to slake his thirst. A hyena that had followed the lion for some time took care of the rest. Capstick and Silent tracked the lion all the way to this point before collecting the remaining fragments of humanity – a bit of lower jawbone and some bone splinters – and returning to the village. It was already late afternoon and neither had any suicide plans: trailing a confirmed man-eater in the gathering dark has only one outcome, and it isn't pretty. Back in the village, Capstick sat up in the open car, with his Evans .470 double rifle for company, and closed in by thorn barriers. The sixth sense of awareness already alluded to in this book woke Capstick, and having heard nothing, he was just settling back when a scream rent the night asunder, followed by three more, then silence.

Racing toward the sound, his scalp crawling, Capstick reached a hut at the far end of the hamlet, the door hanging and its occupant gabbling incomprehensibly in wide-eyed terror. Silent had already identified a lion track outside the hut and after the hunters forced some spirits down the man's throat, he was able to recount the demise of his wife. She had opened the hut door to relieve herself during the night and immediately, the lion grabbed her. She hung onto the open door, suspended horizontally, until the one hinge broke and the lion killed her before making off with the body. Imagine watching your life-partner, or any loved one, killed in this way before your very eyes, the sights, sounds and smells in graphic detail right in your face. The Chabunkwa man-eater's tally now stood at ten.

This illustrates the debunking of another myth about man-eating lions: the frequency with which they kill. The Tsavo lions showed that no rational calculations can be assumed regarding the intervals between a man-eating lion's predations. They can and do kill, and eat, on successive days, sometimes even twice on the same day. It throws more doubt on the revised recent suggested tally of 35 people accorded the Tsavo lions, and supports the arguments of Gnoske and Peterhans that over 100 kills were possible. A lion requires approximately 7kg (15lb) of game meat a day, a lioness around 5kg (11lb) under normal circumstances. In Tsavo, as elsewhere, these figures were constantly far exceeded and could likely be attributed to the opportunistic tendency I've already discussed, that all predators seem to have. Where food is available, and easy to obtain, they will exploit the situation to the fullest. Capstick, knowing this, wisely sat up on the night immediately following a kill and his decision was proven correct.

The men were on the trail before the dawn and followed the tracks into a nightmare of vegetation, the mass of thickets that line the Munyamadzi. Visibility is down to mere feet and hunting lions under these circumstances is sheer folly; the lion has such an advantage that it is almost certain someone in the hunting party will at least be tagged, or worse. This lion was a confirmed man-hunter, an expert killer with no fear of humans and Capstick was under no illusions as to the seriousness of the situation. Impossibly, the cover thickened, and the men moved painfully slowly, making no sound while straining for the noises of feeding. Suddenly Silent froze and stood listening intently, his eyes drawn to something to their left. For what seemed like ages the two men stood, balanced on the cusp of oblivion.

Agonisingly slowly, Silent backed off inch by inch, until after ten yards or so he motioned to Capstick that a woman's hand was lying just off the trail. Both men could now smell the lion, a scent I know well. I have been blessed with an excellent sense of smell and have often smelled them in the bush, then seen them shortly afterward to prove my nose correct. Many people tell me they can't scent them which is amazing to me; lions stay downwind for a reason. They stink, quite frankly. Imagine your cat, and not when its (admittedly seldom but eventually inevitable) bath time nears, try to imagine that it has *never* bathed. Then multiply that by an animal 50 times the size. Factor in that lions are often covered in gore around kills until they lick it off, and put bluntly, old *Simba* pongs.

Capstick knew they were now close, close enough to have to react in a millisecond. That coppery taste of fear filled his mouth as his heart threatened to pound through his chest. Sliding his feet forward in near slow-motion, he discerned a tiny sound to his *right*, and swung around to see the lion already in mid-air and *there*, on him, his brain converting everything to slow motion as it often does under times of chronic stress and danger. He fired - one barrel it later turned out - but it may have been from the impact as the lion barrelled into him, knocking the rifle away and the man over, but taking the bullet through the lower body. Capstick, by now in a dreamy daze, lay and waited for the lion to apply the *coup de grâce*.

Through the fuzz a shout echoed, followed by another as Silent tried to distract the lion with nothing between him and an angry man-eater but his spear. The lion swatted it aside and set upon Silent. The old Awiza tracker fed his hand into its mouth to buy Capstick time, still howling as the white man finally came out of his slow-motion reverie. Tearing through the scrub like a lunatic, Capstick must have felt like he was in a nightmare, that one where the monster is coming and you just cannot move quickly enough to stave off the impending doom, only this nightmare was horribly real. He couldn't find the rifle but his hand settled on Silent's spear. Capstick drove it into the lion's neck as forcefully as he could, the second thrust piercing the spinal cord and dropping the lion dead on the spot. Capstick then tended Silent's mangled arm and after letting the old man drink at the river – a large trauma always inducing a fierce thirst – he carried him back to the village.

*   *   *

The Indian biologist Vasant Saberwal recorded 81 attacks on people by Asiatic lions in the Gir sanctuary between 1988 and 1990, resulting in a "mere" 16 deaths. These figures are however twice as many as those for the previous decade. Apparently, until 1987 the lions were fed meat to provide tourism, and all the attacks were in that area. The comparatively low death rate indicates annoyance to me rather than predatory behaviour. I can only hope the officials responsible for the feeding, and particularly for its subsequent discontinuation, received medals for crass stupidity.

* * *

The southern border of the Kruger National Park is marked by the Crocodile River. Over the river between the towns of Komatipoort and Malelane lies Marloth Park, an area which was turned into a reserve in 1977, and sub-divided for ownership and timeshare. Units are built on 1,500 hectares (18 square km or 7 square miles) and wildlife roams freely between them, including four of the Big 5 (elephants are the exception; originally they came to Marloth too, but the danger and destruction they wrought resulted in them now being prevented from crossing that part of the river). Until *Lion Spruit* was set aside, an area away from the residences bordered by electric fencing to contain the lions, the consumption of people by the big cats was alarming. The animals that come and go between the Kruger and Marloth are fully wild and this was - and still is - part of the attraction to the place. People hand-feed apples to giraffes and zebras; warthogs and bushbuck enjoy being fed sugarcane and other fruit. It's all pretty cool, really; it's also stupid because it's exceedingly dangerous.

Not only herbivores crossed the river; their predators followed suit. Conditioning the herbivores to approach people would merely have brought the meat-eaters closer too. And as we have seen elsewhere in this book, Kruger Park lions have developed a decided culinary taste for *Homo sapiens*. As lions do, they started their attacks on people when they were most comfortable doing so: by night. It became a well-known fact in South Africa that Marloth was famed for the free-ranging wildlife, and that lions had killed some people, but provided one stayed indoors by night, it was still a great place to go. As time passed, the lions realised that people were less active in the night and commenced their depredations in the daylight hours. After rangers shot three entire prides over the better part of a decade, officials decided to fence the lions off from the residents. By then though, it was way too late for several people.

In September 1999, the remains of a man were found near Nyala Street. All the lions had left were a chewed head, one foot (still in its shoe), a baseball cap and a solar panel stolen from a nearby house. It was the fifth attack in that year, but was noteworthy as it was the first *known* fatality. Most of the residents in Marloth were white, affluent and travelled about by car. Not so the rangers, servants and general staff, who almost to a man were black African and traversed the area on foot or using bicycles. Most considered the lions to be good watchdogs, South Africa's rampant crime rate reaching to even this wild retreat. Calls to eradicate the lions of Marloth were met by the (mostly blindly Green preservationist) residents' circulating of flyers calling for the lions to be saved. Without the lions, Marloth is just another place, they argued. As Sydney Maziya said, perhaps they would react differently if the attacks were a little closer to home; in other words, if there were white victims.

It was an inflammatory comment in a country still volatile with racial tension. Maziya, a black Marloth Park ranger, had more leverage than most to make such a statement though. Maziya, you see, was himself attacked in 1998. One evening, Maziya was cycling along Olifant Drive (the main road that runs through the middle of Marloth Park), to relieve a shift worker at one of the main gates. As he trundled along, Maziya heard the sounds of lions ahead, so he dipped down an adjoining dirt road, hoping the shortcut would take him away from any lions. Sadly, for Sydney Maziya, the lions were in the area of the shortcut too. Two lionesses couldn't resist the cycling figure and chased Maziya, knocking him flying and biting him in the left leg. Maziya fought with the strength of desperation and kicked clear. He remembered a swimming pool close by and thought he might be safe if he could just make it to the pool. Against everything he knew and had been taught, Sydney Maziya ran for the watery haven.

In the twinkling of an eye, there were lions all over the ranger, four of them attaching themselves to his still-bleeding left leg. Sydney Maziya realised his number was most likely up. With no other recourse at all, he started to pray; and amazingly, miraculously, the lions suddenly left him. Stunned at the sudden freedom from hideous death, Maziya started to shout and scream for help. To his horror, the lions started to trickle back. Just as he was about to give up, the headlights of a pickup truck pierced the dark, illuminating the grisly scene. The rangers had heard Maziya's cries for help and the lions bolted at their arrival. Maziya spent three weeks in hospital, his left leg well and truly chewed up. Months of therapy and skin grafts followed, Maziya's leg still visibly mangled and sporting huge scars that he will carry for the rest of his life. He was vocal in his calling for something to be done about the lions and was vindicated in the mid-2000s when *Lion Spruit* was fenced off.

In 2005 my wife and I decided to buy timeshare in Marloth Park, and our biggest concern, understandably, was the man-eating outbreak. Happily, the *Lion Spruit* area had been sectioned off, and satisfied that potentially becoming lion food was highly unlikely, we bought a December week. Eventually getting to Marloth Park, we decided to walk the fence. We were horrified to see that warthogs had dug deep trenches to get under the fence, electrified though it was. Suffice it to say that we didn't venture outdoors by night that holiday; the next time we holidayed at our timeshare, the fencing had been vastly improved and was sunken several feet into the ground. There were no gaps dug between *Lion Spruit* and the area of our luxury tent, and the entire fence was bigger and stronger. There was still room for a chuckle at our own expense, although I assure you, it wasn't remotely funny at the time...

It was five years after our first trip; in the interim we had moved to Australia and hadn't returned to South Africa since, save for a busy two-week dash back for a family wedding. We arrived in the night and thus had no idea that the fences had since been vastly improved. As one does from time to time, I awoke in the middle of the night needing to visit the ablutions. We have two luxury tents alongside one another. My wife and I took the one tent – one story off the ground and with ablutions, kitchen and undercover car park beneath the tent – while her parents and our children occupied the other, a ground-floor affair with *en suite* ablutions. For us to visit the ablutions meant exiting the tent and going outside. At night. In Marloth Park. Do you see why my children and in-laws have an *en suite* toilet? Anyhow, sense prevailed and I tried to go back to sleep but, it being our first night, we may have had too much to drink...

Suffice it to say that I couldn't go back to sleep. Although I was very still and quiet, my wife must have sensed me awake, as she awoke too and I told her of my predicament. After a while she too needed to answer a call of nature, so realising that we could just as well go sooner rather than later, we ventured up and to the tent's triple-barrier entrance. After we'd unlocked the padlock and unzipped the two levels, we ventured out onto the timber balcony (the same timber balcony where the patrolling rangers had once seen a mating pair of lions during the quiet off-season, when thankfully no people were around. Mating lions are notoriously cranky). Turning around, I had just zipped the two layers closed again when the roar hit us. The animal was close, maybe 50 metres away, probably

164

even closer. In the still of night, and fuelled by our expectant fears, it was hardly surprising that my wife and I remember the other's widened eye-whites more than anything else!

Armed with the intimidating presence of a foot-long American flashlight – I had sold my .357 Magnum revolver when we left South Africa, a beautiful silver model 66 by Taurus – we made it unscathed to the toilet and back. Rarely have I felt as naked without a firearm as that night. The following day we discovered the strong and unbroken new fence, and the lion tracks – safely on the other side of the fence – were indeed a distance of 50 metres or so away. Funny thing, I don't remember indigestion being a problem for either one of us. We still own the timeshare, returning to this day to enjoy it whenever we are back in South Africa. Oh, and yes; we are fascinated and thrilled to be sharing space with wild lions, even though the Marloth Park lions – at long last – now seem to be definitively fenced off from their potential prey: us.

It is this fascination, this fear and realisation that we have a large belligerent competitor - predator, actually - that provides our obsession with lions, and other large predators. Now - in a situation of rich irony - we just need to ensure there will still be something to obsess over, in twenty years' time…

11   The Spirit Lions – Tanzania today

There has been much study in East Africa in particular in recent years, on man-eating lions. Part of this can be attributed to a recent rekindling of interest in the Tsavo lions – the 1996 film playing no small part – but is much more due to research undertaken by scientists on behalf of the National Geographic and other similar institutions, which keeps the mill going by providing further interest in the documentaries they subsequently air. The Rufiji man-eater, for example, was well-covered in both print and documentary film. Call it the phenomenon of the modern communication age, which has sparked awareness and interest in the most remote places. Extensive interest has been maintained regarding the Tsavo lions and tours now include the den of the man-eaters, which Patterson had found but which had subsequently gone undiscovered for almost a century.

It is Tanzania's ongoing crisis, though, that has seen the most research and coverage as people attempt to deal with, understand and stop the killing. Predation of people by lions has never really gone away from Tanzania, before that known as Tanganyika under British rule and before that, as German East Africa until the end of the First World War, but in recent years it has stepped up markedly. As the human population has increased to the point where Tanzania's wild places are now being inhabited by people, including the massive reserves, some lions have been forced to adapt to an alternative (or is that old but temporarily-forgotten?) food source: people.

The entire southern region of Tanzania is unique in that it is one of the only places in Africa, and thus the world, where wild lions roam free outside of reserves in reasonable numbers. This situation creates its own problems and the burgeoning human population makes lion-human contact a fact of daily life, and will continue to do so until all the lions outside of reserves are caught or shot. There has been an upsurge as populations blow out: between 1988 and 2009, lions attacked over 1,000 people, killing and eating two-thirds of these. And these are just the reported cases. The Lindi area is statistically the worst place in the world for man-eating lion activity. Between 2001 and 2004 there were at least three separate groups of lions on killing sprees in that area, at the same time. In that time the tally was 113 dead people and 52 had been severely injured. There appeared to be a lull in 2005 and 2006 – incidentally when I was in East Africa – but since 2008 especially, the attack tallies have soared again.

In October 2006 National Geographic ran a story by Paul Kvinta, who had gone to help decipher the mess, or at least alert the world to its extent. He headed for Lindi, a coastal town of some 40 thousand people in the South East of the country. On his way there he met with Craig Packer, the world's foremost lion conservationist, in Dar es Salaam, Tanzania's capital. Packer forewarned Kvinta that the lion population in Lindi was on its way out, and the spike in killings just confirmed that to be the case. It's a sort of last gasp, the star burning brightest before it's snuffed out forever. Packer calls it the Njombe effect; I don't think I need to further explain why. In the field and trying to curb the problem are Dairen Simpson, one of the world's foremost trappers, and Dennis Ikanda, a protégé of Packer's from the northern reaches of the country. The problem is serious and extensive, so much so that the people are convinced of another dimension: that of witchcraft.

This has been a recurring theme and the Westerner is almost understandably impatient with this haunted line of thinking. The terror that pervades when man-eating cats have a community in their power is so complete, that one can almost understand this belief. Add in the impossible luck that man-eaters often seem to enjoy and well, things do often get plain spooky. A helpless community will often turn to the witchdoctor, since nothing else seems to help. Sitting in the dark hoping will have no effect; beating on a lion is pointless unless you're using a murderously sharp sword or other weapon. Most villagers are too poor for anything other than the most basic farm implements, and certainly to obtain any type of firearm. In the face of this, where else to turn but the spiritual realm? Circumstances can be manipulated or utilised as if by design, which makes the witchdoctor appear all-powerful, and you have believers. Again, to be fair to the poor souls, you too would gladly clamour for any relief from what must in essence be waiting in utter helplessness for a very unpleasant death. That is, of course, assuming that the witchdoctors don't actually have some effect after all…Africa is a very large and mysterious place. There have been enough situations to at least create doubt in the most sceptical minds. More on this later; for now, a story of an uncomfortable reality…

If Hassani Dadi is still around he's a young man just entering adulthood. But back in 2002 he was a six-year-old, short for his years but otherwise a normal healthy boy. In January of that year he'd gone the short distance to Navanga to help his uncle at his *shamba*, a smallholding producing maize (corn), millet and rice, but this produce tended to disappear down the gullets of bush pigs and vervet monkeys almost as quickly as it could be grown. Indeed, Salum Mohamed, Hassani's uncle, had just moved his entire family – a wife and three children – from their village of Simana an hour away, to help him keep the crop-raiders at bay. It is physical work and with no alternative entertainment available in any case, families tend to rise early and go to sleep early.

One evening, not long before midnight, Salum was awakened from the deep sleep brought about by a hard day's work as a shrill shrieking rent the darkness of his hut asunder. He remembers it being so surreal, that he thought he may be dreaming. But it was all too real; stumbling around inside the dark hut he found his wife and three children all present and accounted for, but his nephew, Hassani forced *into* the wall, screaming fit to burst. Still fighting to get his mental bearings, Salum wrapped his arms around the child and tried to pry him free. The next instant though he was fully awake: a lion's roar sounded through the wall. The tug-of-war lasted just seconds as the child's spindly arm gave way at the shoulder, Salum and Hassani sprawling backwards into the hut's dark interior. Fighting the rising panic in his guts the man managed to get a tourniquet of sorts over the pathetic stump which was gushing blood, horrified at the gurgling sounds the child was making in his arms. Poor Salum then had a terrible choice to make, a choice no human being should ever be forced to even contemplate.

The lions' paws took turns coming through the wall again, reaching for the boy, the arm they had won a mere snack and not quite frankly what they had come for, not enough. They had found the hut's one weak spot, that wall as yet incomplete and lacking its mud coating. The insides of the wall are comprised of branches and grass, and finished with an exterior of hardening mud, usually mixed with cattle dung. Placing the child in a room with four complete walls, Salum shepherded the rest of his family up a ladder and into the rafters. Salum was armed with a machete, and he knew there were at least two lions outside, trying to get in. A machete is known as a *panga* (pronounced puhng-gah) in South Africa, a vicious weapon in street riots and times of unrest when used against another person. Against a lion – not to mention two or more determined man-eating lions – it would be woefully inadequate.

Anyone in this predicament and lucky enough to survive, will bear this out.

One can only imagine how long the night must have been for Salum, and even more so for poor Hassani, lying alone on the floor waiting for death, having just had his arm wrenched off. By morning, as if by miracle, the lions were gone and Hassani still hung on to life. Salum put the child on his bicycle and pedalled frantically down the bumpy dirt road until he reached the tar highway, several miles away. From there they caught a bus to the hospital in Lindi. How Hassani survived is unclear but it beggars belief. Paul Kvinta asked the uncomfortable question; why did Salum not take Hassani up into the rafters with the rest of his family? Was there not enough room? Without directly answering the question, Salum stated that he thought the child would die. In our Western homes, we cannot fully comprehend this horrific quandary, this ultimate human survival dilemma: is your will to live so strong, your terror so great, that you sacrifice a family member to save the rest? What about to save yourself?

Most will read this and definitively state, no way; I will bravely save the family. With a machete, Salum might even have waited for a searching paw to appear through the wall and hack it with everything he had. Most machetes are sharp enough to cause a wound decisive enough to at least make the lion look elsewhere, if not limp off with a serious injury. Even writing this I have that feeling that I could never live with myself later. But how many of us were there? How many have felt the terror in the pitch dark as powerful, deadly animals come to eat you? Our houses have fine, sturdy walls and roofs. Anyone who has lived in Africa will have some idea of the walls that make up most *kaias* and *dungus* in rural areas. Hassani is in no doubt as to what happened that night; as Kvinta interviewed the senior Mohamed, the child - then aged ten - vented his anger at his uncle in no uncertain terms, fully aware that he was the offering that night in 2002. He refused to pose with his uncle for a photograph. One wonders what has happened in this family since.

As the natural prey diminishes and people encroach on the wild lion population in Tanzania's southern reaches, the clashes are inevitable. Dairen Simpson considers it from the lion's point of view: a village is a *smorgasbord*. There are dogs, goats, cattle, donkeys...and people. As Simpson, Ikanda and Kvinta interviewed people in the village of Navanga, the recent nights had been peppered with lion attacks on dogs and goats. This was particularly

169

concerning, as villagers remember the same tendencies from previous outbreaks of man-eating: the lions start on the animals and graduate to people. Tanzania's population in 1988 was 23.1 million people; by 2002 it was 34.6 million. That's an increase of 50 percent in a decade and a half. Small wonder the wild spaces in the South are now seeing habitation where for decades, perhaps hundreds of years, there was none. The population by 2012 was 45 million. Another decade, and up by a third again.

The combination of extreme drought, circumstance and opportunity eventually led to an attack on the night of September 24, 2001. The pride that went on to terrorise the entire region of Sudi-Mingoyo for three years first took an eight-year-old child, Pili Tengulengu, from the footpath as a line of children ran home in the darkening evening. Pili was the last of a string of children. No-one saw anything, but everyone heard Pili's single, shrill scream. Men from the village came looking half an hour later, armed with spears, machetes and lanterns, but had to give up the search as it was too dark to discern anything. The following day a bit of arm bone and Pili's skull were the only remains found. Some seven weeks afterward, a nine-year-old, Maisha Shaibu was killed at the village of Nachunyu. Two months later, Hassani Dadi's arm was removed and eight weeks on from that - in mid-March 2002 - a seven-year-old, Sharifa Magendo was eaten in Hingawali. Each attack brought armed rangers from the Lindi District Game Office to track the pride, with villagers accompanying them or dispatching trackers in their own groups.

It was one such group of villagers that managed to kill two lions in March 2002. Joy was short-lived however; in May of that year an eight-year-old was killed in Navanga and just two weeks later, a twelve-year-old in Hingawali. The pattern was a strange one; man-eating lions usually eat people exclusively once conditioned to consuming us, but this pride continued to kill and eat bush pigs and goats as well. Their attacks on people seemed to resemble smash-and-grab raids, children being far easier to kill and consume quickly. Since a lion has no trouble pulling down an adult human, perhaps these cats were just cautious. Nonetheless it is odd. And the villagers were convinced of witchcraft. They desperately needed a spiritual counter; a witchdoctor, or *mtaalam*.

Traditional beliefs run deep in Africa. Despite many modern political and social structures, Africa is still largely a tribal culture, certainly in the rural areas. The Makonde tribe inhabits a large area that straddles southern Tanzania and northern Mozambique. Since they own many of the small businesses in the towns of these regions, and thus are better-off than the majority of the Mwera tribe, they must have more powerful magic than their rivals; it's as simple as that. Should one require a spirit lion, to punish a rival – he may have stolen from you or engaged in adulterous practices with your spouse, for instance – then a *mtaalam* is your man. For a fee, naturally, he provides some advice and two herbs. The theory is that you take the first herb, and standing in the dense bush near your village, throw it to the ground. A lion appears - literally, in a Cinderella-like flash - and while it executes the assassination you wait in the bush. Freaky enough for you? Now it gets *really* tricky...

Once the animal has killed your rival, the second herb must be employed to deactivate the lion. It returns to you and must *lick the second herb out of your palm*. While you stand there; in the thick bush in the pitch-dark African night; a blood-soaked man-killing lion must walk up to you and lick something out of your hand? Naturally, if anything ever got to this point in the first place, the vast majority of people tend to lose their nerve around this stage and leave before the lion returns. The animal never gets deactivated and a man-eating outbreak is the result. This is what the people in the Sudi-Mingoyo area believed to be the case and the situation was not improving: on June 28 in Simana, the first adult was killed, 58-year-old Juma Musa. The people of Simana pooled their money and contacted Ahmad Msham Namalenga, a Makonde *mtaalam.*

Namalenga is a renowned lion trapper from Mtwara, the district directly to Lindi's South. He specialises in trapping spirit lions, and maintains that his magic confuses man-eaters, which are renowned as having a great ability to sniff out and avoid traps. He placed more than 30 traps in a notorious area to the west of Simana, a patch of dense forest replete with natural springs, a veritable lion haunt fondly named "Baghdad" by the villagers due to the danger it posed. He only managed to catch one lioness that escaped anyway, and the angry villagers killed the two cubs she left behind. In the time since Namalenga's arrival, attacks had actually intensified, five people being attacked of which there were four fatalities. Two of the dead were children. The African like-for-like policy was enforced by killing the cubs.

As the situation worsened, the villagers started withholding information from Simpson and Ikanda, avoiding discussing the lions at all for fear that the spirit lions would punish them. It is much like the situation that George Rushby encountered in Njombe. Then Kvinta realised something quite disturbing; the team were engaged in catch-and-release tactics, relocating lions unless they were positive they were man-eaters. Ikanda had not explained the concept to the villagers, who thought that the team was catching and killing man-eaters, period. Kvinta reminded Ikanda that the community needed to be informed, as a priority; if someone were killed by a collared lion, explaining to the community that the lion had indeed been caught, and collared, and had killed someone, yet was not owned by the team and that they were not controlling it by some high-tech method related to its collar, would pose an interesting problem.

Finally, on 4 August 2003 the well-respected lion-hunter Musa Manga trapped a lioness in a snare. The animal was found dead in the early hours on the path between Hingawali and Simana. A victory after so much suffering; but the lapse was another false dawn. Worse was to follow; far worse. In the throes of celebrating, two 14-year-old friends, Hassan Libanda and Salum Abdala, planned to go up to Hingawali and view the dead lioness. They lived in another village some three hours walk away, called Nkung'uni. Hassan was a very conscientious child, a model elder-brother type that excelled at school and was responsible and diligent. He went to ask his parents if he might be allowed to go, and his father, convinced that the large lioness was the last of the pride, consented. The youths left Nkung'uni at 11am and by mid-afternoon were in Hingawali, where a carnival atmosphere pervaded. The lioness was lain out across the clearing from the market and people were punching and hitting it in the released frustration and fear that had for so long been pent up.

After hanging about for a bit, the boys decided to return home so as not to travel in the dark. They parted at a split in the path a short distance outside Nkung'uni at around 7pm, where the scrub and grass towers 15 feet (5 metres) tall. It was already dark but Hassan was not frightened for the first time in two years. The pride was exterminated, right? But Hassan's uncle witnessed a giant male lion explode from the bush and snatch Hassan in a snarling nightmare of teeth and claws. Yelling to Hassan's father Ahmed, the two men grabbed machetes and raced headlong through the scrub after the screaming Hassan. After some 400 feet (120 metres) or so, the lion dropped Hassan and fled, but the men saw Hassan was dead as they got to him. Ahmed raised an anguished cry to the stars above. The pride was obviously not all dead. On August 10, 2003, Musa Manga tracked the male to a thicket near the village of Nunga. Organising 30 villagers into two equal teams, he set up a classic "beat", the two lines - armed with spears, machetes and anything else they could lay their hands on - converging while making a racket so as to flush the lion. The tactic, while risky, is often employed on big cats, especially on tigers in India, and as so often before, it worked.

Manga was perfectly placed, too perfectly if anything; the huge lion suddenly materialised a mere 8 metres (25 feet) from him and bolted. He shot it in the right side of the neck but his rifle jammed as he tried to fire a second shot. This turned out to be most unfortunate as the lion got away, and in the place of a man-eater, they now had a wounded, angry and maybe physically-compromised man-eater on their hands. And he really cranked up the wick in the months that followed. Between October 2003 and January 2004, he attacked twelve more people, six of these dying. He was snared on 3 February 2004 but escaped to kill a ten-year-old girl in Ruhokwe. On February 12 he was shot again by hunters but survived that too. If anything, it spurred him on still further: he killed seven people in February alone, more than he'd managed in the previous four months. The community was now desperate; the lion seemed unstoppable, a demon carrying his black magic to anyone at will.

In a letter to the District Game Office dated 15 February 2004, the village leaders from the Sudi-Mingoyo area explained their decision to hire three more bush doctors, convinced that the lion had changed tack and now officially become supernatural, citing the sudden illness of "the person who had injured it". The new witch doctors had no effect either though: in March the lion attacked a further eight people; only two of these survived. The *mtaalams* quit and admitted defeat, saying the lion's magic was too powerful. By late May the lion had killed ten more villagers, three further ones left seriously injured. The community was at an all-time low; since October this one animal had a tally of 32 souls, the score since the entire outbreak began a not inconsiderable 54 victims (38 dead, 16 injured). People fled, relocating entire villages in their panic.

But on May 29 yet another death marked the beginning of the end for the lion. Somoe Linyambe was chopping wood in the tiny settlement of Kipanda. As her granddaughter watched from the porch a large male lion tore into her in a growling flash of fangs before dragging her half a mile (some 800 metres) and feeding on her. Somoe's returning husband learned from the child what had happened, although never having seen a lion before, she recounted that her grandmother had been "taken by a cow". Seeing the tracks by the firewood, the man wisely decided against venturing out in the gathering dark. The following morning Somoe's brother, Quss M-bani arrived with some other men and the group tracked the killer.

They found some clothes, then some innards, and finally Somoe's two legs, intact. One of the men suggested poisoning the legs in case the lion returned to them. It was a weighty decision and M-bani consented. When the rat poison arrived, no-one was overly keen on applying it to the remains. So, Quss M-bani knelt down, and with understandable difficulty sliced his sister's legs open, and poured rat poison into the wounds. The following morning the legs had been moved, and even better, had been fed upon. The men couldn't find the lion though, so the following day, assisted by the wildlife rangers, they tracked him down. He was quite dead, a piece of Somoe Linyambe's leg stuck in his throat. The men dragged the lion back to Simana, loaded it on a truck and paraded it throughout the region. The people were overjoyed and thanked M-bani profusely. At long last, the outbreak was at an end.

* * *

Between 2002 and 2004 in Rufiji, Tanzania, a male lion started to consume people at a disturbing rate and managed to kill and eat around 40 people before he was shot; some estimates place his total at over 50. The nature of man-eating being what it is, the higher figure is not out of the question. The Rufiji area in Tanzania is just to the East of the massive Selous Game Reserve and straddles the Rufiji River. It is a finger-shaped area extending from the Selous, marked by the towns of Mloka where the finger exits the reserve, Mkongo on the northern section, Kikale in the North-East, the area's widest point where the river delta starts, Mohoro in the South-East and Utete in the South. The delta mouth enters the Indian Ocean near Mafia Island. Incidentally, the delta contains a mangrove forest surpassed in size only by the Sundarbans, at the south of the India / Bangladesh border.

The area features thick vegetation around the river, thorn scrub and long grass peppered with clumps of banana palms and dominated by the coffee-brown water of the Rufiji River. The typical *miombo* and *mopane* forests so ubiquitous to central and southern Africa are absent here, as are the acacias of the drier regions to the west. From among this thick bracken, people have cleared crop areas and planted the usual Tanzanian subsistence fare of corn, rice and cassava. The farmers erect shelters on the crop fields, called *dungus*, in order to protect the fields from crop-raiding wildlife. The National Geographic researcher, Gordon Buchanan, went so far as to actually sleep in a *dungu*, a crude structure of poles with a floor maybe two metres off the ground, with walls and a roof hewn from natural materials. It is hair-raisingly fragile and in no way sufficient protection against a man-eating lion.

Watching survivors on Buchanan's subsequent documentary recount tales of lions pulling relatives from the *dungus* is humbling, the terror all too real. The locals called the lion Osama, after Osama Bin Laden, who had recently gained worldwide notoriety for the September 2001 "9-11" terrorist attacks on the United States. The big cat's range encompassed eight villages. When he was killed he was found to have a large abscess beneath one of his molars, which was shattered and obviously a source of great pain. Of interest is the fact that he was a mere three and a half years old by the time he was shot, and he had operated for almost two years by then.

It is he that adorns the large billboard warning signs in the region that leave no-one in any doubt as to the problem. Craig Packer considers him to have started his grisly career by mimicking his mother, which is certainly possible, but it could be that he was a young male, cast out of a pride and wandering, starving, until he stumbled across a victim. Being Southern Tanzania, though, where surviving wild lion populations are now being pressured for space by the human population explosion, Packer's theory is the more likely. Man-eating lions there tend to operate in small prides and the conditions are not at all ideal lion country such as that found in northern Botswana, for instance, where there are open spaces, largely free from human interference.

There are references in most of the reports I've read on the Rufiji lion that he was a pride member, and although not the only perpetrator, was the only one caught at that time, and thus became the "fall-guy". Any success during an outbreak of man-eating is welcome, celebrated and paraded for all to see. As illustrated above in the Sudi-Mingoyo region around the same time, the community would do well not to drop its collective guard...regardless, the people can be forgiven for enjoying the victory when the Rufiji lion was finally caught. There is a surviving photograph of him, caged and captured before he was shot. The hatred he exudes is chilling, seemingly dripping from his every pore as he plainly views his watchers as nothing but overdue meals. There is no fear or even mild caution whatsoever in his countenance, although in his defence, the watching crowd were likely shouting, swearing and throwing things at him. The photo of him after he'd been shot is in sharp contrast; he looks almost peaceful and decidedly deflated.

It is a curious thing, how utterly undignified and deflated a lion, tiger, bear, even a Great White shark, appears in death; the animal's magnificence and defiance in life is so contrasted in death, that they appear all the more pathetic and cowed. This beautiful flowery observation, although true, is understandably lost on a community that has been under siege. To their great joy, the Rufiji man-eater could cause the people no more horror, and they celebrated, wildly reviling the dead cat.

When I was in touch with Craig Packer in April 2014, he mentioned that most of the man-eating lions in southern Tanzania had by then been poisoned; this is an understandable reaction from a populace living in mortal danger on a daily basis. It sadly bears out both my prediction as well as Craig's some years before: unless lions are protected from human contact in large, well-fenced reserves and hunting concessions, where their natural prey animals are likewise protected, lions will eventually be exterminated in a given area while a lot of people will be killed and eaten first.

Craig mentioned that many of these Tanzanian people-eaters that covered an area stretching from southern Tanzania to northern Mozambique, survive and continue their predation on humans in Mozambique, mainly in the Niassa area. To underline what both Craig and I have been emphasizing, there is a reserve there and it is a large one, covering some 42 thousand square kilometres (16,400 square miles) and containing 20 thousand elephants; but 40 thousand people live there as well. The outcome is as predictable as it is inevitable.

.

12   The human aspect

So, what about the people? What about the other victims in this scenario? The lions are continent-wide victims and have in many cases been driven to adapt by circumstance; but what about the literal victims, the human beings trying to make ends meet while being subjected to the most banal, base, primal hair-raising horror imaginable? Let's consider the phenomenon of phagophobia. It is non-specific, and applies to the fear of swallowing, of eating or of being eaten. I think this speaks volumes; the fact that it is non-specific means perhaps that in this modern age of defined psychological studies, defined human reactions and the influences that caused those reactions, it is really so long since the vast majority of people had to worry about being preyed upon by animals that it cannot be singled out, isolated in the workings of the mind. But just as likely is the fact that it is so primal that it cannot be satisfactorily identified; it's maybe too close to the bone. There is no real way to study it, as everyone will react so differently and radically when faced with death in such a manner – being eaten by a large animal in a violent way – that accurate study may be impossible. The subject may be killed and unable to provide feedback. Trying to define fear has eluded and frustrated scientists for centuries.

Phagophobia is different to the fear of conventional death. One can perhaps simulate an underground train racing towards the subject and monitor the physical, mental and emotional reactions and changes that the body goes through. It is much more difficult to study an actual near-miss in the African wilderness, or in the sea, or in Canadian grizzly country. As human beings have advanced, we accept a certain amount of risk and danger from such unavoidable aspects of daily life as commuting. Death by car accident is commonplace. Train and aircraft travel are far safer but nonetheless claim hundreds of lives a year. We just don't seem to mind that much. Is it the malice, the perceived anger that makes a violent attack on us by an animal seem so much worse? Why do we care? The victim couldn't give a hoot if they are subsequently eaten; but the family or community do. The mourning over what remains and the process of properly burying, cremating or otherwise disposing of the person form a vital part of gaining closure for the people left behind. But it affects us so much more if a victim is killed and eaten by a bear, for instance, than if the body is destroyed in a plane-crash. Again, it must be the manner of the death and destruction of the body.

The fear of being eaten seems so much more powerful than conventional apprehension that entire communities descend into a depressed and apathetic state from sustained attacks by man-eaters. It has been noted in the vast majority of cases in Africa and India, if not all cases. One of the contributing factors in the massive totals racked up by man-eating leopards and tigers in India and Nepal appears to be the gentle nature of the people. Many times, African tribes are much more aggressive and won't tolerate being eaten. They would go out and swiftly avenge attacks on their number by killing not only the perpetrator but other pride members too, particularly the warlike tribes such as the Zulu, Maasai, Nandi and Dinka. In other less-warlike communities however, the all-pervading blue funk is tangible. Violent retribution just won't happen in many Asian cultures where all living things are interconnected, and should not be killed. Are we, as Westerners, watching part of our ancient, thousands-of-years-ago history unfolding before our eyes over the past three hundred years as we watch communities in the less-developed countries slowly survive by eliminating their large terrestrial predators?

To come across lions on foot and unarmed is to suddenly confront your mortality, and the enormity of that situation is suddenly shockingly real. It is a feeling of sheer body-freezing, soul-destroying terror. I have read it written that your heart drops into your feet. That is aptly described. There is no question in your mind that you are dead meat, should they so decree it. To be so confronted at night is a hundred times worse; it has many times been observed how lions transform at night. In addition, their eyesight is still perfect while ours is severely compromised. The longer the confrontation lasts, the worse it is to those who have studied lions and know the stories. You start recalling all the fun things that appear in this book. The only chance of survival is to freeze, and slowly back off if possible. And yes, Gordon Cundill was right to often quote Kipling: the female of the species is most definitely the deadlier. It's the lionesses that mock-charge; the lionesses that blow the leaves off the surrounding trees with such vehemence and hatred in their snarls. You know when a male really charges that you have a problem, but he's so much less likely to. And I can assure you, having a knife – as Harry Wolhuter did – is still unarmed. Sure, take it away and the last gram of chance you ever had of surviving is snuffed out, but you are in no way in the ascendancy and feeling comfy when armed with a knife, when you come across wild lions on foot in the bush.

African sunsets are legendary; the sky seems impossible, pink and orange streaks slashing almost the entire visible canopy, the clouds made disproportionately dark by the contrasting brightness, as if the light is showing what it can do in a last desperate hurrah. The pervading feeling as the wood pigeons coo in the background is one of peace, and everything in harmony. But it's the time immediately following sunset that can be disturbing in the really wild places; it leaves me with an initial sense of frustration, the ever-intensifying gloom rendering the inadequate human eye increasingly useless. That frustration then gives way to a sense of foreboding, of dread, every thicket filled with gut-churning portent as the bush morphs into the most fantastically-shaped monsters. Worst of all is the *knowing*, though; that the real monsters are out there, somewhere. Just waiting. As Jim Corbett wrote when pursuing the Rudraprayag Leopard in the 1920s in India, the word terror is freely used, but people have forgotten its true meaning. True terror is to be at the mercy – especially when such mercy is highly unlikely – of a predatory animal.

There has been study conducted on the reaction of our minds and bodies to certain aspects of possible predation by animals. The physiological aspects are well-documented but not so well-known are the neural pathways that bring about these physiological changes. Basically, fear is designed to keep the organism – in this case, us – alive and functioning in dangerous situations. Stimuli that warn of danger (from eyes, ears, touch) follow neural pathways to the thalamus, then converge into one and flow to the amygdala, an almond-shaped collection of nuclei in the front of the brain's temporal lobes. The amygdala determines the significance of the danger and triggers emotional responses – such as fight or flight – as well as changes to internal organs and glands. Feelings are conscious, whereas emotions are patterned neuron behaviour. A hyperactive amygdala can result in panic and irrational behaviour. The physical changes brought about by the amygdala are fascinating; it basically readies the body for extreme action. The first reaction is to freeze. If the danger remains, blood glucose levels sky-rocket and the blood vessels dilate in the skeletal muscles, rushing blood there for action.

Breathing speeds up, temperature increases, localised sweating occurs and one's hair stands on end. This last-mentioned is well-noted in all mammals but is clearly visible in cats, for instance, and is formally named piloerection. It basically makes you appear larger and a more daunting target. After this, the body readies the bladder and colon for evacuation, for speed and lightness. Robert Frump wrote most entertainingly on the phenomenon while in Kruger and noted the entire sequence of events in himself, except for the last ones, when he heard the roaring of lions at night. The start of the entire process came when he felt the soundwaves reverberate in his breastbone. Only four big cats roar: the lion, tiger, jaguar and leopard. This ability classifies them as *Panthera.* Animals like the puma are said to scream. Study has shown that one of the very reasons the four big cats roar is to cause potential prey to freeze for that initial split-second. It is often enough to give the predators all the advantage they need.

The best way for humankind to deal with the reality of large predatory animals that want to eat us, is avoidance. If we are able to eliminate ourselves as a prey species as much as possible, the adaptable carnivores will have to look elsewhere. The problems already mentioned in this book mean that our interference and often, just being there, place us in harm's way. This just underlines why all wild lions should be moved to large reserves such as Selous in Tanzania, for their own protection as much as ours. Since the human population explosion is making avoidance all the more difficult – indeed, exacerbating the problem many times over – we should enable avoidance by moving the lions. This takes us back to the situation in place over the last two hundred years, when we started the process of caging the things that bite. We have the benefit over that time of social advancement and the advancement of animal rights, so mere concrete-and-bar zoo cages won't cut the mustard. Properly-run large reserves and concessions are far more realistic propositions, and have the immeasurable advantage of allowing the animals to still literally run wild, with little or no human contact.

Theoretically, that's very nice; if we were to reach consensus on this, several things would have to be in place first. The people in and near the giant reserves would have to be moved out, or understand and accept the dangers. This seems to work for the Maasai in the Mara and the Serengeti, to the extent that if anything, the lions need protection from the people. On the other hand, moving people out doesn't necessarily work, as the situation in South Africa's Kruger Park has so shockingly proven; they may walk back. Add in the reality of unscrupulous sections of the hunting community that don't keep to quotas and stage canned hunting, all to tap the exceptionally lucrative trophy-hunting market, and the net result while time goes by is a rapidly-dwindling lion population. So, it's locked horns, *status-quo* unaltered, Mexican standoff, *impasse*. Meanwhile, communities in northern Mozambique and other places live in daily terror of being eaten by lions. So, what can be done until the world works out its conservation problems for endangered animals?

The realities of Africa in this day and age mean that the current views and agreements of organisations such as CITES are just not integrated into regional and national policies. The sustainable use of lions, for instance, is an inflammatory subject on which there is no consensus at all, not to mention alignment with the conservation strategies of several African countries. Political views in many countries do not necessarily correlate with the views of those countries' own conservation bodies, and those that do, may no longer when there is a government change. An added problem, and it is a large one, is the totally unfounded demand from the Far East for animal parts. Lion bones, for instance, bring a fortune on the black market to the Far East for supposed medicinal value, which has long been proven to be totally without substance. An interesting side-effect of the successful tiger conservation projects, which gained great momentum during the 1970s, 80s and 90s in particular, has been the demand for lion body parts in place of tiger parts. For just about any body part other than the skin, a lion's internal workings will stand in very nicely, thank you.

Corruption, frustration and greed further fuel this trade. The mind-blowing poaching of rhinoceros *inside* South Africa's best-patrolled reserves over the past decade has proven this. Rhino horn – proven to have the same non-existent medicinal value that big cat bones do – is so valuable in monetary terms that even Kruger Park rangers have been implicated and indeed caught for rhino poaching. It is more valuable than gold or cocaine; 2013 figures indicate USD $65,000 per kilogram. All this does is to push the ethical hunting concessionaries into considering unethical behaviour, the canned hunting and exceeding of quotas all too easy to consider when such reward can be had. So, there is the legitimate voice of the preservationist to consider: don't risk any of this by stopping all hunting forthwith. Sadly, again this is a utopia; Africa has proven many times over that the local population – the massively expanding human population is a dire reality – set upon the game animals first. Witness the massive destruction wrought upon the Kenyan elephant population by poaching when hunting was banned there in 1973. I use the word dire because such population growth in already-poor nations means increased poverty, and hunger.

Organisations such as World Vision and UNICEF seem to have hit upon a well-quantified method of seeking relief: for a rounded nominal amount, and in addition to their child-sponsoring program where one commits to an ongoing monthly sum, certain items can be bought for the communities. Examples are a goat, a cow, a market garden starter pack, even an entire stable of livestock, and down to such affordable items as a chicken or duck. Why not cost such items to protect the communities that are exposed to predation by large carnivores in a similar way? Corrals, more steadfast housing materials, audio deterrents, herd dogs and even electrified fencing could be provided in this way. All of these things have been suggested to assist people at the carnivore projects and wildlife conservation network conventions. The pros and cons are laid out and discussed and I have no doubt that many of the good ideas face a few obstacles to implementation, with funding likely the biggest barrier. Why not move onto gleaning sponsorship from citizens of wealthier nations in much the same way that UNICEF and World Vision have done?

I recently received such a pamphlet and the usual reaction of we comparatively unaffected First-Worlders – that of maybe being jaded by a never-ending appeal for assistance – was circumvented in a most effective way. Instead of merely mentioning hunger – which is obviously a far bigger immediate problem to most orphaned children in a war-torn developing country – was the suggestion alongside it that the children are frightened of predation by large carnivores. It got me to thinking. Effective corrals, barriers and fences, not to mention the walls of human dwellings, can greatly reduce the chance of large carnivores reaching people. Similar improvements to their places of work and modes of transport between home and employment will largely eliminate much of the danger, but realistically are a bit of a pipedream at this point. Rural Africa is that spread out that protecting people from home to work and back may be a tad ambitious for now. Strengthening homes and stock corrals is a good first step. As for the rest of the danger, in the case of African countries, take the lions and get them into the large conservation areas and hunting concessions, where humans aren't allowed. There is no other way to ensure the survival of the species, this magnificent beast, this competitor - and hunter - of people.

I pondered various ways to end this book for months; several points have been stressed, several themes emphasised. Wild lion populations are at the critical point and require saving as an urgent priority; conservation – not preservation – is required in well-planned and well-funded joint ventures between governments, communities and hunting concessionaires; and as long as humans and wild lion populations have existed alongside one another, lions have preyed upon human beings. Indeed, as long as they co-exist, lions will continue to prey upon human beings. It is this formidable, wild capability, and often hell-bent intention, that so fascinates us about the big cats.

But I wish to leave the final word to Peter Hathaway Capstick, an excerpt from his 1983 book *Death in the Dark Continent* (St Martin's Press). It is the most appropriate summary on what lions mean to people that I have ever read, and an incomparable full-stop to any work on *Panthera Leo*. In Peter's own words:

...when the fire is low, and the razor blade of moon just a flicker, there's always the cry of the Old Africa, the call that so clearly says that man will never be completely dominant over the ancient but nubile black body of the lady who really controls my heart. The KiSwahili speakers understand the lion's long *UUUUnnnHHHH, Uhhh, Uhhh, Uhhh,* best, I think, interpreting the hollow, echoing challenge of *Simba* that rolls across the liquid darkness of rivers and the muted greenish dun of plain from incredible miles as follows:

"Hi inchi ya nani?" translate the tribesmen with the secret suppression of a shudder. "Whose land is this?"

"Yangu, yangu, yangu."

"Mine, mine, mine."

Believe it, Charlie.

13   Select Bibliography

Game Ranch Management – J. du P. Bothma (ed.) (2002)

The Hunter is Death – Thomas Victor Bulpin (1962)

The Man-eaters of Tsavo – John Henry Patterson (1907)

Death in the Long Grass – Peter Hathaway Capstick (1977)

Maneaters – Peter Hathaway Capstick (1981)

Death in the Dark Continent – Peter Hathaway Capstick (1983)

The Last Ivory Hunter – Peter Hathaway Capstick (1988)

Memories of a Game Ranger – Harry Wolhuter (1948)

Game-Ranger – Hannes Kloppers (1972)

Some lions I have met – Gordon Cundill (2007)

The Man-eaters of Eden – Robert Frump (2006)

The Ghost and the Darkness – Paramount Pictures (1996)

Eternal Enemies: Lions and Hyenas – Dereck and Beverley Joubert (1992)

Hunting the African Lion – Sportsmen on Film (2007)

The Book of the Lion – Sir Alfred Edward Pease (1914)

Maneaters and Marauders – John Taylor (1959)

The Maneater of Mfuwe – Wayne Hosek (2011)

Hunting with the Moon – Dereck and Beverly Joubert (1997)

National Geographic – Man-eating lions: Stalking the Spirit Lions by Paul Kvinta (2006)

National Geographic – Maneater Manhunt documentary with Gordon Buchanan (2012)

National Geographic – Great White Deep Trouble (1999)

Wikipedia – http://www.en.wikipedia.org/lion

http://www.sciencemag.org – man-eating lions attack by the dark of the moon

http://www.smithsonianmag.com – Craig Packer research and Zambian man-eaters

http://www.nwf.org – Mystery of the man-eating lions

http://www.bbc.co.uk – Lion kills woman at California park

http://www.bbc.co.uk – Craig Packer: fencing off lions 'could save them'

http://www.bbc.co.uk – Zookeeper killed by Ethiopian lion

http://www.lindasmith.co.za – Zambian man-eaters

http://www.wildlifemanagementinstitute.org – Craig Packer research: human lion conflicts

http://www.naturalhistorymag.com – Craig Packer: Rational fear

http://www.lionaid.org – charity to protect and conserve lions worldwide

http://www.pawct.org – Protecting African Wildlife Conservation Trust

http://serendip.brynmawr.edu/exchange/node/1749 - fear and the function of the amygdala

http://www.rateltrust.org/library_files - toolkit for human-lion conflict and lion conservation

Some names for lion in Africa and elsewhere:

Afrikaans / Boer: Leeu / Leeuw

Arabic: Sba, Asad, Sab, Sabu, Sibaa

Chinyungwe: Pondoro

French: Lion

German: Löwe

Hausa: Zaki

Hindi: Sera

Hottentot: Gamma

Italian: Leone

IsiNdebele: Silwane

Jalno: Sibur

Kavirondo: Siburr

KiSwahili: Simba

Portuguese: Leão

Russian: Lev

Somali: Libah

Sotho / Tswana: Tau

Spanish: León

Swazi, Zulu: Ingonyama / Imbube / Ilibhubesi

Turkish: Aslan

Yiddish: Lyyb

www.ingramcontent.com/pod-product-compliance
Lightning Source LLC
Chambersburg PA
CBHW051616030426
42334CB00030B/3222